D1449827

MIDDLETOWN

VISUAL ANTHROPOLOGY
A series of books edited by Jay Ruby, The Center for Visual
Communication, Mifflintown, Pennsylvania

This book is part of a series. The publisher will accept continuation orders which may
be cancelled at any time and which provide for automatic billing and shipping of each
title in the series upon publication. Please write for details.

MIDDLETOWN
The Making of a
Documentary Film Series

Dwight W. Hoover

Center for Middletown Studies
Ball State University
Muncie, Indiana, USA

**hp
dp** harwood academic publishers
chur   reading   paris   philadelphia   tokyo   melbourne

Copyright © 1992 by Harwood Academic Publishers GmbH, Poststrasse 22, 7000 Chur, Switzerland. All rights reserved.

Harwood Academic Publishers

Post Office Box 90
Reading, Berkshire RG1 8JL
United Kingdom

58, rue Lhomond
75005 Paris
France

5301 Tacony Street, Drawer 330
Philadelphia, Pennsylvania 19137
United States of America

3–14–9, Okubo
Shinjuku–ku, Tokyo 169
Japan

Private Bag 8
Camberwell, Victoria 3124
Australia

Cover photo courtesy of Bernard Krafczyk, B.K. Photographic Services, Staten Island, New York.

Library of Congress Cataloging-in-Publication Data
Hoover, Dwight W., 1926–
   Middletown : the making of a documentary film series / Dwight W. Hoover.
       p.   cm. -- (Visual anthropology ; v. 2)
   Filmography:
   Includes bibliographical references and index.
   ISBN 3–7186–0543–0. -- ISBN 3–7186–0542–2 (pbk.)
   1. Middletown Film Project. 2. Documentary films--United States--Production and direction. 3. Muncie (Ind.)--History.
   4. Documentary mass media. I. Title. II. Series : Visual anthropology (Series) ; v. 2.
PN1995.9.D6H64   1992
070.1'8--dc20   91–39335
                                                            CIP

To Jan, who has made my life
more interesting than film

CONTENTS

INTRODUCTION TO THE SERIES

Visual Anthropology is a book series devoted to the illumination of the human condition through a systematic examination of all that is made to be seen. It is our intention to demonstrate the value of an anthropological approach to the study of the visual and pictorial world. We intend to present ethnographic studies of the cultural complexities of pictorial media production, analyses of the visible world of nonverbal communication from micro-studies of body movement to macro-views of the built environment, and unique attempts to communicate an anthropological understanding through pictorial means. The result will be a deepening of our knowledge of how visual and pictorial communication functions in our quest to make meaning.

Jay Ruby

PREFACE

I had been thinking about writing this book for ten years, but delayed doing so for several reasons. Among them is, as a professional historian, I believe the passage of time gives one a different perspective than when the actual events occur. Another is that the involvement in the Middletown Film Project was an emotional one for me, and I had hoped that some of the emotion would have dissipated with time. This, however, has not been the case, but I decided to proceed anyway. The result is that this book is not dispassionate; it is not an example of scholarly detachment. I have strong opinions on the subject and, while I have tried to be fair, I have not hesitated to express these opinions. The reader should be advised that there are equally strong opinions held by other participants that are opposed to mine.

This book concerns the making of the Middletown Film series and is written from the standpoint of an academic humanist advisor to the filmmaking process. Very little has been written on film from this standpoint; most of the work has been done by either filmmakers or critics. I hope to remedy this deficiency. Because of my peculiar vantage point, however, I have addressed different problems and asked different questions than those addressed or asked by others. I am particularly interested in how the project came to be, what the original goals were, and how the process of filming affected the individuals being filmed. I am also intrigued by the relationships of persons involved in the project, both with each other and with the finished product. Since I am a historian of the Muncie community, I have a standing and long-term concern with its reaction to being scrutinized once again. I am less interested in the technical or aesthetic aspects of filmmaking, probably because I feel less competent in these areas.

I have taken a severe view of several of the persons involved in the film project, including myself, but I wish to make clear that I do not regret being part of the process. Nor do I begrudge the time I spent on the project. Involvement meant meeting a large number of interesting and different individuals who, despite their shortcomings and weaknesses, also possessed many strengths, not the least of which were a creative spirit and a zest for life. This holds true for both the filmmakers and participants.

I owe a debt to many individuals too numerous to mention. Jay Ruby gave me the incentive to write the book; without him, the book probably would never have been written. Dena Hovis typed the entire manuscript quickly and with good humor. Kirsten Himmelbauer and Holly Meisberger helped revise it. Many individuals have contributed ideas through conversations, comments, papers and articles. Hardly a month goes by without some recollection of the film series between C. Warren Vander Hill and myself. I have benefited from the comments given at the International Association for Audio-Visual Media in Historical Research and Education (IAMHIST), and from K.R.M. Short, who has been so active in the association, and from Peter Stead whose film knowledge is encyclopedic. Brian Winston helped me with his analysis of the film series, though we disagree on certain points. Two graduate students — Esther Yau and Meg McLagan — have taught me much, especially about the aesthetics of filmmaking and about film criticism, of which I am still obviously a novice. Needless to say, none of these persons is responsible for any errors or omissions I may have made.

INTRODUCTION

This is an unconventional book in several ways. I have broken some of the rules normally taught by writing instructors. I have not been consistent in voice nor have I avoided the use of the first person. The book begins with a chapter written in the third person, in a conventional, scholarly way, but then switches to a personal, first person voice for the remainder of the work. There are several reasons why I organized the book in this fashion. The first is that, although I was involved in the Middletown III Project, my participation was a minor one and, of course, I was not in any way connected with the earlier Middletown studies. On the other hand, I was present at the creation of the Middletown Film Project and even claim some paternity. The second reason is that, as the reader will soon discover, I am still passionately engaged with the film project, an engagement that I hope this effort will help break. Such is not the case with Middletown III. I admire the scholars of Middletown III and the intellectual structures they have built, but I have few emotional reactions to those structures. The third reason is that I felt different forms were appropriate for different genres. The sociological studies could be best subsumed in a dispassionate narrative, the film studies in a more personal essay. Although I have attempted to be fair and balanced in all portions of the book, the material on the film project is much more opinionated, a fact I wish to make perfectly clear.

The first chapter, then, is a brief history of the sociological studies of Muncie and the impact of those studies on critics and others, both in and out of the academy. It is a piece I should have written ten years ago as an introduction for filmmakers. It sets forth the conclusions of both sets of studies, emphasizing the seemingly unchanging values in Muncie, which was the major finding of Middletown III. I have intended the chapter to be a background for the rest of the book and pose a question which the reader may wish to consider: How can the data from the Middletown studies be converted into a meaningful and interesting visual form? This question was the most important one in the entire film project and one that, in my opinion, was not well answered. However, if the reader lacks interest in such a question, the first chapter can be skipped or read last.

The second chapter charts the origin of the Middletown Film Project and places it within the political context of the times. It contains a brief discussion of the tensions involved in choosing the director of the National Endowment for the Humanities and in funding projects, particularly media projects. There is a short description of Peter Davis's career and of his direct cinema ideas. The chapter then details the different goals of those planning the series and presents the stories originally conceived as the basis for the films. It emphasizes the tentative nature of the project and of the original treatments.

The third chapter is a narrative account of the background of Muncie politics that is crucial to understanding the surprise ending of *The Campaign*. It then describes the making of the segment that served as the pilot for the series. The chapter outlines the problems encountered in shooting and evaluates the film in terms of its portrayal of the political process in Muncie.

The next chapter, which is quite long, attempts to treat the five remaining films in the series in the same manner that the third chapter treats *The Campaign*. It discusses the subjects chosen for the films as well as the false starts which preceded these choices. It tries to put the films in context by giving a short history of the participants' personal lives, their past experiences, and the social and institutional networks of which they are a part. By so doing, it is designed to clarify scenes that seemingly lack meaning that is, of necessity, lacking in direct cinema films.

The fifth chapter describes the controversy that erupted over *Seventeen* before the series even reached the air. It attempts to document the struggles between Davis and Xerox as well as those between Davis and the Public Broadcasting System. It chronicles the positions of Davis, the filmmakers, Jeff Kreines and Joel DeMott, and Lawrence Grossman, who was then head of PBS, as well as the pressures each experienced in the process. The chapter also delves into the reactions of those Munsonians who attended the private screening of *Seventeen* and the subsequent legal steps taken by parents of Southside students and school board officials to block the public televising of the segment. It concludes with an assessment of why Davis withdrew the film along with asking some unanswered questions.

The next chapter follows along chronologically with the broadcasting of the remaining films and their reception by both the general public and by the citizens of Muncie. It describes the follow-up programs shown on local public television that featured interviews of either participants or of experts on the topic and revealed the reactions of those persons seen in the films. The chapter analyzes the issues raised by *Middletown Revisited*, a locally produced program with Ben Wattenberg as narrator/ commentator, which was designed to replace *Seventeen* in the PBS slot but was not widely seen. Contained within it are the responses of Davis and other filmmakers to criticisms of their work, particularly to the charges of lack of context, and to the imputation that the films portrayed typical behavior. The chapter concludes with selected reviews of the films and of the series, both at the beginning and the end of the screening, showing how critics' attitudes changed as the series progressed and as debate over *Seventeen* became more heated.

Chapter 7 traces the continuing history of *Seventeen* as it journeyed from film festival to movie theater, accompanied by Kreines and DeMott's partisan and self-serving press release that blamed corporate America, Davis and prejudiced Munsonians for blocking the film's appearance on public television. It contains an analysis of that press release that is blatantly skeptical of its claims and critical of both its assumptions and conclusions. The chapter describes how various critics accepted the claims and incorporated them into their accounts of the controversy. It details the conflict between Davis and the filmmakers as he sought to recover the internegative and as they tried to erase him and the Middletown Film Project from the credits, thus divorcing *Seventeen* from its past. The reaction of critics to the film when it appeared in commercial movie houses ends this chapter.

The penultimate chapter is a brief account of the lives of those individuals connected with the project ten years after the filming. The purpose here is twofold: to determine, if possible, any lasting consequences of the experience, and to satisfy natural curiosity about what happened to everyone. Did the filming damage or alter the future of those filmed and had the participants improved or limited their life chances? In answering these questions, the chapter also analyzes the subsequent career changes of several individuals prominent in the project, particularly Davis, who has turned to writing. What elements in common do his films have with his articles and books? The chapter also looks at the changes in attitude and status of the teenagers in *Seventeen* to see if growing older has meant growing wiser.

The last chapter mirrors my thoughts regarding the film project and the technique of direct cinema. It tries to answer the questions of how well ideas can be converted into visual form, whether money spent on such a conversion is better spent elsewhere, and whether federal funding should be used to do this.

Middletown: The Studies

Middletown, or Muncie, Indiana, is one of the most studied communities in the United States. Since the initial research was begun in 1924, the community has learned to endure the probing of numerous investigators, whose many reports have reflected the tensions and concerns of scholars searching for clues to the American urban experience. One might well trace the course of twentieth-century American studies through the Middletown experience.

Ironically, the community was chosen largely by accident, and studied by a person unqualified to do so, with results that did not represent what the sponsoring organization had wanted. When published, however, the report entitled *Middletown* was an immediate success, has remained in print since first issued, and has inspired many successors.

The impetus for the Middletown project came from John D. Rockefeller, Jr. Shocked by the Cripple Creek Massacre, Rockefeller began to search for some ways to alleviate the rancor present in labor-management relations. One instrument he believed would help was religion. In 1919-20, he financed the Interchurch World Movement, which hoped to create the "Church of the Future, whose YMCA-like practical Christianity and social service would, he thought, promote class harmony" [Harvey 1983:339]. The movement failed, causing Rockefeller much pain and financial loss. With the help of Raymond Fosdick, the Interchurch World Movement was dissolved and its assets transferred to a new agency, the Committee on Social and Religious Surveys. Among the assets were field surveys of religious and social needs— *Theological Education in America*, *The Red Man in the United States*, *The St. Louis Church Survey*, and *The Town and Country Church in the United States*—which the committee published [Harvey 1983:339; Fox 1983:112].

In 1923 the committee became the Institute for Social and Religious Research and commissioned new studies with the old goal of unifying all Protestant churches into one vast social service network. The institute managed to complete forty-eight research projects and to publish seventy-eight books in its thirteen-year life (1921-34). Typical of these volumes were those of H. Paul Douglass, an Iowa-born minister. Douglass joined the institute in 1921 and wrote twelve books based on research done there. Among these were *The St. Louis Church Survey* (1924); the *Suburban Trend* (1925); *The Springfield*

Church Survey (1926); *1000 City Churches* (1926); *The Church in the Changing City* (1927); and *How to Study the City Church* (1928) [Haddan 1980:73].

Eventually, the directors of the institute came to believe that the organization should do more than just surveys of churches in particular communities. These surveys were done quickly and were often highly quantitative. Consequently, the institute directors decided to place their major emphasis upon a "Small-City Study" that would analyze the total religious activities in one industrial town. The study would go beyond the usual church survey; it "should ascertain the religious and ethical attitudes and capacities of the people, and the adjustment or maladjustment of the agencies to them. It should stress the intangible psychological factors more, and the external, tabulable factors less than city surveys have done" [Fisher 1924:1].

The institute originally chose sociologist William Louis Bailey of Northwestern University to be the director of the study but soon removed him "on the grounds that while he was a diligent soul he did not have the makings of a personable, insightful participant observer" [Fox 1983:113]. Bailey had already begun to search for prospective cities. Rejecting the two suggested by the institute—Springfield, Massachusetts, and Johnstown, Pennsylvania—Bailey instead submitted a list that included South Bend, Indiana; Flint, Lansing, Jackson, Kalamazoo, Muskegon, Pontiac, and Port Huron, Michigan; Canton, Steubenville, and Warren, Ohio; Racine and Kenosha, Wisconsin; and Rockford, Illinois. The institute accepted the substitution and narrowed the list to five—South Bend, Steubenville, Kenosha, Rockford, and Jackson (substituted for Warren, Ohio, the institute's first choice). The board had set a requirement that the town contain a high proportion of foreign residents; Bailey had set others stipulating that it have a growth rate of at least 35 percent in the previous decade, that it be a county seat, that it be in the east north central region of the United States, and that it contain all the chief religious denominations in the United States [Fox 1983:113; Fisher 1924:1-7].

The man who replaced Bailey was not a sociologist. He was instead a recent graduate of Union Theological Seminary, Robert S. Lynd. Born in New Albany, Indiana, in 1892, Lynd came from an old American pioneering family. His great-great-grandfather had been a Presbyterian minister who had gone to Princeton, but whose descendants had fallen on hard times. His grandfather had been a doctor in Cincinnati but had become an alcoholic. Consequently, Lynd's father had had to leave high school to begin work as a bank runner. He moved to New York City and eventually became, by dint of hard work and ability, president of Manufacturers Trust Bank [Fox 1983:106; H.M. Lynd 1983:30-32].

Lynd went to school in Indiana and graduated from Princeton in 1914. He then became an assistant editor of *Publishers' Weekly* and after that held a variety of publishing and advertising positions. In 1918, he entered the army, where he had an experience that altered his career goals. While ill in an army hospital, he began to tutor other servicemen and decided his true vocation was in human service [Fox 1983:107; R.S. Lynd 1921:82-83]. After discharge, Lynd matriculated at Union Theological Seminary. While there, he managed to take two social science courses at Columbia; these were offered by John Dewey, the great American philosopher, and by Wesley Mitchell, a noted economist of the day. Lynd found Mitchell's work congenial. He particularly admired "The Backward Art of Spending Money" (1912) [Fox 1983:108; Smith 1979-80:99-100], a piece obviously influenced by Veblen's works on human irrationality and conspicuous consumption.

Lynd had another significant, life-influencing experience while attending Union Theological Seminary. In the spring of 1921, he requested a summer job from the Presbyterian Board of Home Missions. The board gave him his choice of preaching in an already established church in rural Indiana or building one in an oil camp in Wyoming. He chose the latter. While in Elk Basin, Lynd worked as an oil field roustabout along with preaching, conducting Bible study groups, teaching Sunday school, and creating both Boy and Girl Scout troops. Out of his experiences came "But Why Preach?" (an anonymous article), and "Crude-Oil Religion," a signed article in *Harper's* in 1922, as well as "Done in Oil," which *Survey* published in 1922 [Fox 1983:108-10].

The signed article, according to Richard Wightman Fox, presages *Middletown*. "Crude-Oil Religion" recounts Lynd's experiences both as a worker and as a minister in Wyoming. "At Elk Basin Lynd had a vision of the *Gemeinschaft*, the supportive integrated community for which he would always yearn" [Fox 1983: 109]. This vision was transposed to the Muncie of the 1890s, the standard against which Lynd would compare the Muncie of 1924. The second signed article, "Done in Oil" was a slashing attack on Standard Oil of Indiana and on John D. Rockefeller, Jr., for the low quality of life in the oil fields. It was, according to Lynd's son Staughton, a polemic that scarcely mentioned religion. In tenor and substance the article described a community that resembled Muncie of the 1920s, causing Fox to conclude "that *Middletown* itself is not so much a comparative treatment of two distinct periods in the evolution of a midwestern town as a description of two conflicting tendencies in its current life" [Fox 1983:110-12; S.Lynd 1979-80:15-19].

Rockefeller tried to block publication of "Done in Oil" when William Adams Brown, a professor of Lynd's at Union Theological Seminary to whom Lynd had sent a copy, called it to his attention. Failing that, he requested space to respond in *Survey* and wrote a reply. He held no grudges, however, and in 1923, influenced by one of his lawyers, Raymond Fosdick (brother of Harry Emerson Fosdick, a minister and another supporter of Lynd), chose Lynd to become the new head of the Small-City Study [Harvey 1983:344-47; Fox 1983: 112-13].

Meanwhile, Lynd had married three days after he returned from Elk Basin. Helen Merrell Lynd was younger than he; she had graduated from Wellesley two years before their marriage. The two had met while hiking on Mt. Washington the summer after she graduated from college. In the ensuing conversation she mentioned that she was reading Veblen's *Theory of the Leisure Class*. This intrigued Lynd, and the two continued to see each other while Lynd was at the seminary and Helen was teaching in a girls' school. After their marriage, they lived with Lynd's parents in New York City while she finished a master's degree in philosophy at Columbia. She, like her husband, was not a trained social scientist [H.M. Lynd 1983:29-33].

When Lynd took over the Small City Study in 1923, he was permitted to choose the communities he wished to examine. He chose South Bend, Indiana, but abandoned his plan in November when he reluctantly concluded that the city was both too large and too ethnic. He then proposed limiting his research to sections of the city populated by the "white-American" stock. This request distressed the directors of the institute and, by mutual consent, they dropped South Bend to look for another community. Lynd then selected a short list of possibilities: Decatur, Illinois, and Kokomo and Muncie, Indiana. He chose Muncie [Fox 1983:118-19; Fisher 1924:14-19].

In choosing Muncie, Indiana, Lynd had effectively eliminated Bailey's criterion of ethnicity. Muncie had a population of thirty-eight thousand, 92 percent of whom were native-born whites. Less than five percent of the population was black. According to Richard Jensen, "no city in the Midwest with as many as 25,000 people was more old stock than Muncie" [Jensen 1979:306; Goodall and Mitchell 1976: 2]. Lynd now described his community as one that would be "as representative as possible of contemporary America, and ... at the same time compact and homogeneous enough to be manageable" [Lynd and Lynd 1956:7]. He also specified that the town was not dominated by one industry, had a "substantial artistic life" not connected to a college or university, and lacked acute local problems that "would mark it off from the mid-channel sort of American community" [Lynd and Lynd 1956:7-8].

The Lynds arrived in Muncie in January 1924. By April the institute had granted them full funding and they hired a staff of three women—a statistician, an assistant statistician, and a stenographer [H.M. Lynd 1983:34; Fox 1983:119; Lynd and Lynd 1956: 505]. The study was underway.

Yet the irony of the situation must strike us even today. Two young researchers with no experience or preparation in social research enter a town that was chosen at the last minute to do a religious study financed by a man whom the senior researcher had attacked. Add to that the fact that the senior researcher has already lost religious conviction, if he had ever had it. [Fox 1983:107-08]. One could hardly have expected the project to succeed even if Lynd had been a compromising person, which he was not.

The Lynds' priority was to devise a method for studying the community. They decided to adopt a scheme developed by the British social anthropologist W. H. R. Rivers to study primitive societies. This scheme divided human activities into six categories: getting a living, making a home, using leisure, engaging in religious practices, training the young, and engaging in community activities. The Lynds collected data in these six categories and analyzed them, using Wissler's paradigm of universal cultural patterns and Radcliffe-Brown's decoding of the meanings of social customs [Lynd and Lynd 1956:4; Smith 1983:n.p.].

There is considerable evidence that the Lynds floundered in the initial stages of the study. Helen Lynd indicated some confusion in her own mind, saying: "So it [the research] was a combination of formal and informal techniques. We would follow up written sources, we would go to meetings, we would later on interview the people, and then we had these informal contacts.

After eight or nine months, the people at the Institute were discontented because they didn't know where the study was going. And neither did we. Something would come up, and that would lead to something else, which wasn't on any chart... But the Institute people saw what they thought was a formlessness with no schedule being followed. I think it was true that what we were doing didn't fit into any category" [H.M. Lynd 1983:37].

The Lynds gradually found their way by a process of elimination and of trial and error. They decided against doing a full historical background and used the year 1890 as a base point instead. They divided the town into working and business classes. (The Lynds based their division on relations to *things* or people [Lynd and Lynd 1956:27].) Their data came from several sources: participant-observation; examination of documentary material (newspapers, minutes of organizations, diaries, and state and local histories); statistics; interviews (these included casual conversations and interviews with six leading ministers and 124 working-class and 40 business-class wives); questionnaires administered to 400 club members, to 700 and 800 high-school boys and girls in so—organizedphomore, junior, and senior classes, and to 550 boys and girls in junior and senior social science classes.

The Lynds did not place heavy reliance upon the last two methods of data collection, saying that the interview groups were too small and the samples were not necessarily representative. The questionnaires were not compiled nor tested for reliability or validity. By contemporary standards the Lynds' empirical and statistical treatments were simplistic [Lynd and Lynd 1956:505-09; Gordon 1958: 64; Madge 1962:135-41].

When the results were analyzed and put in book form, the Lynds had great difficulty getting it published. Raymond Fosdick disliked the book immensely. He had several specific criticisms: It was "scopey" and "its range of ideas and subjects" was "positively bewildering"; it gave an "impression of a confusion of theories and facts—of fragments of reality mixed up with a lot of phraseology which may be scientific—but perhaps not" [Harvey 1983:350]. Helen Merrell Lynd characterized the responses more directly. "They told Bob that they had read it and they thought it wasn't any good, it was unpublishable. They thought it didn't cohere. They'd never seen that kind of book before. They didn't think it was interesting, and they thought it was irreligious" [H.M. Lynd 1983:38].

It was published eventually, not by the institute [Harvey 1983:352; H.M. Lynd 1983:38; Fox 1983:122], but by Harcourt Brace after Alfred Harcourt had read it. It was an instant hit. It received front page reviews in *The New York Times* and the *Herald Tribune*. Helen Lynd was elated to discover that "Brentano's window was filled with nothing but *Middletown*" [H.M. Lynd 1983:40; Harvey 1983:352]. Nor was the success ephemeral. The book is one of the few social science books printed in the twentieth century in the United States that has never gone out of print. Indeed, it is accounted as one of the most significant books in recent American history. In 1970 Robert B. Downs listed it as one of twenty-five *Books That Changed American Society*, including *Middletown* with works by Beard, Thoreau, Addams, Myrdal, and Tocqueville.

Much of the success of *Middletown* was the result of two features. The first was the literary style. As William H. Wilson has perceptively noted: "The Lynds' subtle irony, their unobtrusive methods, their modesty and their narrative power lifted *Middletown* above the relic status of the Yankee City series. Their use of history was greatly superior to Warner's and is, indeed, a model of intelligent sociological-anthropological understanding of the past" [Wilson 1974:117].

Other analysts noted the irony, contrasting it with the style of other contemporary critics of American society. One such is Maurice Stein. "One literary technique they [the Lynds] used for accomplishing this [an all-knowing attitude toward the community] is a kind of dead-pan irony through which they report what the people of Muncie are experiencing while simultaneously critically commenting on that experience. Compared with Sinclair Lewis's cutting use of the same technique in his novels or with Thorstein Veblen's savage ironic manner, the Lynds are distinguished by their restraint, but their technique is related to these other forms of irony" [Stein 1960:309]. The comparison with Lewis is most apt, as several scholars have noted a link between *Middletown* and *Main Street* and *Babbitt*. All three give a devastating picture of life in small towns; all have much in addition to subject matter in common [Stein 1960:3; Fox 1983:126; Lingeman 1981:n.p.]. While *Middletown* on the surface seemed to be a more hospitable place than Gopher Prairie or Sauk Center, it was still not a good place to live. One observer, after reading the book, said "Muncie, Indiana seemed like a stopping point along the way to Dante's Inferno" [Cohen 1975:609].

The second feature was the content. What did the Lynds say in *Middletown*? They said a great deal. The book is full of the details of everyday life: what time people of different classes got up in the morning, who baked and who bought bread, who owned a car, how the car was used, how many persons went to the movies, how the laundry got done, what was taught in the schools, who went to church, what the minister said in church, how many women got married, how many couples got divorced, and what values different class members held. All of these became the stock of social history, a veritable treasure trove of data for further generations of scholars to mine [Stein 1960:3].

In addition to this descriptive material, the Lynds also analyzed the changes that had occurred in the town itself from 1890 to 1924. According to the Lynds, the town had been transformed from a rural, pre-industrial community into an industrial one; the main theme of the book was the impact of modernization upon a community. Starting as a happy town composed largely of skilled workers, Muncie had become a divided one composed mainly of anxious factory laborers caught in the toils of a heartless industrial system. As Richard Jensen has said, "*Middletown* was thus a morality tale. The authors were not poking fun at simple people, they were condemning a civilization. More calmly, they were exposing the contradictions of modernization" [Jensen 1979:307].

What had industrialization done to Muncie? It had resulted in a society divided into classes but not conscious of that division. Working-class neighborhoods had been broken up; families were increasingly isolated. Industrial workers now suffered blocked mobility as skilled workers were reduced to the level of unskilled factory operatives or were never able to struggle up out of that category. The Lynds calculated "that only one factory worker in fifty-three was promoted to foreman in a twenty-one month period" [Jensen 1979:312]. The workers, however, were willing to fit into the system because they had bought into the consumer society. They were willing to work at specialized jobs in order to buy commodities. Munsonians accepted consumer goods as symbols of social mobility, and the most distinguishing feature of *Middletown* was the mass consumption of mass-produced goods [Dixon-Goist 1977:48-9; Fox 1983:123-26]. The desire to consume was common to all levels of society. "The Lynds repeatedly emphasize that more expensive, stylish clothes were looked upon as symbols of social advance, and that the social rituals, particularly in the high schools, required a large outlay to provide the latest in gowns, shoes, stockings, and other adornments" [Hall 1972:492]. But the process was not complete; there remained vestiges of an older, happier time [Fox 1983:123]. This evaluation of Muncie was a significant one, providing a vast treasury of hypotheses and theories to develop, to check, or to reject.

There were, however, difficulties with *Middletown* that were to create severer ones for scholars following the paths first laid out by the Lynds. Because they were amateurs and were gingerly feeling their way, there were many gaps and shortcomings in their work. Perhaps the largest problem was the tendency of the Lynds to state conclusions rather than to prove them. This led to an overemphasis on the speed of social change, the power of the business elite, and the declining opportunities for upward mobility. Contrary evidence in their own data seemed to prove otherwise. For example, working-class politicians in Muncie defeated a city manager plan and a sewer construction project despite the promotion of these ideas by business interests. How could the Lynds claim that the business-class controlled the city when working-class politicians had their way? Nor did the Lynds ask older workers about their mobility, yet it is apparent from *Middletown* that farm boys were pushing these workers up the ladder of mobility [Wilson 1974:117; Jensen 1979: 313-14]. In other areas, the Lynds left out data that might have been useful. They failed, despite their emphasis upon social isolation, to determine household composition or kinship relationships; they barely mentioned older Munsonians; and they failed to show much of the everyday life of the lower segment of the business class, blacks, or even non-industrial workers [Hoover 1976:n.p.; Gordon 1958:24].

Even before *Middletown* had been published, the Lynds had embarked upon new careers. In 1928, Helen Lynd began what was to be a long teaching career at Sarah Lawrence [Fox 1983:122, 127, 131; H.M. Lynd 1983:38-41; Smith 1979-80:100-104]. In 1926 Robert Lynd became assistant director for Education Research for the Commonwealth Fund, and the next year he became acting and then permanent secretary of the Social Science Research Council, largely because of his old teacher Wesley Mitchell. After *Middletown*'s success, he received two offers for tenured professorships: one the

Charles Horton Cooley chair at the University of Michigan and the other at Columbia. He chose Columbia, beginning in 1931 after receiving a doctorate for *Middletown*. (The Lynds blue-penciled out all that Helen had written to make the book eligible as the dissertation.) Before assuming his teaching position, Lynd received another research assignment, however. He joined President Hoover's Research Committee on Social Trends, again largely because of the influence of Wesley Mitchell, the chairman. Mitchell solicited Lynd to apply to the director of the study of consumption, William Ogburn, a sociologist from the University of Chicago, and supported his cause afterwards.

Lynd became the center of controversy again while working for the committee. Assigned to study consumer affairs, he submitted a chapter that stirred up considerable fury because of its critique of the Bureau of Commerce and advocacy of a Department for Consumers. Lynd found himself in a situation similar to that he faced with *Middletown*, as author of a manuscript his sponsors were refusing to publish. Once again, another scholar saved him. Dr. Alice Hamilton, a noted authority on industrial health, supported Lynd, arguing that the chapter was, if anything, not strong enough. Her interference saved his essay, "The People as Consumers" [Smith 1979-80:101-104; Fox 1983:131-32].

Lynd continued his public service in the 1930s while still at Columbia. Although he began two major empirical studies at Columbia from 1931 to 1934, he never completed them. Both showed lines of inquiry he was to follow in his return to Muncie. Lynd wished to determine the impact of the Depression on first, 150 native-born white Manhattan families and, second, 200 business-class families in Montclair, New Jersey. Before finishing these projects, he became a New Dealer. Roosevelt appointed him to membership on the Consumers' Advisory Board of the N.R.A., then chairman of its Committee on Standards, and finally, in 1934, to membership on the executive board [Fox 1983:132-33]. He never was able to finish his research in New York; instead he went back to Middletown.

Lynd returned to Muncie in 1935 to write a sequel to *Middletown*, encouraged by the publisher Alfred Harcourt, who wanted another best seller [Fox 1983:134]. The Institute on Social and Religious Research was not involved; it had closed a year earlier. The change in sponsorship, however, meant that Lynd had less money to employ researchers and would be unable to spend as much time in the town. He came with five assistants but without his wife [H.M. Lynd 1983:37; Harvey 1983:353]. Lynd actually lived only one summer in Muncie; the total time expended by all the researchers on the project was one-tenth that of the original study [Bahr 1982:2-3; Madge 1962:131].

In an interview given shortly after his arrival in Muncie in June 1935, Lynd described his goal as not to write another book about Muncie but, instead, to add an appendix to *Middletown*, one that would outline major changes in the town in the last decade.

In preparing his new study, Lynd indicated that he wanted local residents to critique *Middletown* as well as provide new information [*Muncie Evening Press* 12 June 1935; Fox 1983:129-30]. Lynd had already received both; and, because of his intellectual hegira, had changed his views of what the Muncie experience had meant. Before coming to Muncie, he had been given a graduate research paper, "Muncie and *Middletown*, 1924 to 1934," by a doctoral student in history, Lynn I. Perrigo, from the University of Colorado. Perrigo had been a grade-school teacher and Boy Scout executive in Muncie from 1922 to 1932; he had left the town for graduate study in 1933 [Bahr 1982:5-8]. The paper had not only criticized *Middletown* in general but suggested that it had failed to include any discussion of the influence of the Ball family.

Perrigo was not the only influence on Lynd. For the first time, he had read Marx [Bell 1974:254; Madge 1962:130]. The extent to which the reading of Marx affected him is a matter of dispute. He had become increasingly radical, partly because of his alienation from the empiricism of the sociology department at Columbia and partly because of general disillusionment with the state of American society. He never formally became a Marxist, but remained a native American populist [Fox 1983:137-38; Etzkowitz 1979-80:41-54; Miller 1979-80:58-62] with some Marxist notions.

Other influences on the second study were Lynd's five years of study of consumer affairs, which had given him a low opinion of the rationality of the average American when faced with the power of advertising, and his experience as a New Dealer, which caused him to advocate more governmental protection against corporate advertisers [Fox 1983:132-33]. These experiences led him to a more general questioning of power. As Fox has said: "While *Middletown* noted the strong class basis of life in Muncie, it spent very little time on the questions of who made decisions there, how they were made, and who benefited from them. After his experience as a consumer advocate, Lynd could no longer overlook such issues" [Smith 1979-80:111].

In any case, *Middletown in Transition* was quite different from *Middletown* in many ways. Lynd made no new surveys, and yet, according to one author, his "grasp of what went on behind the scenes seemed much surer that a decade before" [Bahr 1982:3]. Another has claimed that the researchers were able to make a decent study in a shorter time because they had an already established network of informants and used already known techniques—collecting statistics, clipping newspapers, and so on [Bahr 1982:3;

Madge 1962:147-48]. Despite these apologias for the second study, it is obvious that *Middletown in Transition* was less empirical than *Middletown*. Colin Bell has pointed out the problem that this creates. "The really awkward question is whether *Middletown* makes *Middletown in Transition* equally problematic because in the restudy Lynd's theories over-determined his findings whereas by contrast 'data are left to speak for themselves' in the first study. Certainly far less selection and far less argument takes place in *Middletown*" [Bell 1974:254-55].

Given opportunities to change his theoretical framework by using newer sociological ideas, Lynd refused. For example, he derived a sixfold classification of classes in Muncie—one upper, two middle, and three lower—similar to the system of W. Lloyd Warner, but then failed to use it. He did distinguish between those members of the business class who owned the means of production and the cast of supporters of that class, clerical and office workers [Gordon 1958:69; Madge 1962:159; Etzkowitz 1979- 80: 45; Jensen 1979:310-11].

Despite the advantages afforded by increased knowledge of the process of community studies and lack of conflict this time with a sponsor, Lynd did not achieve instant success with his second study. The immediate reaction was less favorable, nor was the long-term reception in the end favorable. The book has not remained in print as long as *Middletown*, fading in and out as demand wells and ebbs. The reasons for this cooler reception are clear. The book is fairly described by Fox as "rapidly thrown together, with much less conceptual, stylistic and organizational care" [Fox 1983:136].

Not all scholarly reviewers have been quite as harsh. Maurice Stein, for example, in his influential and provocative *The Eclipse of Community*, has argued that *Middletown in Transition* was more of a "methodical coup" than *Middletown*. His reason is that *Middletown in Transition* "allows us to see how a historical event, one dominant event in the decade of the thirties, affected the main directions of change in a community where these had already been carefully plotted" [Stein 1960:56]. Stein's opinion, however, is not shared by the majority of critics.

What did *Middletown in Transition* say? The second book used the same familiar six divisions as the first, but within these divisions the authors contracted or expanded the material. For example, in *Middletown in Transition* one chapter is devoted to religion, constituting only five percent of the total, whereas in *Middletown* religion occupies four chapters and 20 percent of the total. On the other hand, the second book spends one-fifth of its space on government, compared to one-fifteenth in the first. Finally, *Middletown in Transition* devotes 10 percent of its space to leisure as compared to twice that in *Middletown*.

In addition to the shift in priorities, *Middletown in Transition* included two completely new chapters that became the most controversial of all. They were entitled "The X Family: A Pattern of Business-Class Control" and "The Middletown Spirit." In the former, Lynd traced the power of the Ball family in Muncie, claiming that it was a "reigning royal family" [Lynd and Lynd 1965: 77; Fox 1983:134]. Lynd then examined the Balls' power using the same categories previously devoted to the study of the community: making a living, making a home, and so on. He concluded that the Balls had increased their power during the Depression because of their financial liquidity and were now the moving force behind the town [Lynd and Lynd 1965:77; Fox 1983:134].

In "The Middletown Spirit," the penultimate chapter in *Middletown in Transition*, Lynd created a list of Middletown values and opposed that list with another list of contradictory values. This eighty-five page chapter, the heart of the book, is a scathing critique of the values of a small-town community. Lynd did acknowledge that Munsonians were friendly, kind, and neighborly; but, despite federal aid during the Depression, they still clung to a vision of the world of self-help that was illusory [Lynd and Lynd 1965:402-87]. They still believed in a social Darwinian system in which individuals rose or fell in terms of their strength and energy.

Both of these chapters created problems for critics, then and now. The first question that naturally arose was why, if the Balls were so powerful, did the Lynds fail to mention that fact in *Middletown*? Lynd's rationale is not convincing; he explains that he had not characterized the Balls, or other similar families, as an upper class because of the belief that these families were integrated into the business class. After the book was written, he discovered that the belief was wrong and, without outside prompting, decided to correct the error in *Middletown in Transition* [Lynd and Lynd 1965:74].

This rather lame explanation omits the question of power. Colin Bell thinks that a discussion of power was included because Lynd was wiser in 1935: he knew what he was doing in the second study, and he had read Marx. But Bell admits there is a problem, saying that *Middletown in Transition* "has a lot to say about what we would call class conflict in the Depression yet their [the Lynds'] first study of only a decade earlier hardly mentions such problems despite being by acclamation a superb de-mystifying account of American small town culture" [Bell 1974:254; Stein 1960: 58; Fox 1983:135]. A more plausible explanation has been suggested by Howard Bahr. He claims that Lynd was only dimly aware of the Ball family and was stimulated by Lynn Perrigo to write a chapter on the X family's power. Bahr's analysis of the structure of Perrigo's paper and the *Middletown in Transition* chapter shows that the latter has taken Perrigo's summary sentences and developed them into paragraphs or pages. The former is the skeleton upon which the latter builds [Bahr 1982:8, 21].

Another explanation is that proffered by Fox, who bases it upon Lynd's own admission that if he had known about the influence of the Balls before coming to Muncie, he would have gone elsewhere. When he discovered their role in his initial visit, according to Fox, he refused to discuss it because it might negate his "argument about 'modern American culture'" [Fox 1983:134-35]. If Fox is, in fact, correct, Lynd was guilty of subjective and distorted reporting in the first instance.

The second controversial chapter, "The Middletown Spirit," is also puzzling. Lynd liked Munsonians. He made friends easily, and, according to Helen, "He always claimed that he could have lived happily in Muncie," whereas she could not [H.M. Lynd 1983: 36]. This claim is substantiated by *Middletown* itself. One of the virtues of the book, in the opinion of Stein, was the personal style, which combined critical detachment with disarming sympathy. "They showed that it was possible for sophisticated intellectuals to root themselves in a community that was alien to their present lives, if not to their past experiences, sufficiently to produce a study of the community which conveyed the inner meanings of its round of life vividly and truthfully" [Stein 1960:312-13]. Why, given the sympathy and insight, did Lynd criticize Munsonians so strongly in his second book? [Fox 1983:130].

Fox argues that this response was a consequence of Lynd's growing conviction that Munsonians were irrational—unable to resist the power of advertisers or the prevailing economic and political system. Nor can Helen be blamed for this chapter; although it probably reflected her view of Muncie, she was not involved in writing it. Perhaps Fox is correct in saying,

"When he concluded in the 1930s that Muncie had indeed succumbed to colonization by pecuniary values, that popular democracy was dead, he issued a biting epitaph for both Muncie and for his own book *Middletown* in the euphemistically titled *Middletown in Transition*. He might just as well have called it *Middletown Interred*" [Fox 1983:111].

What about other changes in Muncie in 1935? According to Richard Jensen, the Lynds found "no new manifestation that had not been apparent in 1924." Modernization had progressed even though social values had not changed to keep pace. The town's appearance had improved, largely because of money infused into the community by the New Deal. Because of the lack of any new general theory, Jensen believes *Middletown in Transition* was a "much shriller book, of permanent interest only in its descriptions of the impact of the Depression on family life and community decision making" [Jensen 1979:310-17]. Stein, on the other hand, thinks the book was revealing because it showed that the Depression had destroyed the community's spirit.

"*Middletown in Transition* reports a final breakdown of any sense of the character or workings of the whole community among most of its residents. It was no longer possible to understand the processes of Middletown life in terms of the functioning of its business class and its working class. Outside forces intervened to disrupt the life activities of both" [Stein 1960:65].

Despite the supposed burial of Muncie in *Middletown in Transition*, the town lived on. Its residents finally took heed of their status as inhabitants of a much-studied town after the publication of the second book. Not that they read it. Perrigo had indicated his chagrin that few persons in the town had read *Middletown* or even heard of it [Bahr 1982:11]. *Middletown in Transition* aroused more interest indirectly because significant readers saw it. Impressed by *Middletown in Transition*, the editors of *Life* magazine decided to show how prosperity was returning to the city, how federal aid had helped, and how the local citizens had voted for F.D.R. *Life* had begun its pilgrimage to discover America in the midst of the Depression; the publication of *Middletown in Transition* had given it a new lead [Goldberg 1986: 188]. It chose Margaret Bourke-White who had just photographed Fort Peck Dam to go to Muncie.

Bourke-White came to Muncie as a tyro photographer and left as a full-fledged photojournalist. Her photo-essay on Muncie illustrated Lynd's emphasis upon class division in a fashion obvious even to nonreaders. "She took a series of portraits of townspeople that had the variety of a collection of 'types': a prissy-mouthed schoolteacher, a fat city father sporting a big grin and a bigger cigar. Most telling were the set pieces of families and clubs, which began with the richest manufacturer in town, who had introduced 'the first pink-coated fox hunt ever to astonish an Indiana landscape,' and ran all the way down the economic scale to two poor hillbillies in a one-room shack" [Goldberg 1986:188-89].

The editor of *Life*, Wilson Hicks, was tremendously impressed, although he thought Bourke-White slighted women and was better with objects than with people. The reaction in Muncie was immediate and negative. Pictures of dirt-floored houses in Shed Town contrasted unfavorably with Ball mansions, and the general tenor of the article was construed to be unflattering. This, combined with the negativism of "The Middletown Spirit," resulted in a general revulsion against all the studies, combined with perverse pride that Muncie was on the map. The latter feeling was accentuated when others took notice. The *Muncie Star*, for example, printed a report on 10 October 1937 that the Scherbaum children of Muncie had received a request from their Viennese uncle to send him information and photographs about Muncie, which he had heard was an ideal and famous city. But such articles gradually faded from newspapers, and the town lapsed into its old ways.

Lynd returned to New York City and to the Department of Sociology at Columbia University after his stint in Muncie. Increasingly depressed and increasingly feeling outclassed by more empirical sociologists, Lynd was unable to complete another major study. His two Depression surveys remained unfinished. In 1940 he published *Knowledge for What?*, a stinging critique of value-free empirical research. By this time, he had "become obsessed with the need to achieve *the* synthesis that would enable him to write the definitive study of power in American society" [Lindt 1979-80:8; Fox 1983:140-41]. He never finished this task either, although he did lecture on the topic to his classes in the 1940s and 1950s. He did write two preliminary pieces that indicate the direction in which his mind was going. They were "Power in the United States," a review of C. Wright Mill's *The Power Elite* in the *Nation* (12 May 1956), and "Power in American Society as Resource and Problem" in Arthur Kornhauser, ed., *Problems of Power in American Society* (1957) [S. Lindt 1979-80:8; Fox 1983:140-41]. When he died in 1971, his aspirations died with him. Nor did Helen Lynd, who died a decade later, continue his quest after his death.

But the impact of the Lynds' work continued to be felt by scholars. Like other classic works, the Middletown books provided much for future researchers. Not only were they a foundation for sociologists; other disciplines used them as well.

Perhaps the first group of scholars to use Middletown materials were social historians. The books contained such a wealth of data that anyone doing a comparison of behavior and attitudes over time almost automatically turned to them for information.

Among the first historians to do so was Frederick Lewis Allen. His *Only Yesterday: An Informal History of the 1920s* [1931] used *Middletown* to a great degree. In his appendix, his first acknowledgement reads thus: "Naturally I have made frequent use, not only in Chapter Five, but elsewhere, of the extraordinarily varied and precise information collected in *Middletown*, that remarkable sociological study of an American city by Robert S. Lynd and Helen Merrell Lynd; I do not see how any conscientious historian of the Post-war Decade could afford to neglect this mine of material" [Allen 1964:298].

In his succeeding volume, *Since Yesterday* [1939], Allen was equally generous to *Middletown in Transition*, quoting his original remarks in *Only Yesterday* and saying "*Mutatis mutandis*, I must now say the same thing of their *Middletown in Transition*.... I have quoted from it more frequently in the present volume than from any other source, and have leaned more upon it than the number of quotations would suggest" [Allen 1961:277]. What had Allen used the most? The answer was information concerning manners and morals, how the automobile changed sexual behavior, and the decline of religious influence, in other words, growing permissive behavior.

Allen's books were not the only histories to use the data, but the data used changed with each generation of historians. The subjects that appear to be of greatest interest at present are women, consumerism, and automobiles. These reflect the growing concern with women's roles, with the increasing commercialization of society, and with the impact of the automobile on the landscape in contemporary America.

A few examples of each will suffice. Linda Hall's 1971 Phi Alpha Theta Prize Essay, "Fashion and Style in the Twenties: The Change," uses information from *Middletown* to show how advertising had changed both the making and wearing of clothes. By the 1920s, fewer working-class women sewed, and all classes were most anxious to be in style [Hall 1972:490, 195-96]. In their essays on women's roles and housework in a 1980 book, Joann Vanek, Estelle B. Freedman, and Susan M. Strasser base their analysis, in part, on the Lynds' studies. Vanek concludes that the description of women's roles in the 1920s was on the mark and holds true for today. "The Lynds' description of the way family roles change remains surprisingly accurate. Although there is every appearance of change today, the patterning of work in the home and in the labor force continues to reflect deep cultural beliefs about the duties and responsibilities of the sexes. As the Lynds observed, change in employment and family roles has not proceeded from diminished support for traditional values. Rather, cultural support for employment of wives had lagged behind actual participation in the labor force" [Vanek 1980:283]. Estelle B. Freedman had earlier made the same point, arguing that the Lynds in *Middletown in Transition* had shown that the need for women to work to augment family income during the Depression, although it confused family roles, actually re-emphasized traditional femininity [Freedman 1974:380-81].

Strasser in her *Never Done: A History of American Housework* quotes the Lynds on the change in dietary patterns from the 1890s to the 1920s, but her major emphasis is on electrical appliance advertising in the 1920s. This advertising capitalized on motherhood sentiments by stating that a good mother put her children first and then arguing that electrical appliances freed the mother for more time with her children [Strasser 1980b:28-9, 78, 97].

The concern with women's roles merges easily with the problems of a commercial society. Rayna Rapp and Ellen Ross in *Ms* magazine used Lynd data to support their thesis that the commercial culture already extant in the 1920s was the greatest barrier to the success of feminism [Rapp and Ross 1983:54-6]. Women bought into consumer society with their desire for new devices that merely extended their traditional roles.

Popular magazines were not the only ones that saw the Lynds as pioneers in the analysis of consumer society. Indeed, serious scholars were beginning to hail Robert S. Lynd as a critic ahead of his time. Two such scholars were Mark C. Smith and Robert Wightman Fox. Smith wrote in the *Journal of History of Sociology* early in 1980, and Fox's important article, "Epitaph for Middletown: Robert S. Lynd and the Analysis of Consumer Culture," was published three years later in *The Culture of Consumption*. Both articles used Lynd's concern with the impact of advertising and consumer behavior as the keystone of their works. Both argued that Lynd had been one of the first to understand the transformation wrought by consumer society.

Certainly a significant aspect of a consumer society such as America is automobile use. Students of that phenomenon also use *Middletown* and *Middletown in Transition* as benchmarks. Both Blaine Brownell and James J. Flink quoted the Lynds' statistics on automobile registration to show the powerful attraction automobiles have always had for Americans. Even the Depression did not cause registrations to shrink as Munsonians continued to prefer automobiles to bathtubs [Brownell 1972:31-2; Flink 1972:451-73]. In addition to these scholars, several journalists also used the Middletown studies as springboards for their works on contemporary automobility. When Leon Mandel was doing research for his book, *Driven: The American Four-Wheeled Love Affair*, he came to Muncie, claiming that he was the first scholar to do so since the Lynds. In a chapter entitled "Middletown Transformed," Mandel argued that the Lynds wrongly characterized the automobile as entertainment when, in reality, it was a major element in the town's prosperity in the 1920s [Mandel 1977:34- 59]. Finally, Michele Krebs, writing in the Centennial Celebration Issue of *Automobile News*, journeyed to Muncie to encapsulate the Lynds' descriptions of the impact of automobiles on the city [Krebs 1985].

Not all those writers who used data from the Lynds searched for role change, consumer demand, or automobile use. Some used them to analyze popular culture. Typical of such attempts was Jill H. Kasen, whose "Whither the Self-Made Man? Comic Culture and the Crisis of Legitimation in the United States" did a content analysis of comic strips and compared the status of comic-strip characters with people in the Lynds' work. Kasen concluded that the Lynds' contention that businessmen had usurped the place of professionals was not demonstrated in comic strips, which showed a pastoral status structure based upon social honor [Kasen 1980:132-35]. On the other hand, Arthur Frank Wertheim used *Middletown* and *Middletown in Transition* in his content analysis of radio comedy during the Depression. The content analysis showed that these programs were designed for family entertainment because of the moralistic overtones, thus confirming the Lynds' argument concerning the increasing role of radio in Muncie life [Wertheim 1976:511-12].

For the "new" social historians who began to write in the 1960s, the rich details of the Lynd volumes were less interesting than their theories, an understandable development in view of these scholars' concern about changes in social structure and social mobility, taking after their sociological colleagues. Foremost among these historians was Stephan Thernstrom, whose study *Poverty and Progress: Social Mobility in a Nineteenth Century City* asked whether there was more social mobility in nineteenth-century Newburyport, Massachusetts, than in contemporary societies. He concluded that there was not. The Lynds' blocked-mobility thesis, according to him, was not proven. The fault lay in inadequate research; the Lynds had not studied the origins of Middletown's labor force: "In Muncie as in Newburyport, it seems clear, the new factories were not crowded with *déclassé* artisans; the factory labor force was made of men who had little status to lose migrants from rural America or the Old World" [Thernstrom 1964:216]. Despite his disagreement with the blocked-mobility thesis, Thernstrom did agree with the Lynds that the advent of consumerism, particularly the purchase of automobiles, signaled an acceptance of middle-class values and gave many workers the illusory perception of upward mobility [Thernstrom 1964:222].

More recently, another contemporary social historian, John Bodnar, has cited the Lynds' insight into the role played by consumer society in helping immigrants adjust to their new life. "In their study of Middletown, the Lynds found that the community's workers were 'running for dear life' in the business of making money in order to acquire more and more of their subjective wants" [Bodnar 1980:46]. This race made immigrants from Europe similar to native inhabitants of rural America.

Whereas historians used the data from *Middletown* and *Middletown in Transition* as a foundation for their specialized studies and attacked the blocked-mobility thesis, political scientists were more interested in the question of who exercised power in the town.

Perhaps the leading scholar in this area was Nelson W. Polsby, who, in the late fifties, attacked the thesis that the Balls ran Middletown. In reaction to such works as C. Wright Mills' *The Power Elite*, Polsby denied that the Balls exercised uniform, constant, and successful influence on the city for their own benefit [Polsby 1959:232-36; 1960:562-603; 1967:14-24]. Using the example of councilmen from the south side of Muncie blocking a sewer construction project favored by the Balls, the Yale-trained Polsby argued that dominating the town was incomplete if the Balls were unable to clean up the polluted river that ran in front of their doors and smelled up their living rooms [Polsby 1960:594]. He argued instead that power in Muncie was divided among competing groups.

The study of power in communities became, in the 1960s, a struggle between those who claimed elite rule and those who opted for a pluralistic model that held that various groups became dominant in the political arena as issues changed. By the 1980s, the struggle itself had been superseded as new interests came to the fore. The emphasis shifted from the question of who governed to an analysis of political culture, focusing on the impact of local policies on attitudes and behaviors [Titus 1981:438]. The terms of the argument on the issue of power were no longer those set by the Lynds.

For most sociologists, the ruling interest was class, and their general opinion of the Lynds' work was that it lacked relevance for those on the cutting edge of the discipline. Stein's description of the use of *Middletown* by sociologists is most apt. "Unfortunately, sociological readers of the Lynd study have simply not been diligent enough. *Middletown* is now read mainly by undergraduates as a sociological classic of the kind everyone should be familiar with even though its significance is primarily historical" [Stein 1960:95].

Yet the Middletown books continued to have influence in the discipline, an influence that extended beyond national borders. Martin Jay has traced the impact of the Lynds on the Frankfurt School and the Institute for Social Research. When the institute moved from Germany to New York City and to Columbia University, it did so in part because of the presence of Robert Lynd. Moreover, its work reflected Lynd's thesis. In *Studien Uber Autoritat und Familie*, the institute acknowledged its intellectual debt to *Middletown*, a debt that was obvious in the institute's conclusions that the bourgeois family was increasingly involved in the consumption of commodities while the proletarian family was being dissolved by external exploitation [Jay 1973:39, 124-25].

The emphasis on socio-economic determinants of the classes with its Marxian overtones that characterized the Frankfurt School and also the Middletown books lost favor in the 1950s as the cold war expanded. Instead, sociologists turned to Warner's definition of class, which was based upon ritual and life-styles, or so said E. Digby Baltzell in 1953 [Bendix and Lipset 1966:266- 67]. Just as the study of power in communities had become less fashionable, so too had the study of class as economically determined.

Despite questions concerning the adequacy of the Lynds' class definitions, sociologists continued to use their correlations. These correlations included those between social class and academic achievement, between social class and membership in voluntary associations, and between social class and parental values. The findings were pioneer ones and adjudged to be valid. Nor were sociologists alone; *Middletown in Transition*'s conclusions even have appeared in the *Harvard Law Review* as evidence that class discrimination was repugnant to traditional notions of equal opportunity [Binford 1971:28; McPherson 1981:709; Kolin 1976:538: *Harvard Law Review* 1971].

As might be expected, scholars expressed continuing concern over the Lynds' research methods. The criticisms ranged from the most minute points to the most general. William Foote Whyte, in a guide to doing studies in the field, criticized the Lynds for not using more local informants in their original study, saying the chapter on the X family in *Middletown in Transition* was much superior because of such use [Whyte 1984:38]. Several scholars from different disciplines found fault with the disguising of the names of Muncie and its inhabitants in both books [Colson 1976: 265; Morriesey 1985:49; Borenstein 1978:58]. Among these scholars were the distinguished anthropologist Elizabeth Colson and the equally distinguished historian Oscar Handlin, who was particularly put out. "The reader knowing something about the bias of travelers compensates for the distortions in the descriptions of society by Peter Kalm or Timothy Dwight; the adjustments are more difficult when it comes to evaluating the useful yet tricky evidence in *Middletown* or in a Harris poll" [Handlin 1979:260].

Still others objected to the failure to put Muncie into a larger national context, pointing out that local residents were losing control over the city's industries and asking why the Lynds had not addressed themselves to that problem [Goheen 1974:366-67]. Not all agree with this criticism, insisting instead that the studies have become metaphors for universal experiences that transcend local specificity. "With this in mind it is easier to understand the procedure of those sociologists who have not set out to 'test a theory' but rather began with an anecdote and then discovered what larger domain it represented. This can be seen in the studies by the Lynds of *Middletown* and by Lloyd Warner of *Yankee City*. Muncie, Indiana, as such, is largely irrelevant to what we learn from the Lynds' study about the *discrepancy* between economic myths and economic realities" [Brown 1976:190].

A final criticism of method will suffice. As early as 1957, John Gillin argued that, although competent studies of modern national culture originated with the Lynds, the Middletown studies were not equal to the best studies of tribal and simple peasant communities because they were incomplete ethnologies. They were instead interactional studies, which lacked the kind of detail expected in the best ethnologies [Gillin 1957:25].

Still the Middletown studies tradition did not die. When Robert Lynd died in 1971, he was still remembered for his work in Muncie. Paul Lazersfeld testified at his memorial service to the validity of Lynd's effort. Lazersfeld even claimed that he had independently established the typicality of Muncie. During the Depression, Lazersfeld supervised National Youth Administration enrollees in New Jersey. Pressed to find work for these students, Lazersfeld assigned them to tasks of compiling cultural profiles of one hundred of the largest cities in the United States. The city that most closely resembled the average was Muncie [Lazersfeld 1975:266].

These remarks by Lazersfeld were curious since he and Elihu Katz had rejected Muncie as the site for their book *Personal Influence* [1955], even though the community was on their short list. The reasons given for their rejection were that it was unwise for sociologists to restudy a community and that the community was a one-industry town [Madge 1962:135]. Others did not agree; as early as 1963, scholars were advocating the restudy of Muncie and, in 1974, Colin Bell asked why replication, which was so central to the scientific method, was so infrequently used in sociology [Bell 1974:253].

The first major replication of the original Middletown studies began in 1975, when Middletown III researchers arrived in Muncie. Fifty years after the Lynds had finished their first field work, new researchers were just beginning a new effort. Financed by a half-million-dollar grant from the National Science Foundation, Middletown III scholars rented a small office near the White River and proceeded to examine the town. The researchers spent more time in the community than the Lynds, more than two years, although the senior researchers spent only about one year each and rotated their assignments so that they were not often in town at the same time. The researchers included some twenty other persons—housewives, doctoral and post-doctoral students, secretaries and interviewers—who spent varying lengths of time on the project [Caplow, Bahr, Chadwick et al 1983:v-ix; Peterson 1982].

There were other differences as well. Instead of unknown and untrained scholars, the three major researchers—Theodore Caplow, Howard Bahr, and Bruce Chadwick—were all professional sociologists with considerable reputations. The senior member of the team, Caplow, had been a student of Lynd in the late 1930s and was Commonwealth Professor at the University of Virginia at the time of the study. He had written many books and articles, including *The Sociology of Work, Two Against One: Coalitions in Triads*, and *The Academic Marketplace*. A man of wide-ranging interests, from theoretical sociology to the sociology of work, social organization, and poverty, Caplow had served as a consultant for several governments, domestic and foreign, and for private industries and had received many grants from a number of funding agencies. Moreover, his basic attitude was quite different from Lynd's. In a book published just before he began research on Muncie, *Toward Social Hope* [1975], he argued that human society was progressing, that social problems were less serious than in the past, and that one of the functions of social science was to publicize those truths. Caplow's optimism was almost the mirror image of Lynd's pessimism; he believed the system was working.

His two junior partners were both Mormons from Brigham Young University. Howard M. Bahr was a professor of sociology and director of the Family and Demographic Research Institute at Brigham Young. He had worked with Caplow in a study of alcoholics in New York City that resulted in a book entitled *Old Men Drunk and Sober* and had written *Skid Row: An Introduction to Disaffiliation, Women Alone, Sunshine Widows: Adapting to Sudden Bereavement*, and *Life in Large Families*. Bruce Chadwick at the time of the study was professor and chairman of the Department of Sociology at Brigham Young University. He had written *American Ethnicity* and co-edited *Native Americans Today* and *Population, Resources, and the Future*. These researchers were older than the Lynds had been during their time in Muncie, more mature and settled scholars. They were also encumbered family men. Together they brought fourteen children to Muncie to go to school, to say nothing of other older children who were living elsewhere [Caplow, Bahr, Chadwick et al 1983:vi]. Finally, to add additional weight to the project, Middletown III had an advisory board of distinguished scholars that included both sociologists and political scientists. They were Otis Dudley Duncan, Jeffrey K. Hadden, Reuben Hill, Charles Hyneman, Alex Inkeles, Sheldon Stryker, and Wilbert E. Moore.

Given the professionalism of the researchers, it is not surprising that the replication was more overtly sociological. Middletown III relied on sophisticated statistical analysis and much more extensive surveying than did the Lynds, while still employing many of their other techniques—newspaper clippings, attending public and private meetings, and interviewing movers and shakers. The group made thirteen major surveys and several smaller ones, compared to the Lynds' three (which were replicated and proved most valuable) [Caplow, Bahr, Chadwick et al 1983:v]. In addition, Middletown III hired the census to "retabulate information about Middletown's population from the original enumerations of the seven decennial censuses from 1910 to 1970" [Caplow, Bahr, Chadwick et al 1983:vii]. Because of the larger number of scholars, the use of more surveys, and the help of the census bureau, Middletown III accumulated much more data than the Lynds.

Unlike *Middletown*, Middletown III findings were published before any book appeared. In a series of papers and articles, participants presented their findings at various meetings and in a number of different scholarly journals. By 1985, these publications had totaled more than fifty. From the first published article, "Half a Century of Change in Adolescent Attitudes: Replication of a Middletown Survey by the Lynds," which appeared in the spring 1979 issue of *Public Opinion Quarterly* [Caplow and Bahr 1979:1-17], the direction the study was to take was obvious. The amount of social change that had occurred in Muncie was less than expected; although technological modernization continued apace, values had remained remarkably stable. This conclusion was to appear again and again.

The high school survey that replicated the Lynds' survey of 1924 first demonstrated that stability. The researchers "were startled by the persistence and prevalence of non-modern attitudes among Middletown's adolescents" [Bahr, Caplow, and Leigh 1980: 223]. Their explanation for this lack of change was intriguing. "The explanation of this peculiar and unanticipated stability is found, we think, in the slowing of modernization, revealed by the telephone data and other series. The forces of change have been winding down in Middletown and will probably continue to do so for some time to come. Middletown adolescents of today have so far experienced less social change than their parents or grandparents, who lived through the cataclysmic transition from a predominantly rural to a predominantly urban society and from an economy based on muscular effort to one drawing on vast supplies of mechanical power" [Bahr, Caplow, and Leigh 1980:231].

When the findings of Middletown III were published as a book, they varied in form from the Lynds' efforts. Instead of writing one book surveying several aspects of Muncie life, the scholars opted for a topical approach: each volume would cover but one subject. The first such volume was *Middletown Families*, published in 1982. Unlike *Middletown*, *Middletown Families* was the product of collaboration of five scholars, Caplow, Bahr, and Chadwick joined by Reuben Hill, a family sociologist, and Margaret Holmes Williamson, an anthropologist. Most of the book was written by the senior authors, but Hill and Williamson wrote one chapter each. Hill's chapter, "American Families During the Twentieth Century," was essentially a historical look at the status of American families in the twentieth century with a review of the most significant scholarly studies on that topic. It placed the Middletown findings in context. Williamson's chapter, "Family Symbolism in Festivals," was an analysis of major holidays in Muncie from an anthropological point of view informed by semiotic theory. Its conclusion was that the focus of Muncie's festivals was now on the family instead of on city or country [Caplow, Bahr, Chadwick et al 1983:225].

Neither Hill's nor Williamson's chapters bore any resemblance to work done by the Lynds. The former chapter compared Muncie with the nation, an effort the Lynds never attempted. The latter chapter also studied subject matter that was ignored by the Lynds. Another new topic was kinship, which was analyzed empirically to determine the shape of families. The senior researchers found that kinship ties permeated Muncie and formed the strongest link between persons in the town except for marriage bonds in combining "normative obligation and personal affection" [Caplow, Bahr, Chadwick et al 1983: 223-24]. These three chapters extended the sweep of the Lynd studies but were not useful in determining changes or continuities in the Muncie family. The other chapters were, however, and their conclusions are contained in the final one. Its title is revealing of its contents. "The Myth of the Declining Family" insists that the Muncie family was stronger in the 1970s than in the 1920s. "Tracing the changes from the 1920s to the 1970s, we discovered increased family solidarity, a smaller generation gap, closer marital communication, more religion, and less mobility. With respect to the major features of family life, the trend of the past two generations has run in the opposite direction from the trend that nearly everyone perceives and talks about" [Caplow, Bahr, Chadwick et al 1983:323; Caplow 1981b:349-69].

The reason why the myth of family decline persisted, according to Caplow, was that it served the purposes of several interest groups—welfare bureaucrats, doomsayers, and so on—which had become dependent upon it [Caplow 1982c]. This essentially conservative conclusion denied the validity of Lynd's prediction that the family was dying.

Equally significant and equally destructive of the findings of *Middletown* was the general trend toward equality in Muncie found by Middletown III. The two classes—working and business—were becoming more alike, as were male and female roles. Men who worked in factories no longer had to rise earlier in the morning than their business-class counterparts, and they often earned more. Their wives no longer had to work longer and harder at housework than their business-class sisters; business-class women now worked outside the home like their working-class counterparts. *Middletown Families* concluded that "Within this dominant life-style, most of the differences that the Lynds observed between business-class families and working-class families half a century ago have by now been eroded away. Working-class people play golf and tennis, travel in Europe for pleasure, and send their children to college. Business-class people do their own laundry and mow their own lawns. Business-class wives with children at home are as likely to hold full-time jobs as working-class wives" [Caplow, Bahr, Chadwick et al 1983:6-8, 15, 18-19, 88-90].

By 1982, when *Middletown Families* was published, work was already almost completed on the second book in the series, *All Faithful People*. Published in 1983, this book's conclusions had also been anticipated by papers and articles. The first article, "Piety in Middletown," had appeared in *Transaction* in the early months of 1981. It was followed by a similar article in *The Public Interest* in the summer of 1982 [Caplow, Bahr, and Chadwick 1981:

34-37; Caplow 1982d:78-87]. Both spoke of religious vitality in the community.

The book on religion, like the earlier volume on the family, relied on multiple authors. In addition to the senior researchers, *All Faithful People* includes essays by three local persons—myself, Joseph Tamney, and Lawrence Martin. I traced the history of churches in Muncie; Tamney, a sociologist at Ball State University, surveyed such practices as private devotions and fasting; and Martin, who was a Presbyterian minister in a prominent Muncie church, reported on his own experiences in that role. None of these topics had been explored by the Lynds in any detail. In particular, the view of religion from inside was new and revealing. All the authors, however, brought more knowledge about and experience in the town than had been possessed by the Lynds, making the historical dimension stronger.

All Faithful People reported that religious life and practice had become less harsh. Munsonians were less conscious of denomination lines, less puritanical, more eager to attend church, and more tolerant of those who had strayed from the way. The book claimed that "divorced persons are admitted to communion, suicides are buried in consecrated ground, and wayward youth are counseled, not excommunicated. Hester Prynne would be welcomed to church supper nowadays and, after a little discreet whispering, would be treated with special kindness" [Caplow 1982d:78-87].

The greater tolerance had resulted in dimunition of belief in certain respects. Faith that the Bible was the sole source of religious authority, for example, had declined 20 percent over the fifty-year period. This decline was less significant than it might appear, however, since it was in part produced by an increase in the number of Muncie Catholics. When that increase was factored in, the decline was only 11 percent [Caplow and Bahr 1979:6]. The major attitudinal changes were the eroding of two precepts: the belief that Christianity was the single true religion and the belief that Sunday should be only a day of rest [Caplow 1979b:4; Caplow 1981a:10].

The decline in these religious beliefs went counter to the general trend, however. The researchers of Middletown III tried to prove eleven propositions that would demonstrate the fading of religious faith as the Lynds had predicted from the vantage point of the 1920s. The propositions were that the following had occurred:

A decline in the number of churches per capita;

A decline in the proportion of the population who regularly attend religious services;

A decline in the proportion of weddings and funerals held under religious auspices;

A decline in religious endogamy, that is, the tendency to marry within a
religious denomination;

A decline in religious endogamy, that is, the tendency to marry within a
religious denomination;

A decline in the enrollment of religious schools;

A declining proportion of the labor force engaged in church occupa-
tions;

A decline in the average proportion of family income contributed to the
support of religion;

The dwindling of new sects and of new movements in existing
churches;

Increasing attention to secular topics in sermons and liturgy;

A decline in the more emotional forms of religious observance;

A decline in private religious devotions [Caplow 1981a:22-23; Caplow
1982b:5; Caplow, Bahr, and Chadwick et al 1983:294-96].

Instead of decline, the researchers found increases in all areas except for
secular topics in sermons. The number of churches per capita about doubled;
the percentage of marriages performed by clergy increased from 63 to 79
percent; donations to the church by working-class families rose from 1.6 percent of income to 3.3 percent (another doubling); and only two sermons of
102 given on a particular Sunday had secular topics [Caplow 1981a:23-24;
Caplow 1982b:6; Caplow, Bahr, and Chadwick 1983:294-96].

Not only had religious sentiments increased; church and state had moved
closer together. Religious groups were more politically active and displayed
more interest in the religious backgrounds of office seekers. Both government and churches showed greater respect for each other's symbols, and government passed fewer laws and regulated religious organizations less
[Caplow 1981a:24; Caplow, Bahr, and Chadwick 1983:296-97].

In concluding, Middletown III researchers claimed that the case for increased secularization was unsubstantiated. "It was this interpretation (that
the super-natural had disappeared from society) of the available evidence
that first started us thinking that secularization might be a myth rather than a
historical process since we have abundant evidence from Middletown and
from every other place in the Western World where religion has been closely
studied within the past few years that the supernatural *is* present as a meaningful reality to a majority, indeed a large majority, of the people in modern
societies" [Caplow 1981a:21].

The reception of *Middletown Families* and *All Faithful People* was less
enthusiastic than the reception of *Middletown* and *Middletown in Transition*;

they did not fill Brentano's windows. Nor was Helen Lynd alive to see either of them, having died one month before *Middletown Families* appeared.

Richard Lingeman, writing in the *Chicago Tribune*, concluded that the strength demonstrated by the Muncie family showed that it had become a refuge from societal problems. Although admitting that his views may have been skewed by the structure of the book, Lingeman suggested that the Muncie family was an evolutionary throwback. "Instead of looking outward and adapting new forms, it has spurned change and adaptation; it is an evolutionary throwback that has developed a tougher carapace, like a horseshoe crab, to enclose it and protect feelings and relationships that are vulnerable in a society that has become increasingly remote, impersonal, bureaucraticized, and threatening" [Lingeman 1981]. Ivar Peterson, writing a pre-publication article for *The New York Times*, offered no judgment on the findings. Instead he highlighted the most significant ones: the continuity of values; the increased tolerance; and the greater egalitarianism [Peterson 1982].

When *Middletown Families* was published, John Herbers wrote the major review in *The Times*. He said, after reviewing the book, that it ignored blacks and the underclass in its treatment of the business and working classes, that, except for the chapters written by Caplow, the book read as if it were written by a committee, and that Middletown III was taking too much time and space in publishing the data [Herbers 1982].

Two difficulties were detected by other astute readers. The first was that the Middletown III books, unlike *Middletown*, were profoundly conservative or, at least, had conservative implications. The second was that they did not reflect the most current sociological interests or methodology. Because of these difficulties, the books did not appeal to either of two articulate audiences—the informed liberal world of the *New York Review of Books* and the scholarly world of academic sociologists, and hence attracted barbs from these quarters.

Conservative accolades, on the other hand, went to *Middletown Families* because it did indeed argue that "moral entrepreneurs" used the myth of the declining family to increase the funding of private or public agencies. A good example of such praise came from Al Moffett, who, in the *Saturday Evening Post*, began his review of *Middletown Families* by saying, "A great hoax would have us believe otherwise, but families are thriving in Middletown, America" [Moffett 1981]. But this conservative use made the book an ideological football.

The reviewer for the *New York Review of Books*, Gerald Weales, an English professor, found the categorization of the helping professions as villains one of the weaknesses of *Middletown Families*. Although the research materials used were the same as the Lynds, he said, information was "filtered through differing sensibilities and intuitions." Caplow and associates, Weales claimed, lacked the satirical sense that could be found in the Lynds, although descriptive passages such as the ones comparing religion to a hot bath and picturing a two hundred–foot banana split made and eaten by a Muncie congregation could be construed as containing a "faint vein of satire." The lack of this sense and the failure to analyze the impact money had on Munsonians made Middletown III research seem cold. "The Lynds," he said, "who distrusted much in Middletown, still managed to convey greater sympathy for the people of Muncie." Beyond this personal difference, Weales found the content disturbing. Characterizing the attack on scholars, journalists, social workers, and government employees as "oddly venomous," Weales concluded that "these books reflect as well as report the new conservatism" [Weales 1984].

The reaction of sociologists was more specific. It came from two professional positions: the lack of interest in community studies and the deprecation of methodology that was not highly empirical. David Reisman, for example, said, "Community studies such as the Middletown project do not have the influence they once had because there is less interest among social sciences in the kind of broad, cross-sectional comparisons such studies yield" [Coughlin 1982]. For most sociologists, the action was elsewhere.

According to others, more serious than the acceptability of community studies were the methods used. Middletown III used the technique because the Lynds had done so. The attempt to replicate had led the later scholars into a cul-de-sac, according to Glen Elder: "By designing Middletown III in terms established by the earlier work, the research team made obvious sacrifices in degrees of freedom from methodological and theoretical innovation. *Middletown Families* does not lay a claim to a place among important studies of the family on the basis of methodology for studying change or on theory regarding family change or continuity" [Elder 1982].

Even more critical than the use of older methods was a failure to meet the standards of contemporary scholarship. Elder, for example, was disturbed that no more than half of the eligible respondents returned the surveys, and the characteristics of those not responding were not described [Elder 1982]. Elder's comments were mild, however, when compared to those of Peter H. Rossi of the Social and Demographic Research Institute of the University of Massachusetts.

Rossi identified the knotty problems faced by Middletown III. The Lynds had not explicitly described the process used in creating and administering their questionnaires, making it difficult to replicate them. When replicated and distributed, only two of the thirteen surveys had acceptable response rates, despite concerted efforts at followup. Rossi blamed the failure to ob-

tain acceptable response rates upon "poorly written questionnaires that pa-
tronize respondents.." [Rossi 1983:n.p.]. Since the questionnaires were
based on those of the Lynds, they constituted a kind of catch-22. To compare
results, the same questionnaire, or one very similar, had to be used; but the
user risked a low return because of the questions asked.

In the end, Rossi credited Middletown III researchers with not computing
any inferential statistics from the surveys with poor response rates, but asked
why the researchers failed to compute them for those with acceptable response rates. He then decided that it probably was not possible "to replicate
what is essentially a qualitative study." Even if this had been done, the study
would not have been very useful since, in his opinion, local studies were not
worth the effort. Instead, the whole United States should constitute the base
[Rossi 1983:n.p.].

Nor was this the end of methodological criticisms, as even more esoteric
points were raised. In response to the article "Christmas Gifts and Kin Networks," Judith Droitcour Miller and Ira H. Cisin argued that Caplow had, by
not adding corrective weights, failed to avoid bias in his derivative samples.
In a response to the comments, Caplow admitted the error [Miller and Cisin
1983:874-76].

On the other hand, qualitative sociologists criticized the Middletown III
books for being too empirical. Such was the tenor of Mark C. Smith's review
of *All Faithful People* and *Middletown Families*. In it, he claimed that "Middletown III substitutes a quantitative, status-quo perspective for the Lynds'
qualitative, activist orientation" [Smith 1984b: 228]. In particular, Smith
contrasted the basic orientation of Caplow and associates with that of the
Lynds. The former viewed the community as insiders, whereas the latter
were more critical. Thus, the Lynds were true social scientists because they
criticized the quality of life in the town in hopes of moving it to a higher
level. Caplow and associates failed to ask questions concerning the quality of
either religious or family life. As Smith says, "Most importantly, Caplow
and his associates never discuss the *quality* of Muncie life. Church attendance, religious weddings, and financial contributions, by themselves, say
nothing about the quality of that religion. In their classic *Middletown* volumes, the Lynds criticized Muncie not so much for its quantitative things but
for its spiritual emptiness. If Middletown III was truly to trace community
changes over half a decade, it should have addressed such issues" [Smith
1985: 64].

As a result, sociological critics tended to view with some skepticism the
claims of *Middletown Families* that the family was alive and well, or the
claim of *All Faithful People* that American society was becoming more religious. Scholars such as Rossi discounted the propositions entirely and even

denied the feasibility of such studies; others less empirical argued that the theses had not been proven. Elder, for example, while critical of Middletown III's methodology, suggested that it would be possible to determine whether change had occurred using a different methodology. "For a study of change, *Middletown Families* follows a strange path by tending to vault over the 40 or more years between the first two projects and the last. We see families and people in the 1920s or 1930s and then again in the 1970s. . . . The study makes no effort to link these different times through the lives of people, families and lineages—to follow their course through retrospective accounts from the 1930s to the Second World War, postwar affluence, and the economic stagnation of the 1970s" [Elder 1982:855]. Even someone as sympathetic to the Middletown III study of religion as Peter Berger was unwilling to accept at full value its conclusions. After calling *All Faithful People* "an example of sociological analysis at its best, which will be a point of reference for the sociology of religion in America for a long time," Berger then said, "The authors evidently believe that their data inflict a mortal blow on secularization theory. That is, in all likelihood, an exaggeration" [Berger 1984:37].

There was a scholarly reluctance to surrender old ideas, to abandon the notion of modernization, or to study a community instead of a nation, despite the obvious problems [Hoover 1987b: 407-51]. Even those uncritical of Middletown III methods maintained that quantitative measures could not capture the essence of changes. Wade C. Roof was one such individual. "Many would agree that secularization is neither as persuasive nor as irreversible as once thought. . . . Yet so complex and multifaceted a phenomenon as secularization is not easily captured by institutional indicators. The persistence of traditional religion does not preclude transformations of its meanings and a secularization of consciousness. Modernity brings about accommodations of religion and culture that are subtle and far-reaching, not the least of which is the privatization of religious realities. . . . What we have in the study is a description of this inner religious world of Middletown, but lacking is an analysis of the structural features of modern society that sustain and complicate it. . . The work is not likely to settle the debate over secularization. . . . Neither are the parameters of secular change fully explored, nor can the conclusions be generalized to America" [Roof 1984].

The fifty-three years that separated *Middletown Families* from *Middletown* had created a severe problem for those attempting community studies. Competition for the attention of a general audience had increased; books such as Davis's *Hometown* or John Baskin's *New Burlington: The Life and Death of an American Village* or Wright Morris's *The Home Place* combined the talents of skilled fiction writers with a sense of empathy and place that sociologists were hard put to match. Unlike the Lynds, Middletown III researchers could not produce a new, fresh work in an entirely different genre. On the other hand, sociological scholarship had become so specialized that attempting a study using surveys and structures from an earlier time was bound to stimulate negative reactions.

What were researchers to do? The compromises they made surely were justified in terms of trying to replicate an earlier study and their argument that the data, though imperfect, were still the best available for analysis of social change is generally agreed to have considerable merit. Sociologists had not been much interested in social change, and historians, whose special involvement was with change over time, usually had far less reliable data.

There is some evidence that the response in the long run to the Middletown III books is beginning to resemble that to the first volumes. Data and excerpts from *Middletown Families* and *All Faithful People* are appearing in introductory textbooks on sociology, particularly those concerning communities and religion. This process has not yet begun in histories, although one might add that there is no Frederick Lewis Allen writing that kind of social history at present. The influence of the more recent study has begun to appear in books written for general audiences. A case in point is Ben Wattenberg's *The Good News Is the Bad News Is Wrong,* which uses Middletown III findings to demonstrate the continuity of values in the United States [Wattenberg 1984:275-76]. Only time will tell if this pattern of use will expand.

The Beginning of the Film Project: National Endowment for the Humanities

In the spring of 1975, I attended a Poynter lecture at Earlham College given by Professor Merrill Peterson, a Jeffersonian scholar from the University of Virginia whom I had met some years before. During the lunch that preceded the lecture we talked about non-consequential matters. Peterson, however, soon attracted my attention when he noted that a sociologist at Virginia, Theodore Caplow, had just received a National Science Foundation grant of a half-million dollars to re-study Muncie. This was news to me.

On my return home I wrote Caplow volunteering my services as a local historian. I received the expected polite letter saying don't call us, we'll call you. Having filed the letter, I promptly forgot about it until the next year when one day Caplow phoned me asking my help in obtaining an historic city map from the Ball State Library. That was the beginning of my involvement with Middletown III. Gradually Caplow found more things for me to do and in 1977 put me in his grant and obtained an appointment for me as Professor of Historical Sociology at the University of Virginia. This was to last until 1979.

Meanwhile, I had also become involved in another project which was to lead indirectly to the Middletown Film Series. In 1975, Paul Mitchell of the Ball State University History Department obtained a small grant from the Indiana Committee for the Humanities to do a public project on work inspired by the section on getting a living in *Middletown*. This was my first acquaintance with any project funded by NEH, but was not to be my last.

The project involved the collection of oral histories from workers in the community and the writing of a series of essays on the topic of work. It also involved a series of planning meetings held late in the afternoons, at night, or on Saturdays. It was at one these meetings that C. Warren Vander Hill, a fellow historian, and I first met Peter Davis.

Davis had come to Muncie to search out "the heart of the heart of the country" He had completed *Hearts and Minds* and had begun to look for a community which he could film and which would reveal the values that he believed had led the U.S.A. into a hopeless war in Vietnam. Obtaining a small travel grant, he, like Lynd before him, visited a number of places: Lowell, Massachusetts; Utica, New York; Selma, Alabama; Santa Rosa, California; Kalamazoo, Michigan; York and Lancaster, Pennsylvania; Denton, Texas; Dubuque and Cedar Rapids, Iowa; and Muncie, Indiana. He had wandered onto the campus and into the office of the Vice-President of Public Affairs who had told him of the group project. He then walked into our meeting and spent the rest of the afternoon discussing with us the character of Muncie. We were excited about the prospect of doing a documentary film on Muncie and urged Davis to select our town. He, however, was reluctant to commit himself and he worried that, because of the Lynds and Caplow, the community had been overstudied. He left Muncie for nearby Hamilton, Ohio, a bedroom community near Cincinnati. We later heard that he had decided upon Hamilton.

Davis was born in southern California where his mother and father worked in the Hollywood film industry. His mother, Tess Schlesinger, was a short-story writer as well. Davis went to college at Harvard, graduating with an English degree in 1957. He worked for one year at *The New York Times* as an editorial assistant before entering the army. Following his service, he went to work in television, first as an interviewer, researcher, and writer for Sextant Productions; he then became an assistant producer of documentaries for NBC and CBS News. In 1968, he wrote the script and co-produced *Hunger in America*, which earned him the 1969 Writer's Guild Award for the best documentary script. In 1970, he produced *The Battle of East St. Louis*, which won the *Saturday Review* Award for the year's best documentary film. These documentaries, although rightly reflecting much credit on Davis, were of course the product of collective authors.

Both films reflected the troubled America of the late 1960s. *The Battle of East St. Louis* featured narration by Hughes Rudd and a three-day marathon encounter group between black and white antagonists. It did not film events as they occurred, choosing to focus instead upon attitudes and opinions of the city's citizens. *Hunger in America* was not as narrow; it documented poor people in four sections of the United States [Jacobs 1979:371]. Both were films that were socially conscious, critical of the existing political and economic system, and emotionally charged.

The reaction to these two films was muted, however, when compared to that of Davis's next two. The first was *The Selling of the Pentagon* in 1971, which Davis wrote and produced. It was a so-called "black film," one which attacked the subject filmed. *The Selling of the Pentagon* depicted the methods used by that agency to present the best possible face; it showed the operations of the public relations division of the Department of Defense which made Pentagon propaganda ubiquitous [Jacobs 1979:518-20; Barnouw 1974:263, 281-82]. *The Selling of the Pentagon* won many awards, including an Emmy, but it stirred up a storm, prompted a congressional investigation, and further added to Davis's reputation as a liberal critic.

His next effort was even more controversial. Obtaining financing from Columbia Pictures, Davis spent one year and a million dollars producing a film on the Vietnam War. His aim was to produce "an American version of *The Sorrow and the Pity*, a compassionate look at the commonplace of everyday life that inspired the people of a large industrial nation to follow their leaders in a war against a remote peasant society far from its shores" [Jacobs 1979:556]. Composed of "interviews, stock footage, [cinéma] vérité, and film clips," the film, *Hearts and Minds*, won a Prix Sedoul, a Golden Palm, and an Oscar [Jacobs 1979:551]. It also created a fire storm of protest, exacerbated by events surrounding the awarding of the Oscar that indicated sympathy for North Vietnam.

We were of course aware of Davis's reputation in Muncie; but since he had decided to film elsewhere and we were already busy finishing our project, we thought little of the consequences of his doing a film on Muncie. We finished our project in 1976 and, after a public forum, reported our findings in *Working in Middletown: Getting a Living in Muncie, Indiana* [1976].

Meanwhile, I had become connected with another NEH project. On 1 June 1976, I became a consultant to the *Ad Hoc* Planning Committee of seven chairpersons of the state-based humanities committees. The reason for the creation of this committee was "to supplement and extend their state-based humanities committees' common purpose, to continue to support and advance the state-based programs in the humanities, and to assume a number of co-ordinating and administrative tasks that were difficult or even impossible for the staff of the National Endowment for the Humanities to fulfill" [Hoover 1978:2]. The reason I was chosen was not because of any great expertise or experience with NEH, but because the chairman of the committee was Martin D. Schwartz, a local businessman with wide-ranging interests in the arts and humanities, who was then chairman of the Indiana Committee for the Humanities. My task was to coordinate the planning committee's work, apply for grants from NEH to finance the operation, create a national federation, have a general meeting and select a permanent director. I rented an office and began work. My experience here gave me considerable insight into the operations of NEH and would later help with the film project.

The impetus for the formation of the Federation of Public Programs in the Humanities had come from John Barcroft, who was at the time director of the Public Programs Division of NEH. According to Michael M. Mooney's highly partisan polemic *The Ministry of Culture*, NEH funded the organization to promote NEH activities in the states and to create an NEH lobby in Washington. NEH made lump sum grants to state humanities councils which Mooney implied were not public bodies at all [Mooney 1980:348; Mulcahy 1982:461-70]. He also questioned the use of public funds to lobby Congress which, of course, would be illegal.

Mooney's confessed partisan account contains elements of truth in it. Barcroft and others at NEH had felt the need for a voice to speak in Congress and were looking for a way in which to do so. NEH had created state humanities councils or committees a few years earlier in part to emulate the state arts councils. The then-director of NEH, Ronald Berman, perceived that the arts councils created a nationwide corps of lobbyists for the National Endowment for the Arts [Berman 1979:48]. Similar groups would be helpful for NEH. Although federal money could not be used to lobby, a federation which relied on dues from state humanities councils that presumably came from private sources could. Moreover, a federation could help member groups improve public programs and fundraising. It was also true that some humanities councils did not have public input; once founded, these tended to be self-perpetuating as members chose successors. In other states, however, the councils had input from the public with members appointed by the governor.

Regardless of the circumstances, NEH was in trouble in 1976, not financial but political difficulty. The original act creating the National Endowment for the Arts and the National Endowment for the Humanities had passed in 1965 as part of Lyndon B. Johnson's Great Society. His administration had not been overly generous to the endowments; however, Presidents Nixon and Ford expanded both exponentially. In fiscal 1976, the budget was $178,000,000 [*Newsweek* 31 October 1977; Mulcahy 1982:71].

Despite the budget increases, Director Berman had problems with Congress, in particular with Senator Pell. Berman was an intellectual conservative who was a Nixon appointee to head the National Endowment for the Humanities in 1971. He had the right credentials, a B.A. from Harvard and a Ph.D. from Yale in Renaissance Studies. At the time of his appointment he was teaching at the University of California at San Diego. His publishing record in his field had been undistinguished: *Henry King and the 17th Century* (1974), *A Reader's Guide to Shakespeare's Plays* (1965), and *Henry V: Collection of Central Essays* (1968). However, his excoriating attack on 1960s excesses, *America in the '60s: An Intellectual History*, won him considerable media and popular attention [*Who's Who in America* 1988-89].

Berman lacked political skills and did not mend his fences in Congress after the off-year elections of 1974. Described by one observer as "a bureaucratic zealot concerned with [the] correctness of a narrow policy viewpoint" and as a "forthright, outspoken, and often combative defender of what he saw as the classical values of the liberal arts," Berman became involved in a battle he could have avoided and was bound to lose. Criticized by Pell as an elitist who fostered a "mandarin culture," Berman persisted in his position and defended the endowment's seeming preference for giving grants to the most prestigious universities in the land [Mulcahy 1982:325].

President Ford nominated Berman for another term in 1976 when I was helping create the Federation of Public Programs for the Humanities, but his re-appointment failed to clear the Senate. In January 1977, Berman resigned, knowing that the newly elected president, Jimmy Carter, would not be supportive.

The position of director of NEH remained open until mid-summer of 1977. The search for a new director was long and difficult, causing *Newsweek* to report that Carter finally threw up his hands and said, "I've been spending more time on the humanities than I have on the SALT talks" [*Newsweek* 31 October 1977]. Finally, Carter announced the name of the new director who was sworn in in October.

The new director was Joseph Duffey and his appointment stirred up another hornet's nest. Duffey lacked Berman's academic credentials. He graduated from Marshall University in West Virginia and received a bachelor of divinity degree from Andover Newton Theological Seminary. He taught for most of the 1960s at Hartford Seminary Foundation and received a Ph.D. from that institution in 1969 while he was directing its Center for Urban Studies. In 1970 he ran for the Senate against Lowell Weicker, but was defeated. Following his defeat he was a fellow at the Kennedy School at Harvard and at Calhoun College at Yale. He remained politically active, supporting McGovern in 1972. In 1974, he became the executive officer of the AAUP. In 1976, he was chairman of the Democratic Task Force on Education and an early supporter of Jimmy Carter. In 1977, he was looking for a more permanent position. He served for a short time that year as Secretary for Education and Cultural Affairs at the State Department [*Newsweek* 31 October 1977; *Who's Who in America* 1988- 89; Mooney 1980:339], but was not particularly happy there nor, according to rumors, was he very keen on heading up NEH.

Duffey soon came under fire from several different sources. A.M. Schlesinger, Jr., a spokesman for the Eastern intellectual establishment, called him hopeless and a "political opportunist" [*Newsweek* 31 October 1977]. He was among those who claimed Duffey would neglect serious scholarship and promote flashy but trivial populist programs. An unnamed source in *The New York Times* pointed out that Duffey was not known "to be an authority on the humanities" [*Christian Century* 31 August 1977]. Those on the right were apoplectic. A *National Review* editorial said that Duffey was a step down in quality, that he was not a scholar but a politician whose claim to fame was his stint as head of the ADA and of Jimmy Carter's Washington campaign headquarters. It claimed Duffey had agreed with Pell's argument that the endowment was elitist and should reach a mass audience. It concluded that "The National Endowment for the Humanities should not be a rest ranch for defeated Democratic hacks, and if the Carter administration intends to make it one perhaps we should re-examine the National Endowment for the Humanities." The *National Review's* suspicions were strengthened later that year when Carter named Livingston Biddle, Jr., Pell's former administrative assistant, as head of the National Endowment for the Arts. The journal said "Tammany Hall would have blushed at anything so crass" [*Newsweek* 31 October 1977; *Christian Century* 31 August 1977; *National Review* 19 August 1977; 9 December 1974].

Not that Duffey lacked defenders. The *New Republic* said he was an excellent choice while at the same time praising Berman for doing a good job despite Pell's attack on quality [*New Republic* 20 August 1977]. The *Christian Century*, obviously pleased that a minister, albeit a non-preaching one, had become head of NEH was even more positive, saying, "Duffey's predecessor—Ronald Berman—was an unpopular unpopulist in the eyes of Congress and much of the informed public. He helped the NEH lean toward subsidizing prestigious schools and programs. Before Mr. Duffey opened his mouth, the elitists were accusing him of being ready to support popular institutions and thus mediocrity—a rather unscholarly judgement to make" [*Christian Century* 31 October 1977].

At Duffey's swearing-in in October, Vice President Mondale said decisions about quality should not be made politically but that grants should be decided upon "publicly by groups which are representative of our whole country." Duffey himself said "What's objectionable in scholarship is self-righteousness, hypocrisy, snobbery, which we mislabel 'elitism.' But in areas dealing with professional scholarship, we need to rely on the judgment of scholarly peers." Following the ceremony, according to *Newsweek*, the crowd ate popcorn and pretzels, drank beer, and listened to foot-stomping country music of the Hickory Wind ensemble [*Newsweek* 31 October 1977; *Horizon* October 1977]. This was not calculated to reassure critics, despite Duffey's compromising words.

During this troubled year, plans for the federation developed and the initial meeting of the new organization was held 6-8 October 1977. The keynote speaker for the first evening session was Duffey. This was his first public address since assuming the office and it attracted considerable media attention. Another significant address was by Congressman Albert Quie who announced his intention to sponsor a White House Conference on the

Humanities in 1978. This meeting signalled the end of my connection to the federation which had come too late to help Berman, but which promised to be of service to his successor. Neither speaker at the meeting said much about the direction that NEH would take in the future.

This was not the end of a connection with NEH, however; although it was unbeknownst to me at the time, it was only the beginning. In September 1976, NEH announced an initiative to bring humanists together with public television stations. Curiously enough, I learned of this not through the Public Programs Divisions of NEH, with which I was in close contact, but from my colleague Vander Hill who in turn had learned about it from the program director of Muncie's PBS station, Ron Wolfe. The latter had gone to a conference in Washington and informally discovered that there would be an opportunity to explore connections. He was technically trained and had neither experience nor inclination to write a proposal for the station.

I did and subsequently submitted one entitled "WIPB and the Humanities," the goals of which were to develop a guide to the humanist resources in the community and to generate three possible program ideas for future use. The proposal was funded for the calendar year 1977 for $13,645. I am uncertain as to why it was funded, but think that there were few applicants since the lead time was about a month; and the fact that WIPB was one of the smallest public television stations in the country made the grant especially attractive. I never consulted with any program officer at the endowment concerning the proposal; I, along with my colleague Vander Hill, did ask on one of our visits to NEH on federation business about the grant's progress. We were told that NEH could not answer that question (and that we shouldn't ask), but that unless the grant proposal were written by monkeys in a closed room we would probably get it.

The project, originally designed for a year, lasted six months more. It had two parts, a series of seminar meetings usually held on Saturday mornings and composed of eight members, plus a planning committee. The former group included one faculty member from Anderson College, a nearby institution, one from Taylor University, another regional private college, and six members from Ball State University by virtue of their positions. These included the Dean of the College of Sciences and Humanities, the Dean of Faculty Development, the Director of Field Services for Continuing Education, the Curator of the Ball State Gallery, the Coordinator of Honors Humanities Courses, and the President of Eastern Indiana Community Television. The planning committee consisted of myself; Vander Hill, Director of Honors Programs, Joe Trimmer, Professor of English; and Ron Wolfe. James Needham, the Director of WIPB, soon replaced Wolfe.

The purposes of the seminars were to develop lists of humanists with their fields of expertise for the station and to generate three program ideas. Following that, the members of the planning committee would take the ideas to larger television stations and to independent film producers to solicit opinions concerning possibilities for filming. The seminars actually resulted in far more than three ideas; there were about 150. Members of the seminar then broke into three groups to identify the most promising ones. The list reduced to "Possibilities of Public Art," "Main Street on the Middle Border," and "Getting a Living in Middletown—Then and Now." Armed with these proposals, members of the planning committee visited Henry Becton, Program Manager for Cultural Affairs, WGBH, Boston; Bill McCarter, President, WTTV, Chicago; Ron Hull, Program Manager, Nebraska Educational Television Networks, Lincoln; and Peter Davis. The reason we included Davis was that we knew him, and we could also visit Channel 13 while in New York City.

The responses from each were quite similar. The first program idea was uniformly rated low because the respondents believed it was only tangentially connected with the humanities and had only local or, at best, regional interest. The other two received more favorable comment, but in the process of discussion, the topic of Middletown invariably arose. Then we felt impelled to discuss Muncie as Middletown, the Lynd studies, and Middletown III. After this discussion, the almost universal response was the recommendation that we do a film series on Middletown, using the third proposal, work, as one of the segments.

Now the question was whether we wished to proceed with the project at all. If we did, we needed to have a filmmaker. We purposefully left our visit to New York City and to Davis until last because we wished to discuss the possibility of his becoming a part of the project.

Davis had not made a film since *Hearts and Minds*. He had chosen Hamilton as his typical city and was writing a book, *Hometown*, for which he had a contract from Simon and Schuster. He had also submitted a $4,000,000 proposal to the Corporation for Public Broadcasting for a fourteen-part documentary with the same title. It was not funded. Although he had originally rejected filming Muncie, he was now enthusiastic about doing so. We agreed to proceed.

Looking back now and knowing now what I didn't know then, I realize what a long shot the chances of obtaining funds for a film were. Davis's notoriety and the problems at NEH were two obstacles, but there were plenty more. The history of federal involvement in the media in the late sixties and early seventies made the odds longer still.

Like the endowments, the Corporation for Public Broadcasting and the Public Broadcasting System were embroiled in political controversy almost from the beginning. Congress authorized the CPB in 1967; and, by 1969, its budget was $5,000,000. PBS began in 1970. Two years later, Nixon, angered by the content of two PBS programs, "Thirty Minutes With" and "Washington Week in Review," which had been subsidized by CPB, vetoed the latter's budget. As a result, the president of CPB resigned in August, 1972, and CPB took all its scheduling from PBS. The following May, the new chairman of CPB agreed that CPB would no longer control programming on PBS but would instead do "Community Service Grants" directly to PBS stations. By 1974, CPB was funding programs again through station program cooperatives. Local PBS stations could create programs, or commission them, with funds from CPB supplemented by grants from the endowments or from private corporations [Mooney 1980:118-20]. Indeed, this was how many public programs came to be created.

Because of the early political problems and because of the nature of the endowments, obtaining grants from them at the time was no easy task. In the first place, the program officers in media divisions were usually not practicing or successful filmmakers. Had they been, they would not have been in the endowments. Their views tended to be narrower and more provincial than those of the creative filmmakers. In the second place, the NEH, in particular, since its charter only allowed it to sponsor programs with humanities content, insured that content by placing humanists, usually college professors of English or history, on grant-approving panels and insisting that they be consultants on the project. Finally, the endowments exercised extreme caution in granting funds. The normal procedure of the NEH was to require four separate grant applications in order to make a film: a planning grant, a development grant, a script-writing grant, and a filming grant. Funds could be granted through any stage but stopped at the next level. The four-stage process could be avoided; the proposer could ask to go directly for a production grant, but we were advised this would diminish our chances. This meant serious problems for any filmmaker, but particularly for documentary filmmakers since they often did not use scripts. In every case, the hopeful filmmaker had to invest considerable time in writing proposals which might or might not be funded and which, in the case of documentaries, would not be used. Still, creative fundraisers could use approved grants at any level to attract other grants, as Mooney points out. "For the few programs which did proceed to completion, experienced public television producers used 'development grants' from the National Endowments as imprimaturs to raise additional funds from foundations, which were often themselves instruments of either profitable corporations, such as EXXON Foundation, or from university-connected systems" [Mooney 1980:124].

Several examples of the filming process will illustrate the kinds of problems encountered with the endowment funding.

The first is that of "The Adams Chronicles," a well-received, non-documentary historical drama/reconstruction series that appeared in the mid-1970s. Virginia Kassel obtained a development grant from NEH in 1970 for $30,375. She conceived of a dramatic series on three generations of Adams, using the editors of the Adams Papers as researchers. In September 1972, she received a production grant of $250,000 for beginning the filming, plus another $25,000 for writing. However, this was contingent upon adding other historians to the project to insure the accuracy of the account. Kassel accepted the proviso, but later argued this requirement lost the single voice of the series and made production extremely difficult. The editors of the Adams Papers checked the scripts after the playwrights had finished and then sent them to the historians whom NEH had recommended. The result was that the project fell behind schedule, the writers were dissatisfied and quit or struck (in August 1974), and the project cost far more than budgeted. Kassel's experience convinced her never to attempt an NEH project again. [Mooney 1980:125-27].

The second case is that of "Understanding the Congress," proposed by Gerald E. Colbert to NEH in January 1976. Colbert wished to show how Congress worked by following the progress of the Clean Air Bill, HR6761, through the House and Senate. Berman gave him a chairman's grant of $17,500, this being a grant given at the discretion of the chairman bypassing the peer review process. Conceivably, this may have been a belated effort of Berman to mend fences in the Congress. A month later, Colbert submitted a supplementary proposal for script and production. He received $272,000 from NEH, plus a pledge to match up to $100,000 in funds raised elsewhere. In September 1976 he succeeded in obtaining $50,000 from Westinghouse, which NEH matched. He chose a public station, WVIA, in Pittston, Pennsylvania, to film what he now projected as a thirteen-sequence series—six on Congressional history and seven on how Congress works. At the recommendation of NEH, he created a board of fifteen eminent political scientists to advise him, but he went beyond that requirement and put together an advisory board of politicians, one which included such powerful figures as Jacob Javits, Clayborn Pell, and John Brademas, all of whom had helped create the endowments. Meanwhile, Colbert had applied to NEA and had obtained a $15,000 chairman's grant, plus $12,000 for writing two film treatments and $3,000 for hiring consultants.

Colbert's film series had several difficulties. The first was the question of whether NEH could legitimately fund a film on Congress without seeming partisan and the second was whether WVIA had the expertise to make the films. Colbert, nonetheless, pushed ahead and asked for $5,000,000 from NEH and a like sum from NEA. NEA denied him funding while NEH finally granted him $60,000 in September to finish two films. The first appeared in April 1979; it was *HR 6161: An Act of Congress*. The second film was never finished, although Colbert did edit another film for the National Park Service [Mooney 1980:91-96]. Such was the fate of a project which had considerable promise but which failed in execution.

A final example of the experience of a documentary filmmaker that ought to have given us pause is that of Donn Alan Pennebaker, a member of the original group of cinéma vérité cinematographers formed by Robert Drew that included Richard "Ricky" Leacock [Jacobs 1979:376; Barnouw 1974: 235]. The group's effort that had the greatest impact on the documentary tradition was *Primary*, a film of the 1960 campaign in Wisconsin between Hubert H. Humphrey and John F. Kennedy. Photographed by Leacock and Albert Maysles with sound by Drew and Pennebaker, the film achieved a considerable reputation.

In 1961, ABC asked Drew Associates to film a series on Latin America. Only one proved acceptable; that one was *Yanki No!*, a depiction of anti-American attitudes south of the border. The result was to paint the associates as being radical; by 1963, it had dissolved and the filmmakers had gone their own ways [Mamber 1974:42-48].

In June 1976, NEA announced a Media Arts Program which would accept bids to produce documentary films by independent filmmakers for public broadcasting. Among those stations that applied was WNET in New York with a proposal to do a film on old age with Leacock and Pennebaker. However, the proposal went nowhere because Pennebaker believed that public broadcasting executives were trying to tell him how to make the film, violating his direct cinema principles [Mooney 1980:282-87].

Secure in our ignorance of others' failures and problems, we plunged ahead. In August 1978, we submitted a research and development proposal to NEH, the second stage of the cycle. I wrote the original proposal; it was refined by Davis and Trimmer. I was the project director; the research office of the university administered the funds. We asked for approximately $50,000 to develop a script on *Muncie, the Town and the Symbol*, in a series to be called "Middletown."

Parts of the proposal were adapted from Davis's unsuccessful scripts for a documentary series on Hamilton, Ohio, but parts were original. The proposal's purpose is best illustrated by these excerpts:

> 'Middletown' will be a television series centered entirely in one community. This series as a whole will constitute a documentary search for the roots of American culture on display in the people and institutions of a single town....The sociological classics, *Middletown* and *Middletown in Transition*, examined the varieties of life and the significance of social custom in a middle-sized American city; 'Middletown,' the documentary film series, will freeze time and place on film as the Lynds did fifty years ago in their books on Muncie. Such a study seems especially appropriate now as we turn inward after Vietnam and Watergate, moving through the Bicentennial in quest of our core.... It will be an exploration of the values which have persisted and those which have faded away....The format of the proposed series is basically that used by the Lynds in their two books and by the University of Virginia sociologists who are now restudying Muncie with the addition of an introductory film which will set the community in historical context of the sociological studies [Hoover 1978:3-5].

The proposal gave a short summary of stories for seven films. It concluded with the revealing statement that "'Middletown' is, rather, an attempt to experience the whole through an illumination of one its parts, a kind of national synedoche" [Hoover 1978:16].

The personnel for the second proposal had changed. While I was still project director and Vander Hill, Trimmer, and Needham remained as the planning committee, the advisory committee was no longer involved. The decision to drop it was urged upon me by the remainder of the committee, with greater or lesser vigor. I did write the advisory committee out, but with some trepidation. I wrote in Davis as a new member to assume the roles of writer and executive producer.

The division of labor was to allow each of us to work to our strengths. In addition to being in charge of financial matters, I, along with Vander Hill, was to do historical research. Trimmer was to rewrite the drafts from our research, while Needham was to evaluate the materials on the basis of their visual promise. Davis's chore was to convert the research materials into shooting treatments (he refused to use the word scripts).

The money requested was to cover the costs of paying us for each day's work, for travel, for graduate assistants, for consultants, and for office expenses. Davis, because of his reputation, was paid $500 per day, while those of us at the university, limited by per diems imposed by its rules, received $125 per day for our work.

We gave ourselves six months to complete the treatment, from 1 January to 31 May 1979. We also programed in travel, three trips for conferences in New York City, and three trips for Davis to come to Muncie, plus trips for the four of us to meet with the consultants we had listed [Hoover 1978: 16-20].

In rewriting the grant, Trimmer and Davis altered it somewhat. They deleted the introductory film which was to furnish context and expanded the number of days each had been allotted in the budget (Davis doubled his and Trimmer increased his by one-third). They named and described in more detail the six films which were now called: *The Job, The Wedding, The Commencement, The Big Game, The Sabbath,* and *The Campaign.* Additionally, they indicated that *The Wedding* would be the pilot film.

The theme of each film was laid out. *The Job* would record the thoughts and actions of three Middletown workers confronting personal crisis. *The Wedding* was to focus on the family through several generations' participation in a wedding. *The Commencement* would portray two rituals connected with public education, commencement and class reunion. The commencement would serve as the principal subject but would be combined with a reunion of graduates from the same school during commencement week. *The Big Game* was to show the final game of the Muncie Sectional Basketball Tournament. This was the "community's preeminent ritual, replacing or subsuming every other ritual in the culture" [Hoover 1978c:17]. *The Sabbath* was to be the most difficult film to make because, according to Davis and Trimmer, religion no longer organized the community's life. This film, like *The Job,* would be a three-person, or rather a three-family, weave. Three different families, one upper-middle-class, another a ministerial one, and a third a working-class one, would be followed through their Sunday activities. *The Campaign* was the last film in the proposal. It proposed to follow a single unspecified political campaign from primary to election.

More significant than these changes was the subtle shifting of the main intention of the film series. My intention was that the series be historical and that it compare the Muncie found in *Middletown* (1929) and *Middletown in Transition* (1937) with the findings of Middletown III. The most recent examination had already cast doubt on the Lynds' prediction concerning Muncie's future and provided, I thought, a theme for the films.

Underlying both *Middletown* and *Middletown in Transition* was the assumption that human values changed in response to industrialization and urbanization, what is now called modernization. Muncie, the Lynds forecast, would become a more secular community with weaker family and kinship ties. They predicted a more rational political system as the tribal politics of the city slowly decayed. Despite evidence to the contrary, the Lynds clung to the idea that the forces of modernization were irresistible.

The findings of Middletown III contradicted that idea: Religion was stronger in 1975 than in 1925, while family ties were at least as strong. Values had changed far less than popular opinion or such works of pop sociology as Toffler's *Future Shock* had supposed. The Middletown III researchers concluded that modernization was slowing down. My own opinion was more radical; I doubted the utility of such a concept and was agnostic about both the rate and direction of social change [Hoover 1987b:407-51].

What I had hoped to do in the films was to document the changes. I had said that: "Just as Dr. Caplow's concern is to compare Middletown of today with that of the 1920s, it is our goal to draw parallels and make contrasts on film" [Davis 1980:14]. But other elements were now added, mythic, archetypal ones.

In the revision of the script-writing proposal and in the succeeding request for money for a pilot film, this statement appeared. "In one sense, Middletown has never been an actual place but an assortment of principles—the democratic ideal, the golden mean, the common man—central to our understanding of the American experience. We have located this **imaginary place** in a middle landscape somewhere between wilderness and metropolis, and we have envisaged it as a middle-sized community, large enough to provide everything its citizens want and small enough to preserve everything they need. In a century of bewildering change, **the Middletown myth** suggests stability. We may never have visited Middletown—we never need to—but the existence of its courthouse square, tree-lined streets, and warm-hearted citizens is fixed in our national imagination because it is somehow important to our sense of security" [Hoover 1978c:5; Hoover 1987c:52-65].

The focus had become fuzzy. Instead of concentrating upon Middletown and its particulars, the search was for the universal American small city. The series was to be more literary and less historical or sociological. Local context was to be ignored in the move toward an American core. In so doing, the popular view of American society was to triumph over the sociologist's analysis of what had happened. This was already apparent in the description of religion in *The Sabbath* as no longer organizing the community's life and the description of the family in *The Wedding*, which quotes the Lynds but fails to mention Caplow.

Why had this happened? There are several reasons for the shift; some were organizational and some were personal. My first great failure was not to articulate my ideas very well. The committee and I had little experience with documentary film making, knowing nothing about the process or of the power of each role in it. I had little idea of what an executive producer did or even what a treatment was. I had less of an idea of how to translate social trends into film. Indeed, I doubted that the whole film series could be done. Passive and shy by nature, I, along with my colleagues, was intimidated by Davis, his literary and television fame. Moreover, in meetings with Davis, I failed to direct our attention back to the main purpose of the project, as I saw it. Nor was I able to persuade Davis or his filmmakers to read or listen to the more recent findings of Middletown III, at least not to my knowledge.

Not that Davis was overwhelming or condescending. He was instead friendly and kind, almost to the point of unctuousness. He declared at a local restaurant that a patty melt was his favorite food and he entertained our ideas with great sympathy. All the while, however, there was an edge to his personality, a vague hint of manipulation, of seduction. I still am unable to decide whether he is the world's nicest guy or one of its more proficient snake oil salesmen.

Davis had, however, great confidence in his ability to produce a film series on Muncie. This was infectious. Once when expressing my doubts about the future of the project, I was reassured when Davis said that if we got the money he would see to it that the films would be made. "I'll make the stories," he said. But the stories he would make were of a different kind. An English major at Harvard, Davis used as his film model *Winesburg, Ohio*, a series of character sketches with no binding connection between individuals except locale, with no great emphasis upon social structure.

Moreover, Davis had little interest in either history or sociology, saying that he did not know how to film history. Nor was he particularly impressed with the historian's fetishes about accuracy or chronological order. Anxious to salvage part of his effort to film Hamilton, Ohio, he regarded the two communities as interchangeable, using elements from one in the other. A comparison of the grant proposal with *Hometown* shows that. A quotation from the sports editor of the *Muncie Star* on the popularity of basketball in Muncie appears verbatim in *Hometown*, but it refers to Hamilton and is attributed to Flatiron, an old steelworker; and the bromides attributed to coach McCollum in Hamilton appear in the grant proposal as attributable to coach Harrell of Muncie. He even used the name of the coach of Garfield High, Don Gillespie, as the coach of Southside High School in Muncie [Davis 1982:40-71]. While this can be rationalized on the basis of economy of effort, it was to bode ill for the future films.

Further complicating matters was Davis's adherence to the technique of cinema direct, modified by his experiences both as an investigative reporter for NBC and CBS news and as an independent filmmaker. From Frederick Wiseman, Davis took the view that the filmmaker need not be an expert in the topic which he was filming; from Drew Associates he accepted the principle that the fictional devices of character, action, and structure could be used in documentary films and that these could be achieved by selecting the story of an individual in a crisis situation; and from Leacock he accepted the idea that the filmmaker should be selective in showing the audience what he wished them to see. Not a purist, he also allowed the inclusion of pieces of interviews juxtaposed and out of sequence with others, staged actions, and used sites that were well-lighted and wired for sound.

He did not allow any more intervention than that, insisting that his "found dramas" needed no explanatory devices—voiceovers, talking heads, or texts—to supply context. Since he had ruled out an introductory film, this meant that none of the insights of the Lynds or of Middletown III would be explicit in the films. These, like the social statistics, would be invisible, and any context would have to be supplied by the viewer from the images.

His vision of the film series triumphed in part because it was one which was thought out and well-presented. The planning committee lacked a clear, articulated alternative. In part this was a result of the make-up of the committee and the interaction of its members. In particular, there was some friction between myself and another committee member, Joe Trimmer.

I had not known Trimmer very long or well when Vander Hill recommended him to me for committee membership. He had not served with the two of us on *Working on Middletown*, but had been a project participant in an earlier one, *Middletown Man: The Human Side of Life in Muncie, Indiana*, sponsored by the Indiana Committee for the Humanities with Vander Hill. Trimmer had come to Ball State University in 1968 after completing a degree in American Literature at Purdue University. He was a bright, energetic, and articulate person who was coordinator of General Education English. He had published a number of articles and edited a major textbook, *American Oblique: Writing About the American Experience* (1976). However, he had a reputation for aggressiveness to the point where he was actively disliked by a number of his colleagues.

Despite that reputation and because of his energy, I agreed to place him on the planning committee. The assignment he wanted and which I gave him was as a writer. He also asked to be the liaison with Davis, citing the need to work closely with him in rewriting. I also agreed to this; but the result was that he became close to Davis and came to act as his agent or representative on the committee, supporting Davis's position in almost all cases. He also visualized the series as a literary rather than an historic one; given his lack of knowledge of the history of the community, this is understandable. In addition, pleading poverty he asked to spend more time than any of the other consultants on the project, a plea which I agreed to honor. But the result was that he gradually assumed more and more control over the information from Davis and, hence, over the project. Finally, because of his energy and his willingness to go into the community, Davis came to rely upon him more than any of the rest of us. This symbiotic relationship weakened the independence of the committee.

A final change also moved more control into Davis's hands. Our link to Muncie's PBS station had promised that it would produce any program developed locally. However, Davis did not like Needham and had a low opinion of both his and the station's ability to mount a major series. He also indicated that he could locate a more prominent station to sponsor the series. Supported by Trimmer, the proposal to change the station connection passed as the rest of us acquiesced.

NEH funded our "Research and Development Grant" for $25,000, half of what we had requested; our travel was severely cut, our consultants eliminated, and our administrative cost request denied. Most of the money left was to go to Davis. Despite this reduction, the success of the proposal filled us with optimism, since we had been asked to provide a full treatment while planning the rest of the series. It was at this point that I began to believe that the project might be accomplished.

Why had we been funded? The answer remains a mystery to me. I would like to think that the reason was that our proposal was so compelling that the review boards immediately put it at the top of their list. That may have happened, but there are other considerations as well. Here are some of them.

Jimmy Carter had been elected in 1976 and his administration had a pronounced populist strain. Duffey had been director of NEH for less than a year, and is supposed to have agreed with Senator Pell that the endowment should reach a mass audience. The political climate was more favorable to a project such as this than it had been in some time. Perhaps our timing was right.

Not that any of us could claim very much political clout, either in or out of the endowment. I had met Duffey only twice and certainly did not know him personally. My major contact at the endowment and the person with whom I worked to establish the Federation of State Humanities Councils, John Barcroft, had long since left for a job with the Kemper Insurance Group. Davis knew no one in the endowment but he had strong connections to the liberal wing of the Democratic Party. His first wife, Johanna Mankiewicz, had been tragically killed by an errant automobile in New York in July 1974, but her brother Frank was prominent in Democratic circles. Associated with the Kennedys, Mankiewicz had been National Political Director of McGovern's campaign in 1972. In 1977, he had become president of National Public Radio. While there was no direct link between NPR and NEH and PBS, such a prominent brother-in-law cannot have hurt our chances.

Vander Hill believes that Davis was the key to our success, not because of his political connections (although he did date Jackie Kennedy) but because of his media ones. He says "Although the idea for a documentary film on 'Middletown' was ours, the level of funding which the project received was due almost entirely to Peter Davis's decision to become the series' executive producer. The Endowment's media staff and the expert readers who evaluated our major funding requests certainly realized that we were making films, not doing research for articles and books. To them Davis was a known quantity. Indeed, at times we felt that the Endowment underwrote 'Middletown' only to obtain Davis's name and reputation" [Vander Hill 1982:50]. This observation may be correct. Certainly Davis was well-known to those in the Media Division of NEH, but he may have been more notorious than famous and given the bureaucratic tendency to shy away from controversy, his reputation may have been a hindrance.

Another possibility which has not received much attention but which might explain our success is the timely return of Middletown to media attention. On 29 June 1978, just as we were preparing the grant proposal, the NBC "Today" show did a feature story on the Middletown III project. We used this appearance to bolster our argument, and I think it may have carried some weight. At any rate, it couldn't hurt.

By late 1978 we were committed to preparing for a film series little knowing what the future might bring.

Seeking the Way

Nineteen seventy-nine was a year with many developments for the Middletown Film Project. We began the research and development phase while at the same time beginning to shoot some footage for the pilot film. Thanks to Davis's energy and effort, the project received additional funding from several new sources. PBS granted us $30,000 in two separate packets in the spring, while NEH gave us $325,000 to proceed with the pilot film in the fall. Xerox corporation pledged $500,000 to be used as a match for NEH and the Indiana Committee for the Humanities.

In January, the members of the planning committee began their work. We were to do treatments which could then be turned into stories for filming. I did background research on several topics—politics, education, and religion. My own efforts were largely in-depth studies of these institutions in Muncie, relying heavily upon printed materials and historical techniques. These were not highly regarded by Davis. He was more interested in stories about individuals. I did find some human-interest stories. My middle daughter was at the time a sophomore at Central High School and, through her, I learned of several individuals, including a nearly blind student, who I thought would be a good subject. These were not accepted. I considered submitting my former office mate's story for possible inclusion in the religion segment. He had been ill for a short time and had just learned that he had terminal brain cancer. This story would have fit in with Davis's idea that religion dealt primarily with death. But I did not consider very long before rejecting the idea, and I am not sorry. One idea I had was accepted. It was to film the mayoral campaign that was to take place that year. I did a piece on the possible candidates and Davis decided to use the mayoral compaign instead of the wedding as the pilot.

The reasons for the switch are unclear. Weddings were still on Davis's mind, but we had no prospects for that segment. We did have a real live campaign in 1979; we either had to film it in that year or wait another four for a municipal election. We could have done a presidential election in 1980 and/or a congressional one in 1982, but neither would have had the kind of local involvement of a municipal election. As a result, *The Wedding* was shelved and *The Campaign* moved to the fore.

This decision created problems. In the first place, we were funded by the research and development grant and had no money for filming. Our production request proposal would not be submitted until June 1979, after the primary election. In the second place, we would be at the mercy of whomever the voters in each party chose. Both candidates could be very dull, making the resultant film a disaster.

We accepted the risk and moved ahead. Davis took the $30,000 provided him by PBS and came to Muncie to shoot the primary. He also had a commitment of $20,000 from WNET in New York City but was reluctant to use it because of fear of being obligated to designate the station as originator. By obtaining vehicles and other support services from the university, we were able to stretch the money far enough to shoot considerable footage, which, however, proved to be of such little interest to Davis that no part of it was ever used.

At the same time, the organization of the Middletown Film Project underwent considerable revision. Davis was unhappy about using the university as fiscal agent. He pressed me to push checks through the bureaucracy. I tried but was never able to hurry them very much; at best, it took about one week from check request to check availability. Davis also wished to have more personal control over the project. For these reasons, he proposed creating a non-profit corporation, Middletown Film Project, Inc., which would have its headquarters in New York City and which would be the fiscal agent. He would assume project directorship and I would become a consultant. None of us were publicly invited to join the corporation as officers, although Vander Hill and I learned later that Trimmer had been privately invited and had accepted.

I opposed the proposed change but was outvoted by the committee. The argument of Davis was persuasive. He said it would be easier to run the project's artistic and financial affairs from New York City; he also offered to pay us a higher per diem than the university would allow. This would make it easier for Vander Hill who, being on a twelve-month contract, could not participate during working hours without violating university rules. Now, reflecting upon the transition, I think I would have tried to retain a limited amount of control over the direction of the films.

Why had I given in so easily? Part of the reason was that I questioned whether I had the ability or the psychic and physical energy to run a project that size. I had a full-time job, was writing a book, and had personal problems. Rationally, I knew Davis was better equipped to undertake the job; however, my demotion still rankled. I had an ego involvement with the project and wanted the films to be a pioneering example of translating sociology and history to the screen. Although he originally supported Davis, Vander

Hill has now come around to my position, saying "Hoover has always viewed this decision as a major error on the part of the academic humanists since, as he has often pointed out, the humanists no longer had any control over any phase of the project. From the vantage point of hindsight, Hoover was right" [Vander Hill 1982:64, fn. 5].

Again, from the vantage point of hindsight, I realize we had failed to discuss other important matters at this particular juncture. Our roles as consultants were not spelled out in any detail. According to subsequent grant proposals, I was to be responsible for two film segments, *The Campaign* and *The Job*; Trimmer for *The Commencement* and *The Sabbath*; and Vander Hill for *The Big Game* and *The Wedding*. Beyond a general reference which said that we would be "involved in all phases of the 'Middletown' series" [Davis 1980:101], there was no indication of what this involvement entailed. Davis had indicated that he did not expect to follow the treatments he had submitted to NEH. Would he ignore us as well?

By this time, I had concluded that my most valuable contribution would be putting events into an historical perspective, since this was what I knew how to do best. On the other hand, Davis seemed to consider the humanist consultants as persons who could locate stories and/or people about whom stories could be made. This, despite the fact that the project proposal included a researcher who would have that responsibility.

My first project, *The Campaign*, badly needed historical perspective. Muncie's politics are tribal and had changed little since the 1920s when the Lynds had been in town. Elements of Muncie's political life are confusing to the uninitiated; normally a Democratic town, Muncie lacks the usual ethnic groups that support the party nationally. It also has a tradition of corruption and personal politics which the Lynds found extremely distasteful. "There is no area of Middletown's life, save religion, where symbol is more admittedly and potently divorced from reality than in government, and no area where the functioning of an institution is more enmeshed in undercover intrigue and personalities" [Lynd and Lynd 1956:322].

An aspect of Muncie politics is the kinship network that persists in the community. Office holders who are no longer eligible for one office run for another. They become professional officeholders; this is their primary vocation. Their sons or grandsons or nephews or nieces run for office as well, leaving it in the family. Old antagonisms persist through generations, as do old loyalties.

Another element that characterizes Muncie's politics is a class division between the working-class south side of the town and the more prosperous, middle-class north side. While this cuts across party lines, it affects the Democratic Party most. In general, the Democrats have tried to appeal to the working-class base by nominating union members for the mayor's office while appeasing the liberal middle class with other rewards. This division has long historic roots, going back as far as the First World War.

The antagonisms are not just the results of personal feuds but involve a real struggle for power. Although the Lynds had predicted an eventual merit system for city employees and on paper such a system now exists, political patronage still plays a significant role in employment and in retention, not to mention promotion, in city jobs. The mayor sometimes controlled the system personally; sometimes it was under the control of the county chairman. Sometimes it was a joint control. Often it was a matter of much contention. When it was, the results were usually disastrous for the contending parties.

A fight over patronage split the Democratic Party in Muncie in 1979. Beginning in 1955, the Democrats had won the mayor's office in every election except for 1963. In that year the incumbent mayor, H. Arthur Tuhey, who had served two terms in office, had strong opposition in the primary. This opposition split the party, enabling John Hampton, the son of John Hampton who served as mayor when the Lynds were in Muncie, to win. Since that time, however, the Democrats had been in firm control of the office. The incumbent mayor was Robert Cunningham who had defeated the party's candidate, the previous incumbent, in 1975.

Cunningham had not been a very successful mayor. Prior to election as mayor he had run a small grocery store in the dilapidated near west side of Muncie, although he had previously worked in a factory and also entertained notions of being a cartoonist. He was folksy but soon earned the reputation of not being effective. Nor was he particularly well connected to the factions within the Democratic Party.

The Democratic county chairman was Ira "Rip" Nelson. Nelson had been successful as a precinct committeeman. One of his long- time opponents calls him "one of the most successful politicians at the grassroots level that anyone could be" [*Muncie Star* 4 November 1979]. He worked as a contractor, but lived in Shed Town, the poorest white section of town, in a large house which towered over the much smaller and modest homes of his constituents. He had won the post in 1978 from Jerry Thornburg, a very bright but controversial Democrat, who had served two years as county chairman. There was still bad blood between the two, but Nelson rapidly consolidated his power and was in control of the party despite sniping from those who had remained loyal to Thornburg.

The Republican county chairman was John Hampton, who had been mayor in the 1960s. While the Republicans had been unsuccessful in local elections, the county chairman's job was a political plum because of Indiana's antiquated law which allowed the county chairmen of the party that held the governor's office to operate the automobile license branches, collecting money for the party and, not incidently, for themselves and their families and friends. Hampton had no strong challengers and the Republican Party was not divided.

The primary election reflected both parties' assumptions about the chances of victory. Ten candidates filed for the Democrats, five for the Republicans, and one for the American Independent Party. Five of the Democrats could be considered serious candidates while only two Republicans were.

The five serious Democrats represented different segments of the Democratic coalition. Robert Cunningham, the incumbent mayor, was one; he represented mainly himself. So did James Carey, but he also had a stronger personal following than did Cunningham. Kent Irwin, a local school teacher, was the best educated and had support among middle-class Democrats on the north side. County chairman Nelson supported Elmer Cox, who was president of the city council. Jerry Thornburg, the ex-county chairman, ran, mostly as a result of long antipathy to Carey.

The two serious Republican candidates were Alan K. Wilson, a local lawyer and deputy prosecuting attorney, and John Jackson, a former auto dealer and conservative religionist. The county chairman remained neutral, but it was obvious that Wilson was his favorite. Neither candidate had run for significant office before, but Jackson's reputation as a car dealer was off-putting.

The two winners were Carey and Wilson. Carey won a plurality of the vote, 2453 out of 8518 votes cast. Three of his opponents garnered about 2000 votes each. Wilson also won by a plurality, 2479 out of 5125 votes cast, but his main opponent, Jackson, was 700 votes behind and Wilson had a near majority [Cunningham 1986:n.p.]. Moreover, the Republican Party was not rent by the primary; the Democratic Party was. The major question was: could the Democratic candidate put the party back together?

Much depended upon Carey, and his record held out hope. Born on Muncie's south side, Carey was Irish, a lifelong Democrat and public servant. He was a Muncie Central Bearcat, lettering in football and basketball. Following naval service at the end of World War II, Carey joined the police force which was recruited mainly from Muncie Central athletes. He rose rapidly. He was the first Muncie policeman to attend the FBI academy; at twenty-eight he became the youngest police captain in Muncie's history. He became deputy first assistant chief in 1958 when the police chief, Jack Young, resigned to run for sheriff. Carey then moved into the chief's slot, a move made possible by his political affiliation. From patrolman to chief had taken less than ten years [*Muncie Star* 4 November 1979].

Part of his success was due to ability and ambition; part was due to political influence and personal charm. However, Carey's career also was touched by scandal. After being chief for slightly over one year, Carey and two vice squad detectives—Claude "Hope" Mullen and Ambrose Settles (a black)—were indicted by the grand jury for malfeasance. The charge was that they failed to enforce the laws against pinball and slot machines, and to stop gambling in cigar stores. Additionally, the grand jury charged the two detectives with malfeasance for failing to arrest Herman and Marie Jeter, the proprietors of the notorious "Chicken Shack," which allegedly sold liquor without a license to nearby black residents. The accused never came to trial; the prosecutor dropped the charges for want of evidence after three years [*Muncie Star* 4 November 1979].

In his own defense, Carey claimed the charges were politically inspired. He also maintained that he had recognized the problem before the indictments had been issued. After he had appointed Mullen and Settles to be a two-man vice squad, he had doubts about their probity and returned them to detective duty. He also said he had tried to persuade the deputy city controller to withhold a restaurant license for the "Chicken Shack," but the latter refused because of insufficient grounds to do so [*Muncie Star* 9 March 1959].

While under indictment, Carey voluntarily relinquished the office of chief and reverted to the rank of major. He became chief again after the charges were dropped in 1963. This service lasted only a year. When John Hampton won the mayor's office, Carey had to vacate the office again to make way for a more politically acceptable person. He reverted to captain and served four years in that position before becoming chief again when Democrat Paul Cooley assumed the mayor's office.

At the same time he was under indictment, Carey suffered personal misfortune. His first wife committed suicide with Carey's own gun and was found by their son who had come home for lunch. Carey eventually remarried a divorced woman who was the daughter of a dentist. A college graduate, she worked as a librarian at Muncie Central High School and lived in the higher rent district on the north side of town. She was protective of Carey and tried hard to overcome his frequent obscenities and coarse language; she was anxious for him to be respectable.

In 1970 Carey retired as police chief and ran successfully for county sheriff on the Democratic ticket. It was his first try at elective office and seemed to prove that he could transfer his personal following into votes. It also meant more money; being sheriff was probably the most lucrative elective office in the county because of the meal allowance paid to the occupant of the office for the prisoners. Carey could add this not insubstantial sum to his police pension. Not only was his financial position more secure, he also received acclaim for his efforts when the Muncie Boy's Club presented him with the 1971 Horatio Alger award for raising himself from humble origins to a position of importance [*Muncie Star* 4 November 1979].

The next year the roof caved in on Carey again. In the summer of 1972 the Delaware County prosecutor, a Democrat, charged Carey with two counts of bribery—one for accepting bribes from a man named Mason who ran an illegal gambling operation in town and another for paying the prosecutor $2,538 to ignore Mason's activities. The case was curious in that the operation was supposedly in Muncie where the city police, not Sheriff Carey, had jurisdiction. Opponents held that Carey had been accepting bribes as police chief and had convinced Mason that he could continue to offer protection as sheriff. Friends claimed he was framed.

Tried in December, the case against Carey looked ironclad. The prosecutor granted immunity to Mason in order to obtain testimony, and had both wired himself to record the bribery conversation with Carey and then marked the bills given him. The case appeared so strong that, according to one witness, Carey had wanted to plead guilty but was dissuaded by his attorneys. Instead, the defense attacked both the credibility and motives of the witnesses, accusing the prosecutor of entrapping Carey "because he's the most popular man in town" [*Muncie Star* 7 and 8 December 1972], never denying Carey's payment to the prosecutor nor ever putting him on the stand to testify in his own defense. The lawyers successfully used Carey's popularity and his supposed stupidity as a defense. Defense lawyer Thomas Cannon epitomized this in his summation, saying "Jim Carey is dumb. Jim Carey made a big mistake. But what honest man has been hurt? I say to you—I beg to you—give Jim Carey another chance. He'll be a better man. Certainly he's suffered enough" [*Muncie Star* 4 November 1979; 14 December 1972]. The jury deliberated less than four hours before finding Carey not guilty of attempting to bribe the prosecutor [*Muncie Star* 4 November 1979; 14 December 1972]. The second charge, accepting bribes, was dropped by the prosecutor by mid-1973. The following year Carey won re-election easily. However, Indiana statutes allow a maximum of only two four-year terms for sheriff, and, in 1978, Carey was out of a job. Having spent his life in public service and lacking prospects for private employment, he naturally turned to the most available and higher office. When he won the primary, he had an unbroken string of election victories.

His opponent, Alan Wilson, was not so lucky. He had lost in two previous attempts to win local elections. Despite these failures, his career had been more upwardly mobile than had Carey's, as he had done all of the things usually necessary for achieving success in America. Born on the north side of Muncie, Wilson graduated from Burris, Ball State University's laboratory school, which, unlike Central which Carey attended, was composed of mainly students from middle-class families. Wilson's father was a mail carrier as was Carey's, but there the resemblances ended. Wilson was non-athletic but was academically talented. He enrolled at Purdue University and graduated as an engineer. He then decided to go to law school giving as his reasons: "I saw it as a chance to work with people and make a better than average income. In addition, of course, law also offered the possibility of a political future" [Vander Hill 1982:52].

After law school, Wilson joined the navy before returning to Muncie to practice law. He was not one of the powerful lawyers in the town; he had not been able to join a prestigious legal firm but instead had opened a small law office with a former law school roommate. His practice was not thriving; he survived in part because of income earned by his wife as a visiting nurse and by virtue of his appointment as deputy prosecutor. His supporters claimed, correctly, that he had never lost a case. However, he had not had many large cases to lose.

Why did Wilson run for mayor? In part he ran because he could use the money; a political win might lead to a more lucrative practice or a higher office. In part he ran because no other serious Republican candidate wanted or believed that the office could be won. Further, the Republican Party believed that he was the kind of candidate who would fit the conservative, low-key image of the party.

This was the situation when Davis came back to Muncie to film the opening of the campaign which traditionally began during the Delaware County Fair in the middle of July. We had a grant request pending at the National Endowment for a pilot film, but would not have a decision until September. Davis came as part of a three-person crew; he filmed these scenes himself; and his sound man was Tom Cohen, who had served in the same capacity in *Hearts and Minds*.

The fair footage appears in *The Campaign* in a series of images near the beginning. These include a shot of Wilson at the Republican tent (each party has a tent at the fair and each has one day dedicated to it), talking to prospective voters and to the fair queen who asks him for a T-shirt. Both encounters show Wilson's character that of a modest, self-deprecating individual who is shy about meeting members of the public, especially nubile young women.

The shots of Carey are taken at the Democratic tent, but the contrast between the two candidates is already apparent. Carey is good-naturedly joking with Hurley Goodall, a black state legislator, and with other political cronies and hangers-on. The immediate impression is of a group of overweight, lower-class individuals who are interested mainly in the free food available in the tent. The music in the background is amateurish in comparison with the professional work of the Republican band.

Beyond those fleeting images of class and character, there is little hint of what form the campaign will take. Nor was there a clear idea of how to proceed with the film, of how to establish a strong narrative line. How could the structure of Muncie politics be revealed in film?

I discussed this problem with Davis and with Cohen who succeeded Davis and eventually directed the film. There were two ideas which occurred to me that might add historical perspective. One was to highlight the emergence of blacks and Catholics into the political mainstream; the other was to emphasize the structure of local politics by focusing upon the continuing inbred nature of Muncie's political leadership.

The Lynds completely ignored blacks in *Middletown* and *Middletown in Transition*, while dismissing Catholics in the latter as "not involved in local politics or any other public aspects of Middletown's life" [Lynd and Lynd 1965:313; Hoover 1987b:56-57]. But times had changed. Both groups had increased in both proportion of population and influence since the 1920s. Blacks now constituted 10 percent of the population, while Catholics made up 14 percent [Caplow, Bahr, and Chadwick 1982:323]. In each case the percentage had doubled and both groups had vastly expanded their political weight. No longer did blacks or Catholics refrain from seeking office; Hurley Goodall, who appeared in the fair scene with Carey, was the first black member of the school board and had become one of the two Muncie representatives in the Indiana General Assembly. Carey was an Irish Catholic who emphasized his Irishness, but he was not the only Catholic in the political arena. John Hampton, the ex-mayor and Republican County Chairman, was a converted Catholic and was a brother-in-law of a Catholic lawyer prominent in the Democratic Party and Carey's campaign.

John Hampton was a particularly interesting example of both the ascendancy of Catholics and the persistence of certain families in Muncie's political life. His father was a furniture salesman and Ku Klux Klansman who served as Republican mayor of Muncie from 1926 to 1930 but, because of scandal, lost in the primary in 1929. He, however, ran successfully in 1942 and served again from 1943 to 1947, although his second administration was also tainted with scandal. Hampton was anti-Catholic, at least on paper. Hampton, the son, had abandoned his father's anti-Catholicism to the extent of marrying a Catholic, converting, and sending his children to a Catholic school.

But the Hamptons were not the only family that linked past and present. Hampton's successful rival in the Republican primary in 1929, Robert Denver Barnes, had a son James who was also a good friend of Carey and whom, despite his Republicanism, he supported. Like Hampton, Barnes had inherited a tradition of political activism; like Hampton, he did not inherit a set of immutable principles. A final example is that of William O. Shroyer who was Carey's campaign manager. An entrepreneur who had two laundry and dry-cleaning establishments on the south side of Muncie, Shroyer had a long-time record of political involvement, and his uncle, Ora T. Shroyer was a Democratic district councilman in 1929.

The problem with exploiting these features of Muncie political life was how to incorporate them into film. Cohen was pessimistic about the possibility of portraying ideas on film, saying that he could produce only surface images. In addition, Davis had an aversion to talking heads and contrived situations. My idea of interviewing persons such as Hampton, Barnes, and Shroyer never was accepted, although I still think recollections of these persons regarding changes of attitudes toward blacks and Catholics, the demise of the Klan, and the tensions between the two sides of Muncie would have provided historical depth and needed context.

Not that there was a reluctance to use the interview technique. There are several scenes in *The Campaign* based upon staged interviews. They include one with Carey and another with Wilson. The Carey interview lasted several hours and resulted in a few minutes of on-screen footage. The same was true of the Wilson interview. Perhaps this caused Davis to conclude results such as these were not worth the effort involved. In any case, there were no interviews of party chairmen in the film.

There were several scenes involving blacks, however, which demonstrated their significance in Carey's campaign. These include the Careys in a black church listening to the choir and a scene in the Rooster-Booster club, a Democratic support group, where blacks discuss Carey's good record as a policeman and indicate their support for him. Curiously enough, there were no scenes of Catholics. Carey is never shown worshipping in St. Mary's; indeed, he appears only in the black church, a scene juxtaposed with Wilson singing in the choir of First Presbyterian Church. One could not tell from the film that there were any Catholics in town or that there had ever been anti-Catholic prejudice.

In September 1979, NEH granted the Middletown Film Project $325,000 to produce a pilot film on the campaign. Xerox committed itself to become the sole corporate underwriter in the amount of $500,000 at the same time. The latter grant was the work of Davis; we had no idea of the provisions of the grant, although we did learn that Davis planned to use these as matching funds for grants from NEH and the Indiana Committee for the Humanities.

Thus was to begin over two years of almost constant involvement of out-of-town film crews in Muncie life. Most of these were recruited from the

East and West coasts and included such persons as Tom Cohen, Bob Brady, Paul Goldsmith, Richard Leacock, and Tom Hurovitz who were in town for varying lengths of time. Among those who arrived was Terry Simon who came to Muncie as Tom Cohen's chief researcher. She began to look for additional stories to film as well as to be a kind of general helper. The Cohen crew located in the Robert's Hotel which was at that time a dilapidated structure with few occupants and those, long-term residents. The team rented a suite for a ridiculously low sum and installed all kinds of equipment, including an editor and a refrigerator. The hotel also had the advantage of providing meeting rooms for the Republican and Democratic Parties on the lower floors.

Then was to start a ritual that soon proved familiar. Film crews would shoot during the day, a driver would drive the footage sixty miles to Indianapolis to be sent to New York City by overnight express, and then the developed film would return soon after. All of this was incredibly expensive and money worries were constant, since the eventual ratio of utilized film to that shot was very low.

The campaign heated up after Labor Day, but the activity did not reveal much of beneath-the-surface activity. Carey appointed a city chairman to run his campaign; this did not auger well for any reconciliation with Nelson for, while it was within Carey's right to appoint such a person, it was an affront to the county chairman. Nor did the choice of city chairman help bridge the gulf with south side Munsonians. He was Everett Ferrill, a professor of history at Ball State University and my former chairman, a liberal Democrat with a personal following on the north side of Muncie, but who had little connection with either Nelson or the south side of town.

Nelson was very quiet as he worked behind the scenes. He was never in Democratic strategy sessions so he was never on- camera. On the other hand, Carey was larger than life and, with the help of his advisors, ran his own campaign. He was extremely cooperative, giving advance notice of all his meetings and public appearances. He willingly helped the filmmakers, even agreeing to work a precinct on Muncie's north side on election day so that the crews could photograph him meeting Wilson, whose precinct it was.

Carey's Democratic opponents either were never asked to appear on camera, as for example Nelson and Thornburg, or refused to do so, probably because of the belief that Carey would win and then exact retribution. We did persuade a local judge, a former student of mine and an ally of Thornburg, to consent to be photographed and to give his very low opinion of Carey. In the actual interview, he had second thoughts and described Carey in glowing terms. This segment went unused; Davis also located a local madam who believed Carey had been instrumental in sending her to prison on an IRS charge when she failed to bribe him. Out of the federal penitentiary, she was a cook in a local nursing home and did not wish to be filmed.

There were two other critics of Carey who appeared on the scene but neither had any political clout. One was an unidentified man in an opening scene at the Workman's Bar, a tavern in the industrial area of Muncie, who called Carey a crook. The other was Anthony Edmonds, another history professor at Ball State University and a liberal supporter of Kent Irwin, who was persuaded to get his hair cut on-camera and to voice his opinions about Carey's past record. Neither represented anyone besides himself, so the strong Democratic opposition remained out of the picture.

The problem with filming the Republican side of the campaign was twofold: Wilson lacked charisma and his managers were very guarded about their strategy meetings. County chairman Hampton and Mrs. Hartmeyer, a campaign coordinator, would not give out information on such meetings or if information had been gained would try to prevent admission. Part of this reticence was because of fears that we might reveal their candidate's strategy and part was because of an innate predilection to secrecy. Matters were exacerbated early in the fall when a member of the film crew inadvertently revealed to the Democrats what the Republicans planned. Wilson's advisors also viewed Trimmer with suspicion because his wife worked in the office of second district Congressman Phil Sharp, a Democrat. This suspicion, combined with his abrasiveness, resulted in them threatening to end all participation if he were allowed to cover their side. His removal further cut our information from that source.

There is one Republican meeting that appears in the film; it is one which the filmmakers stumbled on by accident and which they were able to film. It tends to confirm the fears of Wilson's advisors. In it Wilson receives contradictory advice from a number of supporters. Chic Clark, a leading trial lawyer in town, tells him to shorten his statements and tries to rehearse him for questions he might be asked. Wilson, tired and confused, finally rebels at what he considers to be contradictory advice and leaves the room vowing not to run ever again. The segment makes Wilson appear to be a puppet in his advisors' hands and reflects little credit on anyone involved [Vander Hill 1982:50; Hoover 1988:13].

Most of the film concerned events where the candidates met the public either alone or collectively. These included a race in which both candidates were pushed on beds by supporters during Octoberfest; various meetings organized to present the candidate in a favorable light; scenes with the candidates soliciting votes in either a middle-class suburb on the north side, while walking over what appears to be enormous spans of lawn (Wilson), or visiting in Shed Town to hear complaints about a garbage dump fouling the area

(Carey), and even an interview with a Burris high school class (Carey). The class had decided, with the prompting of its teacher, to make its own film of the campaign. In the case of Wilson, there is also a shot of him taking an elocution lesson so as to make a more effective radio commercial.

By the end of the nine weeks' filming there were few hints of the possible outcome. The film crew, I believe, honestly thought Carey would win, seduced by his charm and by the greater hoopla in his campaign. Perhaps the most spectacular event that contributed to this assumption was Carey's monster rally the Saturday prior to the Tuesday election. The Democrats hired a large hall at the Delaware County Fairgrounds and made it the site of an old-fashioned political rally, the kind that is part of the American mythos. The rally resembled a miniature presidential convention, complete with Carey's picture, name, and shamrocks on balloons, signs, and hats. Visiting dignitaries, including Indiana Senator Birch Bayh (who was himself to be defeated in the 1980 election by Dan Quayle) and Congressman Phil Sharp, lauded Carey and indicated how important his victory would be to the city and to their own campaigns. The scene conveys a sense of excitement and energy which seem to presage a Carey landslide.

To the astute observer of Muncie politics, however, the rally indicated otherwise. Instead of a Carey sweep, the suspicion was that Carey was in deep trouble. What was essential to Carey's winning was a unified Democratic Party with the support of Nelson and Thornburg. He had neither. The large crowd consisted of Carey's supporters; Nelson's minions and Thornburg's followers were not there. Nelson was there; he had to be since he was county chairman. He can be seen sitting on the platform, but he neither speaks nor does he wear a Carey button. Not apparent to me at the time but revealed on the film is a whispered conversation on the platform. "Sparky" Walsh, an old-line Democrat and Carey supporter, agitatedly tells Carey that the firemen want certain promises to be made in order to obtain their votes. Carey refuses, a major error and one that will have ominous results for him.

Local pundits such as Larry Lough, an editor for the *Muncie Star*, had summed up the situation well just prior to the election. While predicting Carey would win, Lough ticked off continuing problems for Carey. "Mayor Bob Cunningham and city council president Elmer Cox seem to remain bitter about the primary results and have been no help to the Carey campaign. Delaware County Democratic Chairman Ira F. (Rip) Nelson, who backed another loser in Cox last spring, still holds a long-standing grudge against Carey, and party efforts on the mayoral candidate's behalf have been minimal. Some even suggest they have been counter-productive" [*Muncie Star* 4 November 1979].

Indeed they were. When Carey predicted that a turnout of twenty thousand voters would assure his victory, he failed to consider what would happen if Democratic voters crossed over. Wilson swept the election although 21,577 votes were cast, winning by a 4,666 vote margin, the third largest in history. He took thirty-two out of fifty precincts, among them many ordinarily Democratic ones. He won five of six precincts in councilman Cox's first district; he won thirteen precincts Democratic Mayor Cunningham had carried in 1975. Nelson predicted before the election that "his" precincts would give Carey on average of 150 votes less than Cunningham. The actual total was 144. This proved, Lough said, that "Rip" could count. Carey said, "I don't like losing to Democrats. Something has to be done. Someone has to take charge of this party who can bring us victory next fall" [*Muncie Star* 11 November 1979].

Wilson's victory was a godsend to the filmmakers. It offered the best possible finish that could have been imagined. This twist would provide a surprise ending, an unlikely occurrence in ordinary life. Now Davis and Cohen had to make a film out of the footage to match the finish. It had to be good because it was to be the base for further financing from NEH and Xerox.

What did the film reveal? It opened with a parade, Homecoming at Ball State in October, and vignettes of drinkers at a bar. It went back to the County Fair in July and forward to the bed race in October. It then gave a fairly straightforward account of the campaign during the next month-and-one-half. It concentrated upon the end results, not the root causes. The film becomes a contest between the ebullient Irishman Carey, champion of the working class and the poor, and the WASP Wilson, the spokesman for rich doctors, lawyers, and businessmen.

This was done with clever cutting and juxtaposition. Scenes of Carey in a black church are paired with ones of Wilson singing in the Presbyterian church choir. Carey is shown meeting with obviously poor people, many of them elderly, while Wilson is shown at a meeting with the governor of the state where one doctor's wife talks of shopping in Chicago and where all are uniformly prosperous. Wilson passes out literature in a middle-class suburb; Carey discusses rats in a poor section of town. The campaign appears to be a clash between rich and poor.

Perhaps the most ingenious cutting is that of Carey appearing before the Burris High School class where, for the first time, he is confronted with questions about his checkered past. Carey begins to discuss his problems with the law, switches to his first wife's suicide and then breaks down in tears. The scene dissolves to his condominium where, clad in pajama bottoms, Carey talks with obvious emotion about what happened to him. The film then returns to the class where, in this person's opinion, obnoxious adolescents pontificate on Carey, accusing him of deliberately faking tears and evading the questions and concluding that the "little people" would be the only ones to vote for him. This Leona Helmsley approach certainly alienated me and inclined my sympathies to Carey.

The ending was also one evoking much sympathy for Carey, and one reminiscent of Hollywood westerns. The camera focuses on Carey who, after congratulating Wilson, moves from the light into the dark followed by a disabled supporter insisting that Jim has really won. It reminded me of the last scene of Shane riding away on his horse as Brandon De Wilde struggled vainly to keep up.

In the teacher's guide to *The Campaign*, Richard Lingeman pretty well catches the spirit of the film. "Consider the two candidates in this film. Hollywood central casting would have been hard pressed to come up with two more contrasting yet emblematic types than Jim Carey, the gregarious, flesh-pressing Democrat,and Alan Wilson, the shy, WASPish Republican lawyer.... Carey seems a holdover from a long line of Irish urban politics, whose last exemplar was the late Mayor Richard Daley of Chicago....Carey does indeed show many of the traits of Frank Skeffington, the Boston boss of Edwin O'Connor's novel. He wears the same big, beating shamrock on his sleeve and has a redeeming concern for the little man....As for Alan Wilson, he is the earnest young reformer, the 'clean' candidate, the rising young deputy prosecutor who goes into politics to make a name for himself....The real issue [in the campaign] is personality, as it is in most small town elections, according to sociologists. People assess each candidate's character in light of their gut feelings, their class backgrounds, their sense of city pride and their economic interests" [Lingeman 1982a]. Lingeman left no cliche unturned in his uncritical acceptance of the stereotypical image of the Irish politician seen in *The Campaign*.

The Campaign had become a psychological drama starring Carey, focusing upon his personality and ignoring the system itself. Carey was not Skeffington, the consummate politician, nor was he much handicapped by his past record. He did not lose because of character flaws, although those did exist, but because of the lack of political skills, because of his failure to unite a badly splintered Democratic Party.

Carey's past misdeeds never were factors in the election as neither the newspapers nor Wilson mentioned them. (It was the stance taken by Wilson's advisors as the one scene showed.) The documentary did reveal the power structure in operation in Muncie, but only indirectly. It was there, hidden in the shadows.

The film was done, for better or for worse. Now we had to wait and see if it was impressive enough to encourage NEH to give us enough money for the remaining five.

Completing the Series

On 16 February 1980, The Middletown Film Project with Peter Davis as project director submitted a proposal to NEH for a series of five additional films. It requested $1,942,208 from NEH, $450,000 of which was to match a like amount from Xerox. It proposed a fourteen-month grant period beginning 1 June 1980, and ending 1 August 1981. The proposal was an expanded version of the earlier development grant; it included a summary of *The Campaign* and a treatment of each of the other five films. It did not indicate which station would originate the program, but WIPB appeared nowhere in it. The pilot film accompanied the grant to be viewed by NEH's media panel.

The panel viewed *The Campaign* and was impressed enough to fund the grant. The work intensified, and Davis's first major task was to find the necessary filmmakers to make the remaining films. As always, his criteria were very high. As a producer he knew that the quality of the films depended upon the quality of the filmmakers. In addition to finding filmmakers, there was still the problem of selecting the subjects for the remaining segments. Only *The Big Game* was partially set; Muncie Central High School Bearcats were to be the main subject, but their opponent was not yet chosen. The others had not even progressed that far. The filmmakers would have to find appropriate stories by themselves with assistance from the rest of us.

The individuals chosen were a mixed bag. Tom Cohen, by virtue of his work in *The Campaign*, had the contract to do a film on *The Job*. His work was well-known to Davis. The person who was to make *The Big Game* was E.J. Vaughn. He was not a well-known documentarian, although he had made a film about the television show "Let's Make a Deal" [Vander Hill 1982:53] which did take a satirical look at the program. Vaughn knew little about basketball, but Davis did not consider knowledge about the topic to be filmed all that important. He was more interested in the product than in its relation to the film's subject.

The three remaining filmmakers consisted of one veteran and a pair of his students. The veteran was Richard Leacock. His students were Joel De Mott and Jeff Kreines. Leacock was a pioneer documentarian, one who could be said to have helped begin the tradition of direct cinema. Born in the Canary Islands and educated in an English school (where he met the daughters of the first great American documentarian, Robert J. Flaherty), Leacock served in the U.S. Signal Corps during World War II. He then took advantage of his acquaintance with Flaherty's daughter to become the cameraman on Flaherty's last film, *Louisiana Story*. Following that experience, he worked as a documentarian for television and for the U.S. government [Barnouw 1974:235-36; Marcorelles 1964:246-49; Leacock 1959:37-38: 1961:23-35]. He was part of Drew Associates in the late 1950s and was, with Albert Maysles, the cameraman on *Primary*. He left Drew Associates in 1963. Unlike the other filmmakers on the project, he had written and been interviewed extensively and had taught several generations of filmmakers at MIT. This meant his views on cinema direct were well-known.

Like other members of Drew Associates, Leacock believed in the use of traditional fictional devices of character, action, and structure. He believed films should focus on a crisis and its resolution. "Situations are selected where a crisis is inevitable, even if the precise outcome cannot be foreseen" [Mamber 1974:118]. Then elements not pertinent to that focus would be edited out, according to Leacock, who never denied this selectivity. He criticized his fellow documentarian Albert Maysles who, he said "was making a religion or a virtue of merely looking" [Jacobs 1979:406]. How Leacock would shoot *The Sabbath*, his assignment, remained to be seen.

His students, Kreines and De Mott, were less well-known. Kreines was a high school dropout who met De Mott, a college graduate and daughter of the noted English scholar Benjamin De Mott (who was to serve later on the board of NEH), at the MIT Film/Video Section taught by Ed Pincus and Leacock. Both influenced Kreines and De Mott, Leacock by his emphasis upon reducing the intrusion of bulky equipment into the filming situation and Pincus with his belief that "filming intimate life was a doorway to filming social, political, economic, and philosophical concerns of the day" [Rance 1986:95].

Kreines came to MIT with a film, *The Plaint of Steve Kreines as Recorded by his Younger Brother, Jeff*, he had begun about his brother, which Pincus encouraged him to finish. According to Mark Rance who studied under Kreines and De Mott, the film was "a home movie, plain and simple, about a twenty-eight-year-old leaving home for the first time" [Rance 1986:96-97].

De Mott had come to MIT with a similar goal: "To create sophisticated documentaries about family life. But Joel was also looking to create a kind of documentary that was like literature, full of twists and turns provided by characters you really get to know by SEEING what they are like. Dramatic film will go through tens of drafts of a screenplay (and tens of writers) to get that effect. Joel was promoting cinéma-vérité/direct cinema to get the very same material" [Rance 1986:97].

Kreines and De Mott got together and shot a film, *Vince and Marianne Get Married,* as their first effort. Their instructor, Pincus, "called it one of the most beautiful documentaries" [Rance 1986:97]. Unfortunately, the wedding was of a couple with Mafia connections so it could only be shown as an underground film.

Their next film, *Demon Lover Diary,* was an account of the duo's experience in making Demon Lover, for "a couple of amateurs, both factory workers, who were, at least in 1975 (when the film was made), movie nuts." The two Michigan sponsors financed this low-budget effort by compensation one had received for losing a finger in an "industrial accident." Unbeknownst to these two, Kreines and De Mott filmed the making of a film. The film, which was not released until ten years later, was, according to Vincent Canby, "wonderful if slightly mean-spirited." At the movie's end, "Mr. Kreines and Miss De Mott flee Michigan, expressing the kind of disdain for the Middle West that Oscar Wilde felt for the entire New World" [Canby 1985a].

Rance has described both the technique and underlying motives of the film best. "Her [De Mott's] film, *Demon Lover Diary,* is more than a home movie, but the raw footage could have been viewed as one. It is loving, angry, playful, vindictive. She never seeks to generalize nor preach about what is going on around her, but to show it as she feels it. (We love baby, so we rush to get the camera to film baby's first steps.) A significant sequence in *Demon Lover Diary* was filmed one afternoon while Joel was aggravated because Jeff was late as usual and she had to kill time waiting. She spotted some children playing with an abandoned refrigerator-size cardboard box. She went over to them and waited patiently, filming them as a parent might film them. The scene obviously had nothing to do with the movie she was shooting, a diary about the making of a ridiculous horror film, and she was down to her last rolls of film, but she shot what she felt like shooting. Her reward: one child finds his father's hidden booze in the garage and proudly presents it to the others. Irrelevant? Hardly. For Joel it struck a chord about life in the Midwest and it is a key to that subtext of the film. It is also a wonderful scene" [Rance 1986:97]. None of us in Muncie knew of the two films that Kreines and De Mott had made. Had we known that they had such a distaste for the Midwest and filmed what they felt, regardless of what the theme of the segment was, we might have questioned their choice.

Davis evidently had no such qualms about hiring them to make the remaining two films: *The Wedding* and *The Commencement.* Davis has given the reasons for his decision to the filmmakers. "Why do you think I hired you? I looked around for quite a while—at a lot of other filmmakers who had studied with Ricky, for instance—before I settled on you. I wanted your tech-

niques and sensitivities to kids for the films that had young people in them"
[Davis personal communication to De Mott and Kreines, 11 October 1984].

Kreines and De Mott came to Muncie and, in keeping with their identification with the working class, claimed to live near their proposed subjects.
They moved to Good Thunder Farm outside of Muncie on the south side.
This was not working-class housing; it was a more up-scale place to live than
the Roberts Hotel where most of the other filmmakers lived. Moreover, it
was in a much better neighborhood since the Roberts was only two blocks
from the railroad tracks and the dilapidated taverns beyond, as well as being
next to the Muncie Mission, a shelter for homeless men.

The search for appropriate stories continued at an accelerated pace that
summer as the filmmakers and Terry Simon spent most of their time interviewing prospective subjects. Only one segment was partially determined.
That was *The Big Game*. We knew that the film had to include Muncie Central High School, since it was the oldest high school with the longest tradition
of basketball victories in town. It had begun its string of state championships,
documented by flags hung from fieldhouse rafters, in 1928. The Bearcats had
entered the realm of myth; their defeat by tiny Milan in the state finals in the
1950s had, in disguised form, been the basis of the film *Hoosiers*.

Moreover, Muncie Central basketball typifies the "Hoosier Hysteria"
which the Lynds noted. They reported, almost incredulously, that such was
the priority given to basketball that the city council voted to borrow $100,000
to build a fieldhouse at the same time that it refused to appropriate $300 to
pay for the continuing service of an assistant in the public library. They also
included in *Middletown* this statement by a minister in a working-class
church. "I have been asked, 'Is it right to pray for the Bearcats to win?' by
one of you who tells me he no longer believes in prayer because he prayed as
hard as he could for the Bearcats and they lost. I believe that prayer should be
used in cases where a moral or spiritual issue is at stake. God *could* favor the
weaker team, but that would be unsportsmanlike of God" [Lynd and Lynd
1956:284-377].

The major question was which other team should be used. In the proposal
to NEH, Davis posited Southside as the opponent, taking as a description of
the climactic game a segment from *Hometown*. He even used a theme from
Hometown. "*The Big Game* is perhaps *Middletown's* closest approach to al-
legory, for in this film an athletic contest symbolizes social and economic
conflict between the upper– and lower–class high schools of Muncie.
Muncie Central serves the high–income northern suburbs, while Southside is
in the heart of slums that come in both black and white. For the players and
their schools, this game is the season, and the season is the cusp of their future" [Davis 1980:77].

Almost all of the descriptions in this paragraph are wrong—Muncie Central did not serve the high–income northern suburbs; Northside High School did. Southside is not in the heart of the slums that are both black and white. It is located instead in a white working–class area of modest and well–kept houses several miles from slums. The poorest whites attend Muncie Central High School which is itself adjacent to an area of decayed housing made into cheap apartments. A game between the two schools would not illustrate conflict between upper and lower classes.

Despite that fact, the rivalry between the two teams is intense, although it would stretch the truth a bit to say that their game makes the season. The teams are not in the same conference nor do they always play each other. They are most likely to meet in the county tourney each spring, but that is not certain either, since such a meeting depends upon vagaries of scheduling and strengths of the teams.

For a variety of reasons, Southside was dropped as the opponent. The focus shifted to a conference game featuring a team from nearby Anderson. Vander Hill had made this decision before Vaughn even arrived in town [Vander Hill 1982:52]. He has detailed his reasons in "The Middletown Film Project: Reflections of an 'Academic Humanist.'" The most important one seems to have been that the Muncie-Anderson game was a home game between conference rivals and was scheduled for January. The contrasting personalities of the two coaches and their coaching styles also contributed. At that time, the two future players, Rick Rowray of Muncie Central and Andre Morgan of Anderson, had not been identified.

In many ways, Anderson High School and Anderson, Indiana, were similar to Muncie Central and Muncie. The school is one comparable in size to Muncie Central, with a mixed population both racially and academically talented—an equally impressive gym, and a basketball record almost as good. Anderson, like Muncie, is an industrial town relying heavily upon automobile manufacturing. At the time, it too had a severely depressed economy and future economic prospects were gloomy. It differed from Muncie in that it had no large university, although it had a denominational college of about two thousand students, and it contained the world headquarters of the Church of God, whose college it was. Neither of the latter two factors really intruded into the high school, the game, or the film.

There were a number of ideas for the film. One by Vander Hill seemed to me to be an excellent prospect for a thoughtful film. He suggested that the impact of basketball on the lives of Munsonians might be best shown by interviews with former Bearcats who had played in college and then on professional teams before returning to Muncie to live. There were several such individuals, black and white, including Bill Dunwoodie who worked as a

community organizer in black neighborhoods and Ron Bonham who ran rec-
reational programs for the city at Prairie Creek Reservoir. These men could
tell about life after basketball. While Vaughn did film interviews with them,
they were never used.

Instead, the film came to contrast the lives of the two coaches, Bill Harrell
of Muncie and Norm Held of Anderson, and the two dominant players,
Rowray and Morgan. There are several reasons for this. The first is that
Vaughn had no clear idea of where the film was going; the second is that
Davis lost confidence in Vaughn and did not allow him to come to New York
to help edit the film. As a consequence, the editors constructed the film without as much input from the filmmaker as might have been hoped.

The lives and styles of the coaches were certainly different. Bill Harrell
was born in the Kentucky coal fields and escaped poverty by going to college
on an athletic scholarship. He became a high school coach where he enjoyed
considerable success, leading Shelby County High School to the Kentucky
state championship. This success earned him the position of head basketball
coach at Morehead State University in Morehead, Kentucky. He was also a
successful college basketball coach but had to resign in the mid-1970s because of conflict over policy with the president and athletic director of
Morehead. He returned to high school coaching at that time because there
was no head coach position at the college level that he was offered, but he
still entertained hope of returning to collegiate ranks.

Harrell was as successful in Indiana as he had been in Kentucky, winning
an Indiana state championship in 1979. The secret to his coaching was primarily mental; Harrell was a student of the game. He fit the game to the players he had, sometimes employing a fast break, but more often a controlled
offense. He stressed defense and the fundamentals. His players rarely made
mistakes, and, as a consequence, frequently defeated teams with superior talent. Harrell's practices were highly organized, with two assistants doing
most of the work with the players and with goals clearly outlined. Harrell
assumed the role of administrator and planner; he rarely lost his temper and
he was not often emotional.

Beyond coaching, Harrell was involved in the community. He was a
Democrat who was interested in becoming county chairman, a post he ran for
but failed to attain. He was not interested in teaching and chafed with spending his time in the classroom, preferring the hardwood instead. He drove a
Cadillac and smoked large cigars; he was an excellent poker player who was
rumored to have won large sums in the games in town.

His opposite number, Norm Held, was different in many ways, although
almost as successful and equally committed to the game. Held was born in
Illinois but went to Milligan College in Tennessee. He originally intended to

become a minister; but because of athletic success, he decided to become a coach. He first coached in Illinois before coming to Anderson in 1973. There, he compiled an excellent record, going to the state finals three times.

In practice and in games, Held least resembled Harrell. There, Held was a stickler for discipline and was highly emotional, resembling Indiana coach Bobby Knight. He berated players and yelled at them. His tactics, according to Vander Hill, were equivalent to marine boot camp.

Off court, Held was a model of propriety, living up to his nickname, "the Reverend Held." He was more articulate, and better educated than Harrell. His language was less riddled with errors, making him a better spokesman for the game. He was no gambler; he sold insurance in his spare time, and, because of his enthusiasm and his reputation, was successful in that as well.

The best players on each team were also studies in contrast. Rick Rowray was a senior at Central; he was white and middle class. His father was director of admissions at Ball State University and his family was intact. He was also an honor student who received much attention from the basketball-mad school, teachers, principal, and students, becoming homecoming king in his senior year.

He had considerable athletic ability, although he lacked certain talents. He was six-feet-four, and was an excellent ballhandler, dribbler, and shooter. He, however, was a half-step slow and could not go to his left. Despite these handicaps, he was heavily recruited by universities, among them Kentucky, Iowa, and Indiana. His obvious intelligence and his other skills made him a likely prospect for both success in college and in life.

Andre Morgan, on the other hand, seemed destined for failure, in high school and beyond. He lived in a black neighborhood in a single-parent family. Morgan was a sophomore at Anderson High School, but he lacked interest in school and showed no motivation to study. His grades were poor, so bad, in fact, that he was in constant danger of losing his eligibility. He was interested in two things, basketball and girls. Because of his basketball skills, he never lacked for the latter.

He was a superb basketball player, one whose natural ability completely outstripped Rowray's. He was smooth, fast, and had a picture-book shot. Unfortunately, he was lazy and did not respond to Held's emotional motivation. Nor did he seem to heed his mother's plea for him to get an education. He was drifting and he knew it. Morgan would not be visited by college recruiters despite his great ability because he was a sophomore and, more importantly, his academic record was so poor that he was a non-predictor, one who would probably fail in college.

The film that Vaughn shot was not complex. It showed scenes from each player's life at home and at school; it showed practices held by each coach;

and it climaxed with the game between the Muncie Central Bearcats and the Anderson Indians. Included are segments showing Rowray being told by his father what qualities are necessary for success, qualities spelled out by Joe B. Hall, the coach at Kentucky, to the Muncie Central principal. The film shows Morgan responding almost not at all to a high school counselor who makes a feeble attempt to attract his attention with remarks about the big game.

Much of the footage, however, involved the players with their coaches, either in practice or in the game itself. Because of circumstance and because the editing was done without the filmmaker, the images of the coaches are reversed. Anderson had a team composed largely of juniors that had loads of talent, enough so that knowledgeable observers believed it was a year away from a state championship. However, it began the season badly and had accumulated a long losing streak before playing Muncie Central. As a result, Held had sunk into a depression and was not his typical, emotional self. In *The Big Game* he appears to be a quiet, patient, reflective person, which he was not.

On the other hand, Harrell also had problems of his own which may have been reflected in his uncharacteristic kicking of the ball and emotional displays, scenes of which editors selected to reveal his persona. In early January, Harrell suspended his three top guards for either violating curfew or not informing on others who broke curfew. This established his stern disciplinarianism, giving an opportunity to see the concerned players who were crushed, and their outraged parents who obviously saw their sons' playing as the ticket to college. It also resulted in film crews being barred from practice for three days, which may have skewed coverage. While the benching of three guards had considerable impact upon the Muncie Bearcats and caused Harrell to bring in younger players he was saving for the following year, it had not ruined the season. Harrell was still winning more than he lost and entertained hopes of going to the state finals again.

The Big Game was a less elaborate film than *The Campaign*, requiring fewer camera crews and less time to film. It was also done on videotape, which made it less expensive. However, the week of the game was a hectic one, with several camera crews in town. It was at this time that I recognized the costs and the lengths to which filmmakers would go to complete a project. Not happy with Muncie food, Davis had a New York City cook fly in for a week to prepare the Chinese cuisine favored by the crew.

The film was one of the less successful ones in the series in my opinion, as well as in the opinion of more informed critics. It had too much basketball and not enough character development. *The Big Game* was too much game. On the other hand, it is difficult to find much character development in seventeen-and eighteen-year-old boys. The film did not show the class difference in high schools as the proposal had said it would, but it certainly did contrast two individuals who had different backgrounds. Still, Morgan's counterpart could be found on the Muncie Bearcats as could Rowray's on the Anderson Indians. But the film did not indicate why the community was so supportive of basketball, showing only how it was such an integral part of the lives of two players and two coaches. It failed to probe the motives of those who cheered on both teams in a frenzy of emotion.

Joe Trimmer wrote the study guide for *The Big Game*, although he was not a major participant in the filming and Vander Hill was obviously more qualified. In it, Trimmer argued that "The big game seems to embody what we miss in our daily lives—order, purpose, fulfillment. A game has a beginning, middle, and end." He also claimed that *The Big Game* is about the value of character. "Coaches, players, parents, and teachers believe that competitive athletics build character" [Trimmer 1982:3-4]. Yet the segment does not show any character being built; Morgan and Rowray have not changed from the beginning of the film until the end. Perhaps the time covered is too short to show character development; perhaps the decisions made on court do not lead anywhere. The film is full of talk about character, but no one seems to know quite how it is to be achieved.

Having said that, I must note two subsequent developments pertinent to *The Big Game*. Its outtakes are the most popular of all those held by the Center for Middletown Studies. Coaches and players want to see the contest. Second, Held reverted to his old persona when the Indians started winning; the team recovered enough to go to the state finals while, ironically, the Bearcats never made it out of the county tournament.

By January 1981, when *The Big Game* was in the can, several developments had occurred regarding the film project itself. Davis had come to rely more and more on Trimmer and less and less on Vander Hill and me. My long background piece on Muncie's schools found no favor from Davis who said he had little use for it and, consequently, refused to pay me for all my time. He may have been right in his assessment of my contribution; Kreines and De Mott were already filming at Southside, a fact which I did not know and of which I was not informed. I had thought the decision about which school to use had not been made. I then offered to resign officially and to send a copy of the letter to the NEH. Davis urged me not to do so and offered to allow me to go to New York City to help edit. I refused, primarily because I knew nothing about editing and because I was teaching full time. Looking back now, I think that this was my second major error, the first being relinquishing project control. Had I agreed to participate in the editing, I might have changed some elements in the films. The offer mollified me, as Davis had expected, and I did not resign. However, I was given no more assignments and received no more pay.

Vander Hill was also being eased out. After finishing his work on *The Big Game* in January 1981, he had little more to do with the remaining four films [Vander Hill 1982:56]. Trimmer, the one humanist who remained active in the project, was the least informed about the community and had no connection with the Middletown III project. He was neither historian nor sociologist. This meant that from this time on, the filmmakers and the producers selected the stories without the benefit of historical or sociological data. The project was no longer ours; although our names still appeared in credits, they gradually receded further and further back until disappearing entirely from *Seventeen*.

Family Business

The film on work had originally been titled *The Job*. The treatment Davis wrote for NEH envisaged a film about workers at Warner Gear, a division of Borg-Warner which manufactures transmissions on the west side of Muncie. He said "This film will pursue the problems and actions of three Middletown citizens as they confront a critical moment at Warner Gear. The conflict and suspense in *The Job* will arise from the dilemma of making choices. A subtle issue emerges from the labor-management dispute. The dispute will be settled, to a large degree, outside Muncie.... The story of our three protagonists will explore a range of themes with regard to American work. Certain values, once so important to our national identity, have been undergoing a significant transformation in our time..." [Davis 1980].

In *Hometown*, Davis devoted two chapters to a strike and its settlement at Hamilton Tool Company. In it, he described the protagonists, their positions, and the reasons for these. In his early thoughts about *The Job*, it is clear that he hoped to film a strike in Muncie and that it did not have to be a strike at Warner Gear.

Two problems prevented Cohen from carrying out Davis's plan. The first was that there was no strike in town in the fall of 1980, nor was there any prospect of one in the near future. The second was that Cohen did not like the idea. While agreeing with Davis that found drama should center on people in crisis, he disagreed about the subject matter. A film on work, he said, should show persons working.

Davis had taken the material on Warner Gear from Vander Hill; we academic humanists supplied between fifteen to twenty stories to Cohen for the work film, but he rejected them all [Vander Hill 1982:56]. Davis next wanted to make a film on the inside workings of a major corporation, something which, according to Davis, had never been done. He had earlier in his career attempted to shoot corporate life at National Cash Register, but had been refused permission [Hoover 1987c:60].

Muncie has a major corporation, one that is on the list of Fortune 500 companies. That company is Ball Corporation, which came to Muncie in 1887 and grew to become a large conglomerate. Although the corporation maintained its world headquarters in Muncie, it manufactured few items in town. It had its major research center, which had developed several products and instruments for aerospace exploration, in Colorado; its container factories were near food-processing and beverage plants and its plastics divisions could be found in several locations around the country.

Ball Corporation, however, had a long connection with the town's history. The Ball family was the *X* family in the Lynd's Middletown in Transition, a family that, according to the Lynds, controlled almost all phases of the community's life. While this claim was exaggerated, in my opinion, in part by the Lynds and in part by the Depression which left Ball Brothers relatively untouched while other companies went under, it did provide a link between the past and present, between business and the town.

There were obvious problems with obtaining approval to film Ball Corporation. The Ball family had reacted negatively to its portrayal in *Middletown in Transition* and had not encouraged public exposure since. It did give generously to the community, but it shielded itself and the business from publicity. It controlled the corporation, although the latter had been public for over a decade, and regarded the business still as a private concern. Further, there was a natural reticence on the part of corporation officials to allow outsiders to create an image that might be, in part or in whole, negative. Why spend millions of dollars on public relations to present a positive image and risk the loss of it all?

Still, there was a possibility of being allowed in the corporation. Ed Ball, a second generation Ball and a man of many interests, had been involved both in NEH and in public broadcasting. He had helped create WIPB, Muncie public broadcasting station. Though no longer directly active in Ball management because of age, his opinion did carry considerable weight. The director of all the public relations programs was John Pruis, a former president of Ball State University who had resigned because of a no-confidence vote of the faculty. He was also a person of wide interest and was on very friendly terms with Vander Hill, a fellow Dutchman.

The film was not to be, however. In meetings with John Fisher, the CEO who was married to a second generation Ball, the filmmakers were unable to persuade him to allow them free rein. Usually aggressive and not prone to pay much attention to power relationships, the filmmakers were awed by Fisher's presence but were unwilling to give in to the demands of the corpo-

ration's legal counsel that the company be allowed to edit the film by deleting segments it deemed unhelpful.

The story for *The Job* film came from Terry Simon who had been searching for leads for Cohen. Among the places she visited was the Muncie Fire
Department School for recruits. There, she met one of Howie Snider's sons
who invited her to meet his father who had a Shakey's Pizza franchise. She
did and, impressed by his vitality and the attractiveness of the family, induced Cohen to meet him as well. As a result, Cohen decided that Shakey's
Pizza was to be the subject of his film.

The decision meant several changes from the original plans. In the first
place, it meant an abandonment of the three-person weave as a technique.
This was not necessarily a disadvantage; using one family as a unit meant a
tighter, more intimate film. Besides, this would provide an interesting contrast to Cohen's first effort, *The Campaign*, which alternated between two
candidates, and Vaughn's *The Big Game*, which also contrasted two players
and two coaches. In the second place, it meant a loss of a historical connection. *Family Business* appears to fit uneasily into the framework of the
Middletown studies. The Lynds had neglected small businesses in both their
books, preferring instead to focus upon larger industrial enterprises. This
was a result of their intellectual framework which held that a consequence of
industrialization was a division between large businesses and labor. Middletown III scholars had followed suit, contrasting the lives of factory
workers with those of the business class, although they recognized the
growth of service industries in the town. Neither had really analyzed the
hectic world of a small business such as Shakey's Pizza where a whole
family worked in what seemed to be a cottage industry. But there was an
upside to this choice as well. The growth of franchised outlets was a significant feature of Muncie's recent history, reflecting indirectly a change in the
employment structure noted in *Middletown Families*. Increasing employment of women outside the home provided families with more money and
less time, thus creating more opportunities for fast-food outlets. Finally, by
emphasizing the central place of work in the lives of the Snider family,
particularly in Howie, *Family Business* articulated one of the most striking
elements of the continuing Middletown spirit.

Cohen took a chance in *Family Business*. At the time he decided to film the
Sniders there was no apparent crisis such as Davis believed necessary as the
hinge for documentary films. Perhaps Cohen believed that one would inevi-
tably develop, given Snider's personality and the tensions that came from
parents trying to be both parents and employers, and from children trying to
achieve personal autonomy.

Certainly the Snider family was an unusual one. Howie was a Muncie native and a Catholic, a fact that would set him apart from others in town. He had attended seminary with the intention of becoming a priest before changing his vocational goals to become a pilot. He joined the Marine Corps and rose to the rank of lieutenant colonel, serving in various places in the United States and overseas, including Vietnam, and, at the same time, getting married to Judy and having eight children. After twenty years in the corps, he retired to Muncie where his parents lived, with no intention of going into business. Instead, he planned to get a master's degree in journalism at Ball State University and to teach. He took classes there and even taught advertising on a part-time basis. But soon after returning, he met two other retired veterans like himself who wanted to go into business. He agreed to become a partner and took on managerial responsibilities of the Muncie Shakey's franchise. The partnership later opened a branch in Anderson, the home of Andre Morgan, which proved very unsuccessful and which was bleeding the original store quite badly. (Oddly enough, this fact never appeared in the film.) The two other partners became interested in different projects and left Howie with the major responsibility for the pizza parlor. He then used his family as the basic work unit in order to cut labor costs.

Howie and his partners had made several bad business decisions in addition to opening another branch. They were undercapitalized and they were in the wrong location. Shakey's Pizza was on Kilgore Avenue, a part of Indiana 32, a state road that led to Indianapolis, but it was an isolated restaurant located next to a plant nursery and across the street from a monument outlet. Customers had to make a special effort to get to Shakey's or else they had to be drop-in customers. There were few of the latter. Unlike hamburger row on Wheeling Avenue or on McGalliard Extension, where one fast-food outlet crowded another, the street lacked hungry customers cruising by looking for a place to eat. Howie had to entice customers to his place of business. He tried all kind of ways to do this and to overcome the fact that the food was not very good. He advertised widely on the radio and in the newspapers, using his considerable skills in marketing. He provided live entertainment, playing the banjo and having sing-alongs. He recognized people's birthdays and he ran many specials, most of which emphasized a great deal of food for little money—all you could eat for $3.29.

Cohen and Howie hit it off from the start. Howie, like Jim Carey, had few inhibitions about being filmed and, like Norm Held, was quite curious about the entire process. Cohen was honest with Howie (in my opinion, Cohen was the most open and least devious of all the filmmakers) and spelled out what his filmmaking principles were. According to Howie, "Well first, Cohen told me initially he wanted to be objective. He said he was a man of many preju-

dices and biases. But he knew what they were, and he could deal with them."
Later, when discussing editing decisions, Cohen told Howie that he chose
"truth over fact." He also said that the Sniders would be "presented fairly—
no better, no worse than they are" [Cox 1985:1, 16, 17].

The major problem facing Cohen was how to make a story out of random
happenings. Two things helped him to do so. The first was a fortuitous occurrence and the second was a willingness to violate cinema direct maxims.

Three weeks into the film, Howie received a letter from the franchise
headquarters demanding payment of back royalties. Howie has given an account of what happened then. "When I got the letter I didn't know whether to
show it to Tom or not. Then I decided that not showing it to Tom would be a
violation of the relationship, the trust we'd established .... When I handed
him the letter, I didn't say anything. He read it very calmly. He stayed very
cool. He looked up at me. Even under his coolness, I could see he was jump-
ing up and down saying, 'Thank you God for giving me a story for this damn
thing'" [Cox 1985:14]. Thus did Cohen get the hook for the segment, the
struggle for the family to keep the business afloat.

Having determined that this was the story, Cohen then was willing to suggest scenes or activities and to rearrange the order of events to fit into a more
dramatic narrative. Several examples will suffice. Cohen suggested that the
sons go to the Indianapolis mall instead of going to work; en route he also
suggested topics to discuss, saying "If you wouldn't mind, sometime, could
you please talk a little bit about your father and the business?" When the sons
return anxious and guilty, they are confronted by their angry father. Yet since
there was only one film crew, the two events could not have been filmed at
the same time. One had to be staged afterwards [Cox 1985:13-14]. Finally,
the climax of the film, which shows the dramatic family conference, was out
of chronological sequence, but was made the end because of its emotional
intensity.

By making the theme of *Family Business* the struggle to save the business,
the filmmaker achieved unity at the expense of complexity and character development. By concentrating upon the pizza parlor, the filmmaker overem-
phasized the isolation of the family from the larger community. Most of the
scenes take place in Shakey's Pizza, a large, cavernous hall which, though
rigged for lights by the crew, still seems dark. Most of the shots are at night,
adding to the gloom. Rarely do we see Howie, who is the centerpiece of the
film, outside the restaurant. We do not see him teaching a class; we do not see
him going to church on Sunday. We do not see him drinking, although he was
by his own admission hitting the bottle heavily [Cox 1985:15].

Moreover, because most of the shots were of the pizza parlor and, hence,
public, certain of the participants who were more private rarely express their

true feelings. This is particularly the case with two persons, Lee, one son, and Judy, the wife, neither of whom appear in many of the scenes but who, according to Howie's own testimony, were probably the most important persons in the Snider family, Lee for his work and Judy for her emotional stability which held the family together [Cox 1985:15]. "You don't see a lot of Judy in the film. And when you do, she's in the background. That's true to life in a way, but then it isn't.... Tom (Cohen) told me, 'I think I got a one-man show here, Howie.' I told him he couldn't be further off. Though it may not always come across, Judy is the real strength of this family, especially as mediator between myself and the kids" [Cox 1985:16].

Beyond that, the failure to probe deeply into Judy's character leads to misinterpretation of her actions. A case in point is her reaction to Howie's crucial telephone call to the franchise headquarters. In this scene she is sobbing quietly while Howie is trying hard to persuade his creditors to extend his payments. The viewer assumes that as a supportive wife she is crushed by the prospects of business failure. Such, however, was not the case. "Where she cries, after I'm on the phone with Shakey's Corporation, that cause-and-effect, the way the film makes it look, is not the whole story. Judy was hoping in her heart of hearts that we'd go under. She'd had it with the film crew—they'd been there nearly a month. And there I was, getting up a new head of steam to keep it all going" [Cox 1985:16]. This hope for failure is nowhere even hinted at in the film.

Despite these omissions, *Family Business* was a powerful film. It is, in my opinion, the best in the series in terms of human interest and dramatic power. Viewers would want Carey to win the election, but knew if he didn't that he would survive and that Muncie might be a better place if he lost. Howie's failure meant the failure of the family and the defeat of what appeared to be a really good guy. That led to deep empathy for the Sniders, one that became obvious immediately after *Family Business* was aired.

Having said that, I must also say that *Family Business* failed to illustrate the place of work in Muncie and it failed as a portrait of an American family, substituting myth for reality. The meaning of work is not clear in the film, partly because the film isolates the pizza parlor and Howie. The viewer does not have any good idea what work means to the other members of the family—to Judy or Lee or Lloyd. They sometimes verbalize about what they think work means to Howie but they do not reveal why they work so hard.

Perhaps a broader view of the significance of Shakey's Pizza might have come from a closer scrutiny of all of the family or even of the customers who ate there. We catch a veiled hint of a problem from Liz when she says that the worst part of working behind the counter were the customers on the other side. Looking carefully at those customers, we can see that they are not members of the town's elite. Certainly they are lower middle class at the most; many are working class. What service does Howie provide them? Are they there for a cheap meal and free entertainment? Are they college students out for a change from their residence hall dining rooms? In short, how does Howie's place fit into the structure of community activities?

Nor does *Family Business* show an unvarnished view of family life. Some parts, such as Howie's drinking, are left out. Even Howie's most often repeated story about his own behavior, a story that tells us much about Howie's exhibitionism, failed to appear in the film. After the four-hour family discussion that provided the climax of *Family Business*, Howie and Judy climbed the stairs only to discover that the film crew had followed them up the stairs to their bedroom which the crew had lighted earlier without telling the Sniders. Howie admitted he didn't know what to do. They got in bed and Howie had to go to the bathroom. Remembering the injunction to be natural, Howie left the door open while urinating even though he knew the camera was on. Being very uncomfortable, Howie finally thought of a way to end the scene. He snuggled up close to Judy and asked, "You horny, hon?" [Cox 1985:19].

The Snider family we see takes on a kind of archetypical air. It became, like Middletown as described in Davis's grant proposal, a mythical entity, one that each of us wants ours to be and never is, containing the kind but demanding father, the supportive mother, the loyal and well-behaved children.

That this was the case is evidenced by the public response to the film when aired. The telephone at Shakey's Pizza rang off the hook as callers from every part of the country wanted to know how the business was doing and to encourage the family to persist. Business increased by 30 percent as interstate travelers went out of their way to stop to see Howie. Some even drove from as far away as Chicago just to meet members of the family. In a burst of entrepreneurial enterprise, Howie ordered T-shirts with his picture on it to sell to his customers [Vander Hill 1982:57].

Among those who called in the euphoria after the airing of *Family Business* was Henry Winkler, then starring in "Happy Days" and a producer on the lookout for new ideas for TV series. Winkler signed an option to turn *Family Business* into a series and, in discussing with Howie the response to the film, gave as good a reason as any for the reaction. When Howie asked why people called him, Winkler responded: "'Communication, Howie.' That was Henry's answer. He said people want to believe a family like ours can exist, a family where people can communicate" [Cox 1985:18].

Alan Trachtenberg, who did the teaching notes for *Family Business*, was at a loss as to how to describe the film. Like Cohen, he focused upon Howie, asking the question "What drives Howie, and how does one measure the 'value' of his business?" Trachtenberg was unable to answer his own query, turning the drama into a commentary on contemporary American society. Howie works because of "a traditional American ambition: personal freedom based on economic independence" [Trachtenberg 1982:6]. From there Trachtenberg segues into a discussion of changes in American society that have made Howie's vision seem old fashioned. No longer is Howie a sole entrepreneur nor is the business a family business because of obligations to an impersonal corporation. But work is not the final meaning of *Family Business*, according to Trachtenberg. It is, instead, the conserving of family values. "By the end of the film, 'family business' appears as something larger, more inclusive than the running of Shakey's; it has become instead the means of preserving certain values. The title finally reveals the meaning of the film to be the expression of a family spirit *in spite of* the business of Shakey's" [Trachtenberg 1982:7]. Although they took different routes, Winkler and Trachtenberg ended at the same place. Work was incidental to the meaning of the film.

Community of Praise

The film on religion had not been decided upon when Leacock and his young assistant and student Marissa Silver arrived in Muncie, although it was extremely important. In my mind, religion was a key to understanding not only the community but also the Middletown way. After all, *Middletown* had begun as a survey of religious practices and the second Middletown III book, *All Faithful People* (1983), devoted itself entirely to the subject.

The original research on the religion segment was done by me and by Vander Hill. We hoped to tap the rich vein of history in the community and, in particular, the significant findings of Middletown III, which by 1980 had already appeared in articles and papers. These included the fact that religion, at least as evidenced by both public and private practices, had not vanished nor even weakened as the Lynds had predicted. Instead, in both the working and business classes, Munsonians were more religious than ever, measured in such tangible terms as church attendance and financial support, and in such intangible ones as more private devotions and higher appreciation of religious participation.

Like some of the other films in the series, the original treatment, entitled *The Sabbath*, called for a three-person weave. Religious practice would be illustrated by events that occurred in the lives of members of three churches. We had even picked out the churches to be used: High Street Methodist Church, a mainline Protestant church which was the first choice of the business class when the Lynds studied Muncie; Grace Baptist Church, a recent addition to Muncie's religious scene which was fundamentalistic, had established the only Christian school in town, and was the fastest growing congregation in town; and an unnamed storefront Pentecostal one [Hoover 1986:61; Vander Hill 1982:55].

There were several reasons for these choices. The first was that Muncie was, and is, a Methodist town. It is a Protestant community and the largest group of Protestants are Methodists. Further, High Street Methodist was the first church in Muncie. It was still a downtown church while others had moved to the suburbs. Finally, it had a strong congregation. When leaking gas exploded in 1978 wrecking the church's interior, the members pledged enough money on one Sunday to repair the damages.

The second was that Grace Baptist Church illustrated a trend that Middletown III had uncovered, the growth of Baptist churches since the 1920s. By the 1980s, there were more Baptist churches than any others in town, although there were fewer Baptists than Methodists. Moreover, the growth had been, in a significant way, from the South and from congregations that were independent and not connected to the larger Baptist conventions. The pastor of Grace Baptist Church was Collins Glenn, who illustrated that phenomenon in his own person. Born in Thomasville, Georgia, Glenn was a farm boy who entered his parents' feed and grain business after high school graduation prior to going on the road with Ralston-Purina. He had a vision of Christ while travelling and, as a consequence, entered Bob Jones University. He came to Muncie in 1967 and used his sales techniques to increase the membership of the church from eighty-five to twelve hundred by 1980. In doing so, he created a church which had both business class and working class members.

The third church had not been chosen but the preference was for a Pentecostal one, perhaps a black one. While Muncie does have a Pentecostal tradition, Pentecostals do not dominate the community's religious life. Still, the number of Pentecostals was growing and, unlike the two other churches chosen, they were more likely to represent the working rather than the business class.

When Davis wrote the treatment for The Sabbath, however, he deleted High Street Methodist Church. In the two-person weave, the crisis was the impending death of two of the members, a young married woman in Grace Baptist Church and an elderly man in the black one. Davis conceptualized the meaning of religion to be contained in how people face death. This is quite clear. "We see that religion is still at the center of the community's fears about death and speculations about afterlife. Through these two ministers and their congregations, we will participate in the quest for faith....In each of the preceding *Middletown* films we have seen how Americans live; in *The Sabbath* we have seen how they die" [Davis 1980:106-107].

Of all the films, *The Sabbath* was the least thought out prior to the actual filming. Davis was not religious and his treatment reflected a very limited perspective on the phenomenon. The treatment was the last he wrote; it was also the shortest and the least satisfactory.

The treatment had no appreciable impact upon Leacock or Silver, neither of whom was religious nor even knowledgeable about Protestant Christianity. They could not distinguish between evangelicals and Pentecostals; they did not know the theology that separated one congregation from another or Christians from non-Christians.

They rejected both the three- and the two-family weave; they rejected the churches that we had suggested. Vander Hill has indicated why. "Leacock and Silver wished to focus, for reasons of intimacy and scale, on a single family rather than on three families and their churches. They also wanted to work with a family which had been influenced by the contemporary charismatic movement, a family which saw the Lord's presence in every area of human endeavor.... To Richard Leacock, three families in three congregations must have seemed to be a suggestion designed to make his task increasingly difficult. And besides, as Leacock himself confided to one of the academic humanists, any film on the institutional church these days would have to reveal the hypocrisy of so much of contemporary mainline Christianity" [Vander Hill 1982:55].

Leacock had narrowed the focus considerably; instead of a film about a group of believers, it was to be of one family. Instead of being about *The Sabbath*, it was to be about one family's search for religious faith. The new name, *The Community of Praise*, fit the film quite poorly.

Leacock and Silver began at square one in their film, discarding any previous leads. They attended religious services of all kinds and even filmed three. Eventually they found the family they wanted at a charismatic service at the office of a local veterinarian, Dr. Haggard, where worshippers spoke in tongues, cast out devils by vomiting and belching, and attempted to heal sick or injured members. This was the Tobey family.

The family belonged to no church at the time of the filming, but was seeking a new religious home after being expelled from a Methodist Church in Dunkirk, a small town near Muncie. They did not live in Muncie but rather on a small (35 acre) farm outside the city where Phil Tobey earned a living by welding. The family was a composite one; both had been divorced before; the children were hers and not his. Phyllis Tobey had lost a second husband to cancer before marrying Phil. The family also had considerable problems. Phil had been a hard drinker and had tried his hand at a number of other jobs before becoming a welder. Conversion to Jesus had ended his drinking but had not changed all his behavior. He was a stern step-father who believed in corporal punishment and an angry husband who had left his wife several times before. His wife Phyllis was better educated than he, having graduated from the University of Michigan with a degree in psychology in 1956, but she was a deeply troubled person as well. Given her experience with men, one can understand her saying that she found Christ to be "a more perfect lover" and that she trusted the Lord "for my every need." She was protective of her children and worried about their relations to their step-father and their spiritual health, which is to say their willingness to obey their parents and to submit to God's will. Her approach was more intellectual than Phil's, more dependent upon books and less on experience.

Her three children all had problems, or what appear to their parents to be problems. Chris, the oldest son, had gone to jail because of "drinking a lot and not going to work and messin' around." There, according to his mother, "he finally asked the Lord to come into his life" [McQuade 1982:6]. Rebecca, the daughter, had a physical problem, scoliosis, curvature of the spine. She was the most submissive child and the one who seemed the most accepting of her parents' faith. However, she faced the problem of achieving self-identity during the troubled adolescent years with the handicap of physical disfigurement. Her hope was to be normal and pretty. Noel was a rebel, but not in an invidious sense. Donald McQuade, who wrote the teaching notes for *Community of Praise*, has described him best. "Noel, the youngest, is essentially an unconverted presence in the midst of the family's struggle to take, as his mother notes, 'authority over the powers of darkness in this house.' He debates with his father about doing chores; he teases his sister; he spars verbally with his mother. Most often we see him playing or working alone. If there is a rebellious spirit still loose in this house, his parents fear that it is Noel. He is, as he says, 'not willing to be willing.'"

Although the family faced no immediate crisis, it was apparent that it was full of tension and that perhaps it might break apart at any time. Leacock took a chance in choosing the Tobeys and in a sense he lost. There were no major crises in *Community of Praise*; there was no denouement as in *The Campaign*; there was no game to win as in *The Big Game*; and there was no threat of economic disaster as in *Family Business*. Instead there was a series of minor problems, and a sense of foreboding about the future. Noel cuts his finger, but the wound is not life–threatening. Although always under pressure, he never agrees to religion's discipline. Chris is a shadowy figure who fades into the background or is not there. The depth of his conviction seems shallow; he is not struck down as others are by the charismatic leader in the Full

Gospel Men's Fellowship meeting. Unlike the Sniders, there seems to be no unity of goals in the Tobey family.

Nor are the Tobeys part of one religious community. It is here that the film is most confusing and lacking in context. There is no attempt to identify the various groups to which the Tobeys go in their search for a community of believers, but there are at least three. The first appears early in the film; it is a charismatic congregation that meets in the office of a Muncie veterinarian. This group casts out spirits which it believes can cause epilepsy, alcoholism, and smoking. The film lingers on these weird practices, not, I think, in search of spiritual truth but rather in fascination with the odd behavior. The episode adds little to the film, reinforcing my belief that it was included for its shock value. The second is another charismatic congregation in Hartford City, a small town near Muncie. This segment is not sensational nor is it prolonged. The third shows a meeting of the Full Gospel Men's Fellowship where the leader speaks in tongues and anoints with the spirit. Here the film documents the members of the congregation who were stricken by that spirit. However, the groups do not overlap insofar as membership is concerned nor do the Tobeys technically belong to them. They are still searching.

The film intermixes these scenes of worship with those of domestic life: taking care of chores, having a festive meal, going to school, visiting a grandparent living in Florida, and discussing problems in the kitchen or in a car while doing errands. There is no need in this film to alter chronology or to do staged interviews. This is Direct Cinema with all of its strengths and weaknesses.

One strength is Leacock's desire to intrude as little as possible by using hand-held cameras and no extra lighting. It was shot during the winter in a house that was not too well lighted, resulting in underexposed film. This underexposure fits, in my opinion, the somber theme of the film. It shows in the harsh daylight and stark darkness a world of contrast, of sin and devils fighting the light. The darkness Phyllis feels in her home is visually represented. On the other hand, the film does not capture the tension among members of the family very well. Phyllis and Phil speak of domestic problems but there is no confrontation between the two so the viewer cannot know how serious or recent these difficulties are. Nor does the viewer really understand exactly what the Tobey family believes. All is surface testimony. Perhaps that is the extent of Phil's faith, but what about Phyllis? And what do the children believe? For a common anchor, their religious beliefs seem uncommonly hidden.

A more significant weakness was what the family was supposed to represent. Were the Tobeys typical of religious developments in Muncie? While the answer is not a simple one, on balance it must be no. The fact that the

Tobeys belonged to no church and yet attended services is atypical. Their preference for Pentecostal experiences was not a majority preference among Muncie worshippers. All the Pentecostal sects combined in Muncie attract fewer members than the mainline Methodist, Baptist, or Roman Catholic churches, ranking fourth in the community. While the number of Pentecostals had increased in Muncie, they were by no means a large segment of the population. Davis was wrong when he defended the choice of the Tobeys by claiming the family represented one of the fastest growing religious groups in Muncie or American society.

Davis's claim was echoed by Donald McQuade in the Teaching Notes for the film, but his interpretation was somewhat skewed by the fact that both assumed that the Tobeys were evangelical Christians without recognizing they were charismatic Pentecostals. McQuade said that "once perceived as a movement of marginal importance in American life, evangelical Christianity in recent years has gained wide respectability and new leads of popular support by rebuilding values at the center of our culture such as earnestness, self-discipline, and private enterprise." McQuade then further confused the issue by listing Robert Schuler and Jerry Falwell as charismatic ministers along with Oral Roberts and Jimmy Swaggart, and by lumping Gerald Ford and Jimmy Carter together as part of the same movement [McQuade 1982:5]. His effort to make sense of the Tobeys' experience was unsuccessful; the teachers using these notes would be quite unenlightened.

Community of Praise was to become the second most controversial film in the series. It offended many religious Munsonians who believed, correctly in my opinion, that the Tobeys were not typical of Muncie's church members and reacted negatively to such sensational scenes as vomiting out the devil. Less involved viewers disliked the technically poor film quality because of inadequate lighting. No one, except some film critics, was to be very enthusiastic about the segment.

The Second Time Around

The Wedding had been much on Davis's mind from the earliest beginning of the project. In his conversations he had indicated that he was much impressed with Robert Altman's *The Wedding*, or at least by the issues Altman raised. In his proposal to NEH, Davis began his treatment thusly: "*The Wedding* will basically follow the progress of a young man and woman on their wedding day. There will be 'flashbacks' of the type used in conventional fiction movies, and these will serve two purposes. The first is to probe the sensibilities of different members of both families—parents, grandparents, aunts, uncles. Through their relatives we will perceive the ways marriage has changed over the generations, and how it has remained the same. *The Wedding* is enriched by a variety of relationships in a single family—the aunt who lives in Boston with someone she does not want to marry, the uncle whose two marriages have failed, the brother and sister-in-law who cannot have children. The second purpose of the 'flashbacks' is to enable us to show the rituals that add tension, depth, and complexity to the impending ceremony" [Davis 1982:43-44].

Davis projected that he would film two families, the bride's and the groom's, for two weeks prior to the ceremony, thus gaining the opportunity to catch them "in intimate moments of reflection" [Davis 1982:44]. He then went on to describe a possible scenario for the film, although there was at that time no couple identified as the subject of the film. The scenario is an interesting mix of fact and fiction. Davis named the florist Barbara Rae, although that shop was primarily a bridal one; he named the photography shop Paul's Quick Photo Shoppe, although Paul's was a flower store. He identified the O'Rourke Travel Service correctly, but listed the travel agent as Suzanne Hunnicut, a disguised name for Babe Swartz, an ex-madam who claimed to have bribed Jim Carey. The minister of the service was to be Collins Glenn, pastor of the Third Presbyterian Church, which in fact did not exist. This segment of the treatment shows Davis at his most playful and shows how little he regarded accuracy in his treatments. It also shows how lightly Davis took his obligation to NEH or to Muncie reality.

The Wedding was not to be a picture of harmony, however, as Davis envisaged a reception at the film's end which would expose all of the pitfalls of marriage. "If, in nuclear terminology, the wedding of Bob and Nancy Jackson could be called fusion, the reception at the Roberts Hotel after the wedding would have to be called fission. Families, in-laws, generations and individuals all seem to divide, even to come apart. Virtually nothing is as it seemed at the wedding" [Davis 1982:55]. It is apparent from the treatment that Davis wished to dispel any romantic notions about life after marriage, for the remainder of the treatment recounts the disappointments encountered by sundry relatives. Two issues suggest themselves from the treatment of *The Wedding*. The first is that the proposed use of flashbacks in a documentary film done in the Direct Cinema tradition was unusual, to say the least. How could Davis have done this? He might have found home movies of relatives' weddings, but these, if found, would be unlikely to contain reflections of the kind Davis wanted. Moreover, the use of flashbacks would violate the chronological sequence of life as lived. The question is moot, however, since Davis did not use them.

The second issue is the one of privacy. As Esther C. M. Yau has said, "... by giving filmmakers an almost unconditional admittance into the privacy of their lives, most subjects in *Middletown* unknowingly condone the exploitative aspects of direct cinema filming. Specifically, in *The Second Time Around* a trace of voyeurism becomes evident as a result of Elaine Ingram's naive receptiveness of the filmmakers during the critical moments of her life" [Yau 1983:8]. The planned invasion of privacy was already more evident in the treatment for this film than in any of the others. *The Campaign* was to explore the structure of politics, *The Big Game* to trace interschool rivalry, *The Sabbath*, the impact of religion on three families, and *The Job*, the conditions of industrial life. None of them had proposed to explore as deeply the layers of private emotions as had *The Wedding*.

Given the assumptions of Davis, both artistic and technical, the selection of the couple to be photographed was crucial. All of the consultants participated in the search. We asked our friends about their children's wedding plans, looked for wedding announcements, and, in the case of Trimmer, hung out at bridal shops trying to find likely candidates. Many were asked but few chosen.

De Mott and Kreines finally picked a couple, an eighteen-year-old boy and a sixteen-year-old girl. They filmed for a month before abandoning the project for a variety of reasons. Among these were the facts that the wedding would have been held in Ft. Wayne and not Muncie and that a maiden aunt interfered constantly and prevented the team from filming what they wished [Vander Hill 1982:57; Hoover 1983b:n.p.]. Consequently, the filmmakers gave up on the wedding film by the spring of 1981 and devoted their full time to finishing the high school film which was far behind schedule, leaving Davis the task of finding a couple and filming them.

By this time, Davis had become convinced, perhaps by his own experience, that remarriage of older persons was most representative of modern Muncie. I tried to convince him, based on Middletown III evidence, that a younger, previously unmarried couple would be more representative but failed. The median age of first marriage in Muncie had not changed in fifty years (men married when they were a little over twenty-three while women averaged two years younger). Moreover, the divorce rate in Muncie in the late 1970s approximated the 1920s rate, although in fairness it must be noted that the latter rate was much higher than the national rate at that time [Caplow, Bahr, and Chadwick 1982:114, 305].

Davis soon found the couple he wished to film; they were David Shesler and Elaine Ingram. Both had been divorced and were in their late thirties; both were attractive and articulate. Both were lower-middle class, but with middle-class aspirations. Both had graduated from Southside High School, Muncie's most working-class school, which was the setting for *Seventeen*. Both attended Ball State University, he part-time and she full-time. She lived in an apartment in married student housing while studying industrial education, while he lived in an apartment in town and worked as a minor city employee in charge of the street department's sign-painting shop. She had a number of relatives in Muncie; he had only his mother who taught in the Muncie Community Schools. If a family network were to be done, it would have to be Elaine's.

David and Elaine had known each other for seven years prior to the film. This fact and age made them untypical of Muncie's marriages, in my opinion. My colleague Vander Hill has disagreed with this assessment and has argued that "they certainly fit a typical national model" [Vander Hill 1982:57].

On the other hand, they fit perfectly the description of the series' participants made by Ralph Janis. "The lives portrayed were those of average people—the middle strata of Middle America. Davis's America is just 'folks,' as the saying goes: neither poor nor rich, neither fools nor villains. One suspects that Robert and Helen Lynd, the authors of the original Middletown series, would have argued that the center of the series hit just below the middle of Muncie's classes on that hazy line where white collars show some blue. Thus, the series is not best seen as finding the heart of middle America—lower middle would be more accurate" [Janis 1982:347].

The film itself is a study of the few weeks leading up to the wedding which serves as the end piece. There is no reception seen afterwards nor are there many revelations concerning relatives' views of marriage, nor are there flashbacks. There is little indication of any kinship network in which David and Elaine were involved, the kind of kinship network which *Middletown Families* said was so important in the town [Caplow, Bahr, and Chadwick 1982:195-224]. The two appear to exist in social isolation with no one but each other in whom to confide. Only in a few scenes—choosing the color of the bridesmaids' dresses and participating in the bachelor party—is there a sense of a larger world of others. David's mother is the most visible relative; she talks of his first marriage, of his father's death, and of her feeling about black bridesmaids' dresses, but says little about her own marriage. Elaine's mother is nowhere to be seen; her father, one assumes, leads her down the aisle but he does not have a speaking role. Nor are her children much involved; they are topics of conversation rather than subjects in their own right.

The film achieves a sense of intimacy by narrowing the focus to the engaged couple and limiting the context. David and Elaine discuss many of the questions that concern those about to be married: "Should the wife work? How can middle-class couples afford to purchase a home? Who does the housework? And perhaps most importantly, why get married at all?" [Vander Hill 1982:58].

In answering these questions, David and Elaine reflect some of the Middletown III findings, namely that modern Muncie marriages are much more companionate than those in the 1920s and that women's liberation has had little effect on the propensity to marry [Caplow, Bahr, and Chadwick 1982:34-35, 114-15]. David and Elaine discuss whether to start another family, a topic the Lynds said was not discussed in the 1920s. David, the more materialistic of the two, wants to know whether Elaine will continue to work so that they can reach agreement on where to live. Elaine, the more stubborn of the two, wants to know whether David wants children. In addition, the film explores both work and household roles, showing that the amount of housework done or planned to be done by men has changed little.

As far as purchasing a home is concerned, the film suffers from what was a unique situation in 1981. In order to curb inflation, interest rates had risen to about 18 percent on house loans, making it almost impossible for David and Elaine to buy a house, at least not the kind they wanted. In their search for the right place, they rejected living on Muncie's south side from which they came and aspired to live on the more prosperous north side. The film does not show how futile the search was; David and Elaine move into his apartment instead of buying a house. This ran counter to the proclivity of Munsonians to own their own homes.

Finally, the question of why get married at all is never answered adequately. Indeed there was worry that the wedding might never occur. The edited film omitted part of the tension between Elaine and David, particularly in the counseling sessions insisted upon by the minister at College Avenue Methodist Church. Such were his misgivings that he doubted at times that the wedding should go forward, and at the wedding predicted the marriage would last no more than a year. Both participants were independent, Elaine especially so, and both seemed unwilling to make the concessions necessary to allow marriage to work.

None of this is evident on the wedding day, and the wedding itself appears picture perfect with only the weather threatening to put a damper on the festivities. Because of that, the church was as well-lighted as a Hollywood set [Vander Hill 1982:58]. Elaine looks beautiful as she dresses for her wedding (her only concern about the film was the shot where she was seen in bra and slip that would be viewed by her sons). Even the bridesmaids in black did not lend a funereal air. The film ends as the happy couple exits the church.

The Second Time Around deviated as much as any film in the series from original plans and, yet, in many ways it came the closest to capturing the changes in Muncie from the time of the Lynds to Middletown III. It shows, indirectly, changes in attitudes toward marriage and the family as well as changes in roles and role expectations. This is shown in the *Teaching Notes* written by Alice Trillin which, in my opinion, were the most perceptive of all. In them, Trillin emphasized how times had changed but also how they had not. She noted how much women now expected to work, using statistics from Middletown III. She pointed out how attitudes toward marriage had changed in Muncie from the Lynds' report "that a high degree of companionship is not regarded as essential for a marriage" to David's statement that his "friendship with Elaine is his most important reason for getting married." Finally, she noted that Elaine did not hesitate to discuss business matters as women in the 1920s did. (Trillin, however, failed to list the new open attitude toward family planning that Caplow and associates had found.) On the other hand, she found that romance was still alive in *The Second Time Around*, as witness David's labeling of Elaine as a romantic and, despite his self-classification as a realist, his insistence on a church wedding and the enraptured look on his face as Elaine walks down the aisle. She also noted that although there was more sharing, it was still not complete. David vacuums the rug but won't cook dinner; Elaine will not help pay for the house. Trillin concluded that David and Elaine's "belief in marriage and romance may not be so different from the beliefs that were at the center of the silent marriages of Muncie 50 years ago" [Trillin 1982:8-9].

The Second Time Around was a happy film, happier than any of the others. There were no major crises, no lost election, no fear of losing the family business, no hint that life might be downhill after being a basketball star, or that religion might fail to heal family tensions. It was a smaller, more intimate film; it did not violate the principles of direct cinema except for the well-lighted church and yet, for this viewer, came closer to what the original intention of the series was than any other. Perhaps this showed that the microscopic approach was the most appropriate means to demonstrate macroscopic development.

Seventeen

The school for *The Commencement* had not yet been chosen when Kreines and De Mott arrived in town. The consultants had looked hard for stories in several of the schools, but the decision was complicated by two factors: the earlier decision to make the Muncie Central Bearcats the focus of *The Big Game* and the history of schools in Muncie.

When the Lynds first studied Muncie in 1924-25, the city had but one public high school—Muncie Central. While Ball State Teachers' College built a laboratory school, Burris, in 1929, the town did not add another high school until the 1960s despite the pressures of a post-war baby boom. Although students in the 1950s had to attend Muncie Central in shifts, the school board failed to open another high school at that time, according to popular belief, because it did not wish to break up winning basketball teams. In the 1960s, however, it could no longer resist and built two new high schools: Southside in the early 1960s and Northside in the late 1960s.

Each of Muncie's schools had a different character based upon its history. Muncie Central had the longest tradition of any high school, one dating back to the nineteenth century. It had the most heterogeneous school population, drawing upper middle–class students from outlying residential areas, working–class and lower–class ones from deteriorating white inner–city neighborhoods and nearby black ones. It had the highest proportion of dropouts of all schools, but the second highest percentage of those attending college.

Burris students consisted of professors' children, plus others from surrounding neighborhoods, city and region. It had no school district and had a waiting list for entry. The school had a local reputation for snobbery; it was a small school with a permissive atmosphere and a student population motivated to attend college. It lacked a football team, had a mediocre basketball team, but an excellent girl's volleyball team.

Southside, on the other hand, was a school with a reputation of being tough, although the only murder in the town's schools had occurred in Burris. It was the school with the largest number of working-class students; it also had a significant black population, but no more than the other city schools, except Burris. Southside had the worst race relations in town. Shortly after it had opened the students, with the tacit approval of the school board, chose the name "Rebels" and made the Confederate Battle Flag their school emblem. The school attracted students who found such a tense atmosphere congenial, and had the only racial riot in Muncie schools in the 1960s. The teachers and administrators at Southside did not share the student values. They were sensitive to the school's reputation and struggled hard to overcome it by emphasizing middle-class values. Southside was also heterogeneous; it had a black girl who went to MIT, a board member's son who was accepted at Columbia, and the son of a Ball State administrator who won a tuition-paid scholarship to Dartmouth.

Northside was the newest and smallest city high school, built because of pressure from real estate interests to locate a high school adjacent to the rapidly expanding northwest side of Muncie. It had the fewest black students, the most sons and daughters of professionals, the highest SAT (Scholastic Aptitude Test) scores, the highest percentage of college-bound seniors, and the fewest dropouts. It had the most traditional and academic curriculum.

In the treatment for *The Commencement*, Davis indicated that Muncie Central was to be the locale and that the focus was to be on both commencements and class reunions. *"The Commencement* will focus on both the senior class at Muncie Central High School and on alumni who return for their tenth, twenty-fifth and fiftieth reunions. Hopes and expectations of several yesterdays will be compared with those of today.... This film will portray two rituals often identified with public education in America, the commencement and the reunion. In addition to its identification of the graduation ceremony, the film's title implies that everything happening in school represents a beginning, an opening up, a preparation for life. The reunion will be integrated into our story to provide a reference point, a vital link to the past" [Davis 1980:64-65].

Davis's plan here resembled that for *The Wedding*, using a crucial ritual as a pivot to connect past and present and representing the past by using recollections from older generations. The treatment included both actual and fictive people. Davis had a segment on a high school history teacher at his twenty-fifth reunion; a fictive bike race; a senior prom with a band led by a defector to Canada during the Vietnamese war, another fictional creation, during which students take a pot break; and on four graduating students, one of whom is a black basketball player, another of whom is going to Northwestern as a way station to Florence to study the quattrocento, another who is going to Purdue, and a final one with aspirations to become a lawyer. The commencement he envisaged was an odd one, with addresses by Mayor Alan Wilson who has just won election and Hurley Goodall, the black state representative from Muncie. The created situations, however, were not the main point, or so Davis claimed. "Although *The Commencement* may at times seem to be preoccupied with the ambience of high school, its major concern is to inquire into the meaning of education. What have our graduates been taught? Will their education enable them to reach out for their expectations? Will they repay the community's investment in their training by leaving town?" [Davis 1980:72].

Taking this as our base point, we explored the possibilities of filming at Muncie Central. I compiled a list of stories that my daughter who was a junior at the school told me. Joe Trimmer continued to research class reunions, interviewing former scholarship winners and class presidents. Kreines and De Mott visited the high schools as well in order to gain a sense of atmosphere.

Not only we humanists but the Muncie School Corporation (the legal and administrative agency controlling the Muncie public schools) believed that the film was to be about education. Davis and Trimmer had a series of meetings with school administrators and the corporation's legal counsel. According to Vander Hill, "Differences of opinion eventually resolved based on a fair amount of give and take on both sides, with the result that the project received fairly open access to most secondary school activities. A few areas received an 'off limits' designation but none proved to be a barrier to filming. However, there is no question whatsoever in my mind as I reflect on these meetings that school administrators and counsel believed that the education segments would provide viewers with a broad examination of life in at least one of the city's high schools" [Vander Hill 1982:58]. The agreement outlining the expectations of the Muncie School Corporation confirms Vander Hill's supposition:

> Middletown Film has been formed to search for continuity and change in American life as embodied in the people and institutions of a single community.
> Middletown Film is convinced that high school—and, in particular, the senior class—will be the right place to put its efforts in the area of education. Middletown Film will make a good faith effort to achieve a fair balance of coverage among Southside, Central and Northside high schools and to portray participation in high school athletics as well as in academic and social settings.
> While neither time nor funding is sufficient to cover all schools and sports in Muncie, Middletown Film is confident that its concentration will convey the essence of what teachers, coaches, and students are striving for and that Muncie will be proud of the results.
> The film on seniors will seek to present the pivotal points in the year before graduation. It will seek to portray their attitudes, concerns and feelings when they are deciding what to do with their lives, what their relationships to the adult world are likely to be, whether they are headed toward college, a job, marriage or the military.
> Middletown Film and the Superintendent, or his designees, will meet monthly, and at such other reasonable times as either of them may request, to review the program to date, to discuss the implementation of the principles herein stated, future activities, and any other matters either party reasonably requests [Hoover 1987d:167].

The agreement was an omnibus one designed to cover both *The Big Game* and *The Commencement*. As is apparent from the text, the school corporation believed *The Commencement* would be about a school, that it would have considerable footage of teachers, that it would be flattering to the school, and that it would culminate in graduation. Further, the corporation expected that there would be monthly meetings between filmmakers and school officials where progress would be reported and where the corporation would learn what was happening. None of the conditions were met: There was no input from teachers; there were no meetings between filmmakers and the superintendent; and the film was not one of which the school corporation could be proud.

Early on, Kreines and De Mott chose Southside High School as the locale. It is my belief that they chose it deliberately because it was a working-class high school and had a rebellious reputation. (Kreines and De Mott consciously identified with the working-class, wearing faded jeans and eating biscuits with sausage gravy at the Pixie Diner.) They chose Southside without consulting the humanists, but with the approval of Davis. He has explained his reasoning. "I was uneasy about Muncie Central because I knew we were going to shoot another film there, at least in part, and you (Kreines and De Mott) were even more uneasy though I very much liked the girl student you introduced me to there. Northside provided an atmosphere that none of us found congenial to directness and honesty, and films about those kind of teenagers have been done a great deal. In addition, we had already used an important sequence from Burris High in *The Campaign* and Burris is very similar in its student body to Northside. When you decided, therefore, to concentrate at Southside, I was ready with strong encouragement" [Davis personal communication to De Mott and Kreines 11 October 1984].

The selection of Southside radically altered the nature of the film. It meant the abandonment of any attempt to connect contemporary Muncie with the Lynds' Muncie. Southside had fewer than twenty graduating classes so no reunion would have members over forty. It also meant the film would lack the sense of tradition in Muncie.

Kreines and De Mott made several false starts before finding their subjects. Initially, they began shooting the story of a wrestler who, because of a heart condition, faced problems during the season and the hard decision to have open heart surgery at the end of it. This story leaked out to school authorities who were not meeting regularly with Kreines and De Mott and who were quite pleased with the topic. However, the filmmakers dropped this story because the boy and his parents openly discuss his sex life, or so they claimed in their press release after *Seventeen* became controversial. They said, "His frankness didn't dismay the filmmakers—his parents accepted it, with only a rare tut-tut, but it *was* atypical" [Kreines and De Mott n.d.:14].

Whatever the reason, the wrestling story gave way to the Lynn Massie one. Behind schedule because of the abortive wedding film and the false start, the filmmakers pushed ahead to shoot footage in the early months of 1981. They continued on into the summer and were the last to finish filming. The *Second Time Around* had been started later but finished sooner.

Seventeen is a difficult film to analyze because of the furor which it aroused. It has become an object of controversy whose artistic merit has been sidetracked while opponents quarrel over the way it was made, the ethics of using students, the legality of the releases, and the intent of the filmmakers.

The filmmakers have not explained why they chose Lynn Massie to be the centerpiece of *Seventeen*, but the viewer can assume several reasons. She is attractive and she was rebellious. She also evidently formed a close bond with De Mott as several scenes in the film show her looking to De Mott and in one actually talking to her. Perhaps she was, like Howie Snider and Elaine Ingram, willing to "turn herself on" for the camera. She also shared the quality noted by Esther Yau, ".... in *Seventeen*, the young and inexperienced teenagers expose their youthful rebelliousness without any inhibitions, being totally ignorant of the implications of letting in an omnipresent camera" [Yau 1983:8].

Kreines and De Mott did, however, rationalize the choice, not of Lynn, but of someone like her because they believed the Middletown Film Series had ignored issues of class, race, and sex. Whether this rationalization was after the fact or was part of their original motivation is difficult to determine. After attacking the "falseness of the cultural details" in the treatment of *The Commencement* without recognizing that Davis had created it, as he had the others, as a kind of fiction designed to obtain grant money from NEH, Kreines and De Mott say they deliberately set out to counter the rest of the series. "There—without support from the Middletown Project for their contention that the series was grossly out of balance—the filmmakers of *Seventeen* determined that the protagonists, that the resultant scope and emphasis might counterbalance the rest of the series" [Kreines and De Mott n.d.:16].

They also set themselves apart from the other filmmakers in their technique. Convinced that direct cinema could only be accomplished by drastically reducing the size of camera crews, Kreines and De Mott developed their own method. "About a dozen years ago, Jeff Kreines and I designed a sync system for shooting solo—no sound recordist, no lights, no crates of paraphernalia, no crew: the filmmaker works by himself. The one-person rig is a 16mm camera/tape recorder combination that weighs about twelve pounds, sits on the shoulder, records double-system sound, and shoots color film under extremely low light—less than a footcandle" [De Mott n.d.:1]. Whether it is possible to see let alone film on less than a footcandle, De Mott does not say. They were openly contemptuous of the other filmmakers in the series with their lighting, elaborate equipment, and large crews. Even Leacock, their mentor, had used Silver as his sound person. Moreover, because of their belief that the filmmaker should not attempt to hide his/her presence, they refused to use zoom lenses. "We each use only a ten-millimeter lens—which means we ordinarily shoot within a foot-and-a-half to three feet of people. That distance allows no ambiguity: The filmmaker is there and playing unaware is inconceivable when you can reach out and slap someone. The filmmaker's closeness makes it clear he expects people to recognize his presence, just as they would any other human being in the room" [De Mott n.d.:6]. Their emphasis upon interaction, as opposed to the Direct Cinema maxim that the filmmaker should be a "fly on the wall," had several consequences. It meant, as we have seen, interchange between filmmakers and protagonists. It also meant that scenes which included conversations between people at some distance could not be made unless the cameraperson switched from one to the other. (Critics of *Seventeen* were to claim that much of the students' impudent behavior toward Mrs. Hartling took place outside her line of vision and earshot, but that editing made it appear she saw and heard everything but did nothing.)

There were other consequences as well. Much of the finished film is underlighted. Despite this attempt at purity, principles of Direct Cinema were ignored. The film has sequences which scramble chronology (the fair scene occurs in the summer of 1981 after the commencement). Moreover, according to the testimony of some of the participants, Kreines and De Mott staged at least one scene, the beer party, and paid for the liquor.

In any case, the film was an ambitious project, one which took many months to finish, and which attempted to do much more than any of the others. It did not feature a particular crisis in anyone's life, unless Lynn's senior year could be construed as one, or the impact of Church Mouse's death on Keith Buck as another. It has no strong narrative line, no sense of beginning or end; it only opens and closes. The lack of a strong narrative line is curious since De Mott, according to Rance, had no prejudice against one. Indeed, she wished to create dramas. Perhaps she and Kreines allowed themselves to be distracted by "interesting" segments. It also switches protagonists; most of the time it focuses on Lynn, but part of the time it focuses on Keith Buck and, at another time, the center of attraction is Robert House.

The number of persons who appear in the film is overwhelming. There are at least three dozen who have speaking roles. The main characters are Lynn Massie who has a black boyfriend, John Vance, who plays on Southside's basketball team, but there is also Robert House, a black basketball player who is in Lynn's home economics class and whose black girlfriend Kim Moore is pregnant with, and has, his baby. There is Keith Buck, a white boy who has grown up with Lynn and spends much time at her house, but whose girlfriend is Dana Minnick. Lynn has a white girlfriend, Amii Reinke, who dates Daniel Vance, a black student who is John Vance's cousin. She also has two black male friends, Terrell Smith, who likes Lynn and tries unsuccessfully to warn her about John Vance's intentions, and David Branson, Terrell's best friend. The latter two are on friendly terms with Shari Massie, Lynn's mother who is thirty-four, and often visit her house. Lynn's father, Jim, is thirty-eight and works as a construction laborer. The family also includes T.J., Lynn's sixteen-year-old brother who rarely appears, and Robbie ("Rod"), her thirteen-year-old brother. An uncle, Ron Massie, can be seen at

Lynn's party at her house. Finally, Penny Shaggs is a white girlfriend of Lynn's whose house is the refuge for Lynn when she stalks out of her home and with whom she smokes pot in the last scene.

There is very little in the film concerning Southside High School and only a few teachers and administrators can be seen. The most prominent are Mrs. Hartling, a home economics teacher, and Mr. Gorin, a black sociology teacher. Lynn attends both classes as does Robert House. There is a short scene with Mr. Showalter, a dean of boys, to whom Robert is sent for a rule infraction, and another with Mr. Robbins, the coach of the Southside basketball team on which John and Robert play.

With such a large cast, sorting out the players becomes quite difficult and identifying their attitudes and values even more so. It is obvious that the Massies and the Bucks are working class. Lynn's father works construction and Keith's cleans septic tanks, but the black protagonists are less easy to identify as to class. One is a minister's son whose ambition is to attend college and several of the others are middle class as well. Michael Gorin, the black sociology teacher, was a graduate of Ball State and a student of mine, as was his wife Carnice who teaches history at Muncie Central. They are aspiring persons who are certainly middle class.

The film opens with a segment on Mrs. Hartling's class where the students are obviously rebellious and learning little. Mrs. Hartling seems particularly ineffective, in part because she attempts to become involved in her students' lives and because of her exaggerated gestures of annoyance at cooking failures and surprise at learning of Kim's pregnancy. She mouths cliches that she is trying to teach her students about life, but her students rightly recognize that she didn't teach them anything about cooking.

Gorin's class is more effective; he obviously struggles to teach citizenship and he relates well with his students as witness the final day's classes when all gather to have a picture taken. Still, his lectures seem far removed from the life of the students. In the library on assignment Suzie Granger talks to Lynn about pornography while ignoring her assignment, and the students lack interest in writing a letter to the president. Both these glimpses of academic life at Southside show the school in a bad light, with a teacher who is silly and students who are bored with school. Moreover, there is an implicit assumption that high school counts for little.

This assumption is reinforced by the rest of the film which, except for the basketball practice and game, is set outside of the school. There are various scenes involving Lynn and her boy-friend John. In these Lynn and Amii discuss how their association with blacks causes them to be ostracized by other whites. There are several parties shown. One is at the apartment of Neal King, a black, where Lynn and Wendy Gregory, a white girlfriend, smoke pot and Wendy kisses her black boyfriend in a long and sexually provocative way. Another, and an equally controversial one, is in Lynn's house. There, partygoers congregate to talk, drink beer, and smoke pot. At the party, Lynn's youngest brother "Rod" drinks beer and apparently smokes pot as well. The party lasts all night; the police are called; and it ends with Buck drunk and devastated with the news that his best friend, Church Mouse (Tim Barton), was killed in an automobile accident. For a time, the camera lingers on Buck and his grief, ignoring Lynn, as he gorges down food and is comforted by Mrs. Massie.

A persistent theme in the movie is racism and threats of violence. Black girls call up Lynn to threaten her for her involvement with Vance; white racists burn a cross in the Massie's yard. Buck and his friends, including "Rod," gather at a nearby park in preparation for a gang fight in response to the beating of Mike Barton, Buck's friend, and cousin of the dead Tim Barton. Nothing materializes but it is an opportunity for much strutting and macho behavior.

The reaction of Lynn's parents to events is a mixed one. Her mother and father cannot be called civil rights liberals; they, particularly Lynn's mother, accept Lynn's boyfriend, although he does not appear in the house, but they also distinguish between good and bad blacks. Lynn's mother is particularly exercised about black girls' threats to her daughter and shows Lynn a gun which she encourages Lynn to use if necessary. They, like other whites in the area, would not approve of blacks and whites marrying.

Several episodes show generational conflict; Lynn fights with her mother, often about money, and bullies her into buying her clothes, just as one boy bullies his mother into more money for his prom date. Fathers appear to be less involved with their children; they certainly do not supply them with money.

Toward the end of the film there are two episodes which were later to cause controversy. Neither are directly connected to Lynn. In one, House goes to Ball Hospital to visit his son. While there he shows considerable pride of parenthood, although he has taken no responsibility for the baby and has even told Mrs. Hartling that he wasn't going with Kim when she got pregnant. Further, he claims his mother is happy about her first grandchild rather then upset about the child's illegitimacy. In the second scene, Bill Slavin, a white boy of seventeen, recounts his sexual exploits to Buck in graphic detail while Debbie Minnick, the younger sister of Buck's girlfriend, listens unbeknownst to Billy or Buck. Neither scene seemed integral to the film but both challenge conventional morality.

Seventeen ends after the commencement which is not seen, and with no class reunions. It concludes with Lynn and Penny Shaggs buying some pot, and smoking it while listening to music as they drive away in Lynn's car. Lynn does not then or ever reflect upon her future, neither her expected one nor her hopes. Will she continue her part-time waitress job, will she leave home, will she marry John Vance? All is still unsettled.

The film lacks continuity and a strong story line. It is episodic and reflects an aesthetic that does not value coherence, but this aesthetic is entirely the filmmakers. Kreines and De Mott reserved the editing for themselves as had Leacock, but it was obvious they had difficulty in that task. In over a year of shooting they had accumulated sixty hours of film which had to be edited down to two hours [Kreines and De Mott n.d.:14]. They had finished shooting in the summer of 1981 and had to finish the film by March in order to make the series deadline.

No one in Muncie was privy to what the filmmakers were doing; as far as the school authorities and the humanists, except for Trimmer, knew, the film was to be *The Commencement*. Indeed, the releases which parents and other individuals signed still bore that name. How much Davis was involved is a matter of controversy. Kreines and De Mott claimed that Davis had given them complete autonomy. Davis denies this, arguing that he was always involved. After the film had aroused much ire and the filmmakers had issued a press release in which they made this claim, Davis responded. "Now it suits your interest, apparently, to claim I was 'detached'... but my detachment led to our talks—endless talks—about the film that began in May 1980 and continued until March 1982. Was I more detached during our screenings of dailys or did this not truly express itself until we were screening out portions of the film?" [Davis personal communication to De Mott and Kreines, 11 October 1984].

In any case, the filmmakers barely made the deadline. They made a trailer for Davis to use in promoting the series, but by 8 March 1982, when PBS downlinked *Seventeen*, the editing was still not complete. The version lacked final touches, and the filmmakers continued their work until early summer.

It was the still incomplete version that Trimmer used to write the teaching notes for *Seventeen*. He made a valiant effort to tie the film to *Middletown* by quoting a portion of the latter book to the effect that parents did not want to know what their children were doing nor did the children want them to know. What this had to do with the film is difficult to determine. Lynn did not conceal her activities from her parents; as a matter of fact, they encouraged her rebellious behavior, allowing her to drink at home, a violation of Indiana's drinking laws. Nor does Robert conceal his child from his mother. A good deal of the action of students of the film is open and done with parental knowledge. Then Trimmer shifts the thesis of the film from its announced one. It is no longer about education in school; it is instead about being young and seventeen. "*Seventeen* is about being in between. If sixteen marks the end of innocence and eighteen the beginning of maturity, then *seventeen* is characterized by indecisiveness. Too experienced to be adolescents, too childish to be adults, the seventeen year olds in this film seem simultaneously in search of and in retreat from the responsibilities of relationships" [Trimmer 1982:9].

Thus does Trimmer change the emphasis from an examination of institutional education to a psychological analysis of what it means for Lynn, Robert, and Buck to be seventeen. No longer is the film about Southside High School; it is one about Lynn Massie and her growing-up pains. Trimmer devotes about half of his discussion to events in Southside High School although, as we have seen, these only occupy a small portion of the film. He argues that Mrs. Hartling's claim to be teaching "Citizenship, how to be a good person, to be honest," and the student's reply that "you ain't teaching us to cook" establishes "the tension in the film between what teachers are teaching and what students are learning, both in and out of the classroom" [Trimmer 1982:9], thus missing the point that there is little evidence in the film that Mrs. Hartling is teaching either citizenship or cooking. There is one paragraph devoted to Lynn that concerns her learning about shifting loyalties of groups. There is another about Buck's reaction to the death of his friend Church Mouse. There is no overt reference to anything else, but Trimmer concludes that "*Seventeen* presents serious problems for parents who would protect the young and for teachers who would direct them. It may even present serious problems for students who are used to being protected and directed. The young people in this film exceed the limits of acceptable language and responsible behavior in almost every scene. Many viewers may respond to this activity by questioning the morality or typicality of this group of seventeen year olds.... We can fuss about the language or behavior in *Seventeen*, but if we do we will fail to notice the film's basic truths" [Trimmer 1982:10].

Trimmer anticipated the storm that was to follow, but underestimated its intensity.

Things Go Sour

From September 1981 until March 1982, Davis busied himself with innumerable details of finishing the series and putting it on the air. He had many problems trying to hold the corporate sponsors to their commitment, problems that he did not succeed in solving. These problems, however, were behind the scenes and had not yet reached public notice.

The major problem was with Xerox. The corporation, as we have seen, pledged $50,000 of its grant to support the teaching guides for the series. The remainder was a match for NEH funds and had been spent for production costs. Xerox, as the corporate sponsor, was also to promote the series. It had hired two public relations persons, Wachsman and Boren, to publicize the series [Davis personal communication to De Mott and Kreines, 11 October 1984], the corporation's major public television effort for the year; it was particularly interested in the education film and wanted to push it quite hard.

Early in the fall, rumors of the content of *Seventeen* had reached Xerox. It is a mystery as to what Xerox representatives heard or who told them. Kreines and De Mott claim in their press release that Xerox learned "from Middletown, not the filmmakers that the film contained an interracial romance and four-letter words" [Kreines and De Mott n.d.:1]. It is unclear what they meant by Middletown. The only person who met with Bob Schneider, Xerox's representative, was Davis [Davis personal communication to De Mott and Kreines, 11 October 1984]; Schneider had no contact with any of us in Muncie and he certainly had no contact with Kreines and De Mott.

Davis has denied revealing anything to Schneider, and I believe him to be truthful in this matter. There are several possible explanations. Perhaps the public relations persons who interviewed Kreines and De Mott for publicity releases somehow, intentionally or unintentionally, revealed aspects of the film. Perhaps one of the persons viewing rushes or the work print tipped off the corporation. The rumor we heard after the fact was that a woman involved in the project in New York City who was quite religious saw parts of the film and became concerned. She was the one who disclosed the material to the responsible individuals in the corporation.

In any case, by October 1981, Xerox began having doubts about the film. The corporation was not, however, sufficiently concerned to refuse Davis's request for a last-minute loan to continue editing the films and to cover other costs [Davis personal communication to De Mott and Kreines, 11 October 1984].

In November, Schneider went to PBS and to NEH to voice the corporation's concern with *Seventeen*. He, according to the filmmakers, inquired of Steve Rabin, then head of the media division of NEH, if the Middletown Film Project would be delinquent if it failed to screen the last film. Rabin responded that it would not [Kreines and De Mott n.d.:1]. His trip to PBS alerted the network to Xerox's uneasiness and was to lay the groundwork for a later confrontation between Davis and Lawrence Grossman, the head of PBS.

There is no evidence that either NEH or PBS at that time exerted pressure on Davis to change or censor *Seventeen*, although Kreines and De Mott believed that PBS's attempt to move the deadline for delivery ahead was a deliberate attempt to disqualify the film from showing [Kreines and De Mott n.d.:1]. The filmmakers were still not finished and were going to have difficulty meeting the original deadline set by PBS.

Meanwhile, Davis was trying hard to convince Xerox to remain as a corporate sponsor. He pled with Schneider "not to make up his mind on narrow commercial grounds... but to wait and see what the series' reception would be and what kind of praise his company would get for backing it." The question by December was whether Xerox would pull out of the series or just pull out of *Seventeen*. Schneider at that time favored the more limited action while another executive, Michael Kirby, argued for dumping the whole series. Schneider, who had been ill with heart problems, told Davis in late December that *Seventeen* was definitely out. Davis's final plea for *Seventeen*, written on New Year's Eve, was not heeded [Davis personal communication to De Mott and Kreines, 11 October 1984].

Early in January Davis took action, which made him vulnerable to criticism, both from PBS and Kreines and De Mott. He showed a final cut of *Family Business* to a number of people—none from Muncie—including representatives from PBS, from WQED Pittsburgh, which was the station Davis picked to originate the series, and from Xerox. He then took the three Xerox executives to a cutting room where he screened a rough cut of the trailers for all the films. Davis has explained his action. "The reason for this, as I explained to Larry Grossman, was that Middletown had no money to finish these trailers, and WQED had refused to provide it. I was therefore in the position of needing to raise money just to get the trailers done. So I had invited Xerox to look at what we had of the trailers—about thirteen minutes, a couple of minutes or so on each of the six films—and tell us whether they'd (sic) put up money so we could finish them. Particularly since, in the corporate underwriting sense, Middletown was Xerox's series" [Davis personal communication to De Mott and Kreines, 11 October 1984]. According to Davis, he succeeded in obtaining the necessary money from Xerox to finish the trailers and for promotional materials for them. The only mention of *Seventeen* was by one executive, Joe Cooper, who expressed his liking for the trailer and his sorrow that Xerox did not wish *Seventeen* to be a part of the series. At this time, both sides understood that Xerox had dropped *Seventeen*. The question was still the fate of the series.

Xerox asked Davis to eliminate *Seventeen* from the series, but he refused. Xerox then took the corporation's name off it and off the series as well, and canvassed the other corporate supporters to do likewise. "Xerox agreed to pay production and advertising costs up to that time, but would not allow its corporate name to appear in any post-January, 1982, advertising, except as mandated by FCC requirements" [Vander Hill 1982:59]. The disagreement with Xerox had several pernicious effects. It did not cost the Middletown Film Project $500,000, since most of that was money already spent. It did mean that other sources had to be found for last-minute production expenses, that another group would have to pay for the teaching notes, and that the publicity for the series would be drastically reduced. Of the three, the last was probably the most serious blow. The other funders continued their support; and, after all, Xerox's share of the total cost was less than 20 percent. Trimmer persuaded the Sachem Fund and the Indiana Committee for the Humanities to grant enough money to complete the teaching notes [Vander Hill 1982:59; Davis personal communication to De Mott and Kreines, 11 October 1984]. However, since the public relations firm was just preparing to release material on the individual films and filmmakers when the decision to withdraw was made, this publicity never saw the light of day.

Beyond this loss were psychological and emotional repercussions. Since these decisions were largely the product of negotiations between Davis and Xerox and were never made public, they created a major crisis in confidence for Kreines and De Mott. The filmmakers were later to charge collusion between Xerox and Davis to prevent *Seventeen* from being shown, claiming that Middletown Films had informed Xerox of the content of *Seventeen* and that Davis had shown segments of the film to Xerox representatives in violation of filmmakers' ethics. Grossman was also to use Davis's showing of the trailer of *Seventeen* as a breach of ethics, saying "Disgraceful. Peter Davis used to work for CBS News. No one there would show a program to an advertiser before it was completed. It certainly violates our regulations. By breaking a strong professional code he has brought the trouble on himself" [Kreines and De Mott n.d.:3]. Moreover, the contretemps had alerted PBS to the possibility of further trouble and would result in close scrutiny of *Seven-

teen. The network whereupon asked Kreines and De Mott to submit a rough cut of the film for viewing; this viewing caused a reaction that both Davis and the filmmakers regarded as PBS's attempt to block the film's showing [Kreines and De Mott n.d.:3; Davis personal communication to De Mott and Kreines, 11 October 1984].

In retrospect, the clash with Xerox shows the corporation to be unethical in its attempts to pressure other backers. It could have withdrawn from the project without comment and without efforts to close it down. Yet the corporation's position is understandable and Davis was not as angry with it as he was to be later with Grossman and PBS. "To me, their [Xerox] dropping of the series' ancillary publicity and even their canvassing of our other support had never seemed as villainous as what PBS did. I am very familiar with the loss of sponsorship for controversial films. It happens every day and has happened to me a number of times. Corporations see themselves as profit-making machines, and anything that threatens the profits has to go. Xerox was never all that comfortable with the Middletown series from the outset, but they (sic) needed something on the air in the spring of '82; they (sic) wanted to keep up their PBS visibility. At first a couple of their executives seemed to like me, though one never disguised his hostility. We had an uneasy, interesting relationship, and they (sic) did give the series extra money, not once but twice, even after they (sic) knew *Seventeen* was going to cause them problems" [Davis personal communication to De Mott and Kreines, 11 October 1984].

Davis, on the other hand, can be faulted for his continued efforts to persuade the corporation not to abandon the series. Showing representatives the trailer was probably an error in judgement because it could be, and was, twisted by the filmmakers and PBS to make Davis appear too close to the corporation. Yet Davis can be excused. He desperately needed money, and he did not show the program to advertisers. He only showed the trailers.

At this point, all was not lost. The media did not know of the decision, and money had been found to complete the program. The next hurdle, which proved an even higher one, was PBS.

One does not have to be a bureaucrat to understand the position in which Grossman found himself. He was serving in an administration which was overwhelmingly ideological and which was anti-government in both rhetoric and action, except in the case of defense. Reagan was in the second year of his tenure and had succeeded in imposing his will on Congress. There was a real chance that PBS might find its funding more drastically reduced or even eliminated if it presented a program that pictured American high school students in a very bad light; for, despite proclamations to the contrary, the agency, like NEH, had been highly politicized. Further, what about public support outside the Beltway? April was when *Seventeen* would be shown; that was also the month that many stations had fund-raising drives which were vital to keeping them on the air. What would happen to receipts if a film which flaunted conventional mores were shown in the middle of a drive? Finally, Grossman had personal ambitions; he was soon to move up to the position of news director of NBC. Why risk your career for one film?

In any case, March was the crucial month. On 8 March 1982, PBS broadcast *Seventeen* on a preview feed. This feed was out of chronological order; it was the second segment to arrive at stations although it was the last scheduled to be shown. At the same time, *TV Guide* appeared with a story on the series which contained news of Xerox's withdrawal, its reasons, and a statement from Grossman reflecting the official and negative position of PBS. The article was devastating; Xerox said the film was "something we could not suggest students and parents view in their own homes." Grossman argued that "there are some things you cannot do on TV," and called several segments not acceptable and "ghastly" [Kreines and De Mott n.d.:3]. At the same time, Grossman castigated Davis for improperly showing portions of *Seventeen* to Xerox, a twisting of the events as we have seen.

The response to the film and the attendant publicity was very negative. According to a reporter at a Chicago convention of public television broadcasters, there was a unanimous rejection of *Seventeen*. WTTW told PBS it would not show the film; Nashville's public television station even cancelled the whole series because of *Seventeen* [Kreines and De Mott n.d.:4- 5].

The reaction to the controversy was intense in Muncie. For the next three weeks, the town's populace talked of little else. The two local newspapers— the *Muncie Star* and the *Muncie Evening Press*—provided a blow-by-blow account of the situation. (Both papers, incidentally, are owned by the Pulliam family, and Vice President Quayle's father was the publisher for a time.) While most of the town remained ignorant of the film's contents, others were more informed since Jim Needham, station manager for WIPB, had invited members of the school board, along with the humanists, to view the downlinking. He then arranged for another showing for Southside teachers and parents and, according to Kreines and De Mott, videotaped participants in *Seventeen* while questioning them about their participation [Kreines and De Mott n.d.:7].

Reporters interviewed the principal of Southside, James Hedge, and Davis. Hedge reflected the anger of the school authorities. "They did us in. Just did us in. It's ironic what they told us they wanted to do. They wanted to depict high school life, especially the senior year, and follow that year through and include athletics, homecoming, prom, commencement, and everything in between. They said they wanted to depict education through the eyes of a senior student, to make a film which former students could be proud of. They filmed everywhere but none of the positive aspects are shown" [*Muncie Star* 12 March 1982]. Hedge represented accurately what he thought the agreement with the Middletown Film Series said. His was not a minority opinion. Tempers ran high in Muncie and while we humanists were not threatened, we kept a low profile (later Kreines and De Mott left town partly because of the town's anger). One story that circulated did quote an unidentified school official who lived near Trimmer as saying that he wouldn't mind running over him if the official saw the latter out running. Apparently he didn't.

In an interview, Davis maintained that the quarrel was the result of "an unfortunate misunderstanding," saying *Seventeen* was not about the Muncie schools. "It's about 17-year-olds. That's why we called it that" [*Muncie Star* 12 March 1982; 19 March 1982]. Yet in another interview, one with Arthur Lubow in *People* later that month, which citizens of Muncie read, Davis said "It's like bringing specimens back from the deep....You can't believe you're seeing it" [*People* 29 March 1982]. That this was a distortion of a quotation from Freud and had universal application to all the films escaped notice. What Davis really believed the film's subject to be is difficult to determine. Later, in 1984, he represented the film to European audiences as being about education. "*Seventeen*, which is the Middletown film on education and youth, explores the anguish, joy, despair and struggle in the lives of a small group of working class teenagers in Muncie, Indiana. We focus especially on one highly energetic girl (Lynn Massie) and her friends, both black and white, as they navigate their final year of high school. They are learning and the school is teaching, but what they are learning is not what the school thinks it is teaching" [Davis personal communication to De Mott and Kreines, 11 October 1984].

Davis's protestations did not alter the attitudes of the school board, Southside teachers, and parents who saw the film. Feeling betrayed and believing that the filmmakers had deliberately distorted scenes, they hired lawyers and began collecting affidavits from both participants and parents. Among the charges made in these affidavits were that parents and students were deceived, particularly by releases bearing the name *The Commencement* which led them to believe that the film was about that event. One of the affidavits was from Lynn Massie saying that she had been induced into behaving as she did; others claimed that the filmmakers had furnished liquor and pot to the participants and had allowed them to use their car.

Two different groups hired attorneys: one was the school board; the other consisted of participants' parents. On 18 March 1982, five Munsonians flew to Washington, D.C., to confer with PBS officials. They included Needham;

John Beasley, the attorney for the Muncie Community Schools; Robert Beasley, his son who was also an attorney; Sam Abram, assistant superintendent for secondary education and the highest ranking black in the school system; and John Hedge, the principal at Southside. The superintendent for the Muncie Community Schools, Don Slauter, and Franklin Brinkman, an attorney retained by Southside parents, remained in Muncie, but retained a keen interest in the proceedings and were to be much involved later.

The delegation to Washington presented its case to PBS, arguing failure to obtain proper releases, manipulating and enticing students into certain behaviors, staging scenes, and deceiving parents and students [Vander Hill 1982:60; Hoover 1987a:37]. The representatives also claimed that the film defamed Muncie Southside, the school system, and that it identified a female student who had been promiscuous.

It is difficult to determine the impact that the delegation had in Washington. Grossman has maintained that the visit had caused PBS lawyers to become quite concerned about the legality of the releases and that Davis could not assure them otherwise. He also claimed that he had not been approached by Xerox or anyone else, except of course Davis, about *Seventeen* prior to this visit [Grossman telephone interview, 11 April 1986]. This denial runs counter to Davis's statement that Schneider had visited PBS in November.

Meanwhile, matters between Grossman and Davis had deteriorated. PBS had demanded a mixed and printed version of *Seventeen* in final tape transfer two-and-a-half months prior to broadcast. The network accepted, however, a final edited tape off a work print, which it previewed in February [Kreines and De Mott n.d.:18]. Kreines and De Mott have argued that the pressure to produce a version for in-house viewing was an attempt to kill the film. "That the PBS staff's demands were arbitrary, capricious and unreasonable was clear. So was their determination. If PBS could disqualify *Seventeen* from broadcast on some technical grounds—like the date of delivery, the form of delivery, the length of the film—PBS could accomplish suppression quietly" [Kreines and De Mott n.d.:19].

Davis and Kreines and De Mott agree that the preview of *Seventeen* made a significant impression on PBS. Davis said that "one of the executives had told me previously the film had jarred her so much she went home and smoked the best, most exhilarating dope she had had in years" [Davis personal communication to De Mott and Kreines, 11 October 1984]. The filmmakers also quote Davis's report that some of the PBS viewers thought the film was wonderful [Kreines and De Mott n.d.:19].

But Grossman was not impressed. According to Davis, "He obviously hated it every way he could." Grossman, however, encountered opposition from his staff against killing the film, enough so the film survived, but PBS

insisted that the turtle-sex segment be deleted. Davis discussed the issue with
Kreines and De Mott and arrived at a compromise with Eric Sass, the sched-
uler for PBS. This was that the five-minute segment be cut from the main
satellite feed, but that the uncut version be made available to any station that
wished it. Sass sent Davis a telegram saying that PBS would agree to broadcast the film if the cut were made. Davis then assented [Davis personal communication to De Mott and Kreines, 11 October 1984].

This then was the situation when the Muncie delegation arrived in Washington. At that point, according to Davis, Sass and Grossman broke their
agreement and asked for further cuts [Davis personal communication to De
Mott and Kreines, 11 October 1984]. According to Kreines and De Mott, the
original request was for eight major cuts but was later reduced to three: the
kiss between John and Lynn, "Ron" Massie smoking a marijuana cigarette,
and the county fair sequence [Vander Hill 1982:60; Hoover 1987a:59].
Davis refused to make the cuts, although he informed the filmmakers of the
situation. He said that he never suggested that he or they would agree to the
cuts and that both the lawyers for the Middletown Film Project and PBS
thought them to be unnecessary [Davis personal communication to De Mott
and Kreines, 11 October 1984].

On 30 March PBS announced that Davis was withdrawing *Seventeen* from
the series. In the press release, Grossman stated: "PBS offered Mr. Davis the
opportunity to make certain changes in the program in light of questions
raised by several minors concerning their participation in the program intact
and has withdrawn it" [*Muncie Star* 31 March 1982]. On the other hand,
Davis claims that Grossman cancelled the segment after "he had created a
sort of open season on *Seventeen* both in Muncie and among his affiliates"
[Davis personal communication to De Mott and Kreines, 11 October 1984].
Nowhere did either Davis or Grossman mention pressure from Xerox.

Indeed, Davis's main ire was directed at Grossman and at PBS. He believed that Grossman had lied to him and had pandered to both the conservatives and liberals. According to him, Grossman "had hated the film so much
that he lashed out in every direction, signalling to all his affiliates that it was
open season on *Seventeen*" [Davis personal communication to De Mott and
Kreines, 11 October 1984]. Not that he was any easier on PBS. "PBS, on the
other hand, is not supposed to be there for profit or even respectability but for
the presentation of material the commercial networks are too profit-orien-
tated, craven, dull, or cowardly to broadcast. In the case of *Seventeen*, PBS
proved far more cowardly than any network I've ever had experience with.
Larry Grossman did his job against us so well he now gets to run a news division for NBC; obviously I don't believe the one—suppression of *Seventeen*—led directly and unstoppably to the second, but there is no doubt NBC

knew they were getting a protector of institutions and not a defender of original work when they hired him" [Davis personal communication to De Mott and Kreines, 11 October 1984].

Kreines and De Mott also lambasted Grossman, calling attention to the mission of PBS. "In fact, in his tirade against *Seventeen*, Grossman lost sight of his mandate from Congress: in return for public monies, public television must broadcast a diversity of views; in PBS programming, independent voices, as well as the corporate voice, must be heard. But the President of PBS made his allegiance to the corporate voice a matter of public record. He never defended any aspect of *Seventeen*, even privately" [Kreines and De Mott n.d.:4]. Discounting their own simplistic division of American life into corporate and non-corporate voices, the filmmakers did lay their fingers on a real problem with PBS. What obligation did it have to broadcast controversial materials?

But Kreines and De Mott did not stop there; they also began to blame Davis. For them there were many villains; there was Xerox, there was Grossman and PBS, and, finally, there was Davis and the Middletown Film Project. Their reasoning was that Grossman had intended to torpedo the film all along but had to do it cleverly to avoid the appearance of censorship. This he did by attacking both the film and the producer, the former for its rough language and sensational theme and the latter for showing portions of *Seventeen* to Xerox. Thus, the filmmakers concluded, Grossman caught Davis in a trap.

They said Davis should have admitted that he had shown a trailer to Xerox and that he did it without the consent of Kreines and De Mott. But Davis would not do this because he then would have had to admit that he was "completely removed from the making and shaping of the film," and that he did not know what form *Seventeen* would take when he showed the trailer. Thus did Kreines and De Mott declare their complete autonomy from the Middletown Film Project. "The filmmakers' role was to complete their work in Muncie, without outside aid or interference. The executive's role was to complete negotiations, on Middletown's behalf, with PBS, CPB, WQED, NEH, ICH, and Xerox" [Kreines and De Mott n.d.:21]. If Davis had done this, the filmmakers claimed, everything would have been all right. "Such an explanation," they said, "would have cleared *Seventeen*, by establishing that its creation was immune from any improper influence from Xerox itself, or from an executive sensitive of Xerox's desire" [Kreines and De Mott n.d.:22].

Davis did not make such an announcement, and from the viewpoint of hindsight it is difficult to see what such an admission would have gained, even if it had been true (Davis claimed it was not and the evidence seems to be on his side. According to his testimony, he viewed dailies, looked at cut portions, and participated vigorously orally and by mail) [Davis personal communication to De Mott and Kreines, 11 October 1984]. If Davis had made such an admission, would that have changed Grossman's opinion about *Seventeen*? Would Grossman not have eliminated the film on the basis that it was made under false pretenses? If Davis had no control, would the series have been a series? The answer is of course no.

Kreines and De Mott then argued that the failure of Davis to give them full credit was because of an enlarged ego. "What Grossman had gauged correctly was the vanity of the man: Davis was incapable of publicly admitting any act—even the lesser sin of trailer showing—that might tarnish his image. Upright, courageous, uncompromising those labels became less easy to attach to a guy who gave his corporate sponsor a review of potentially controversial material" [Kreines and De Mott n.d.:22]. They then accused Davis of failing to be truthful concerning the film by claiming he had not shown any film of *Seventeen* to Xerox (this accusation is not quite on the mark, although it must be admitted that Davis was less than candid about what he actually did). Tom Shales of the *Washington Post* quoted him as saying on 23 March that he had not screened the completed film for Xerox and that, when asked by Xerox officials if there were rough language in any of the films besides *The Campaign*, he warned them "about the authentic but potentially offensive glossary of profane and scatological expressions in *Seventeen*" [Shales 1982a]. Davis failed to mention the trailer nor did he say when he showed *The Campaign* to Xerox (if he did).

From this lack of candor to the press, Kreines and De Mott decided that somehow Davis and Grossman were in cahoots, that both were protecting Xerox. They thought Grossman knew why Davis had not mentioned showing the trailer. Like Grossman, Davis wished to keep funding for the series' public relations campaign, "an effort that amounted, in practice, to the promotion of himself, as filmmaker and writer" [Kreines and De Mott n.d.:23]. In other words, they said Davis had been bought out. "Though Xerox had signaled its fury over *Seventeen* by withdrawing its advertising campaign and denouncing the film publicly, a gentleman's agreement between Davis and Xerox remained in effect. The agreement, common in public television annals, was that no attempt at interference, no assertion of editorial control by a corporate sponsor, would ever reach the press. Brutally put, the price of financial support is silence. In this case, in return for not mentioning Xerox's unethical activities to the press, Davis could expect Xerox to continue to pay for his promotional campaign" [Kreines and De Mott n.d.:24]. This compromise, according to the filmmakers, was also designed to give Davis more credit for the film they had made.

Again, Kreines and De Mott are wrong in their facts, but Davis's actions and words had given them a base for suspicions. He did receive a loan, never paid back, for finishing the trailers and he did not criticize Xerox severely for pulling out of the project, calling Xerox's actions understandable.

Another person against whom the filmmakers railed was Jim Needham, general manager of WIPB. They have this to say about him. "It should be noted that Needham was a long-term advocate of censorship. A Moral Majoritarian, he made a practice of suppressing films whose viewpoint differed from his own. Example: In place of nationally scheduled *Song of the Canary*, an investigative report critical of big industry, Needham ran propaganda for prayer–in–schools movement—*Let Our Children Pray*, starring Art Linkletter" [Kreines and De Mott n.d.:5].

Needham did decide what programs the community should watch, although he was also sensitive to community pressure. He became too involved in the *Seventeen* affair and took it upon himself to act as spokesman for those hoping to stop the film's showing. He was quoted in the *Indianapolis Star* the day after the withdrawal of *Seventeen* that "Many elements in the Muncie community are convinced that public presentation would have involved substantial legal difficulties and would violate the rights of students and others included in the program. Some of the participants have retained legal counsel to protect their rights in this matter and we are pleased that this controversy has been resolved" [Inman 1982]. His participation in the trip to Washington did not go unnoticed locally or regionally. Although the board of WIPB took no action, mainly because he did not bother to inform it, either before or after, of what he had done, the Indiana Associated Press Broadcasters Association censured him on 3 April at its convention in Fort Wayne. By an interesting coincidence, the president of the association was a Muncie man, Jack McQuate, who was public affairs coordinator for WBST, Ball State's campus radio station. The association had a near unanimous vote to censure, with only one member voting against the resolution. McQuate indicated that the problem was one of prior censorship, holding that it was inappropriate for a station manager to support a group advocating either editing or suppressing the film. The incoming president, Linda Losch, who was news editor at WOWO in Fort Wayne, also stated, "It was wrong to censor it, even if the content is not journalistically correct or if it is unethical" [*Daily News* 16 June 1982].

Needham received no reprimand from the station nor was the Association's reprimand general knowledge. News of the action did not appear in city newspapers and the whole controversy never reached the board level at the station.

Kreines and De Mott also included the community in their attack, calling what happened in Muncie a "witch hunt," claiming that the entire community somehow succeeded in suppressing the film. They maintained that parents, lawyers, newspaper columnists, community leaders, and Needham joined in the pressuring of *Seventeen* participants [Kreines and De Mott n.d.:6-8]. They were particularly exercised by an article that appeared in *The Nation* on 12 June 1982, "Muncie Protects Its Own," which was the most detailed account in print of what supposedly happened to *Seventeen*.

Richard Lingeman, executive editor of *The Nation* had come to Muncie in April at my invitation to deliver a Center for Middletown Studies lecture. I invited him because of his book, *Small Town America: A Narrative History, 1620–The Present*, and his obvious knowledge of American towns. He had never met Davis and he met Caplow for the first time there. Caplow had come to town to celebrate Middletown Week, which featured one of the Middletown films and the publication of the *Middletown Families*. After visiting Muncie, Lingeman wrote an article on his perception of what had happened to *Seventeen*.

What bothered the filmmakers in the article was his judgement that the issue was not censorship, "at least in any dire sense" He, like Grossman, said the determining factor was the threat of lawsuits by the attorneys for Muncie Community Schools and Southside parents. He repeated some of the charges which had appeared locally. "The Muncie papers played up stories quoting students who said the film crews were so disruptive that they took to covering the omnipresent lenses with their hands; there was an implication that the students who cooperated (and ended up in the film) were the 'show-offs.' There were also charges of the 'Chinese' shooting—employing a camera with no film in it—in the school while the raunchier extracurricular scenes were assiduously recorded. Participants in some of the scenes—notably the 'kegger'—said they had not realized that footage taken would be part of the final film" [Lingeman 1982b]. He also noted that while a sociologist had told him "that the way Muncie suppressed the most unflattering film of the six without stirring up a censorship fight was a remarkable example of community action" [Lingeman 1982b]. The community as a whole was not unanimously in favor of the withdrawal of *Seventeen*.

He was right; the protests came from school officials, parents of participants, participants, and Needham. Many in the town opposed withdrawal. Among them were Mayor Wilson, the winner in *The Campaign*, and Hurley Goodall, a black state representative who was a member of the board of WIPB and who told *The New York Times* that "if the efforts to prevent the showing of the film were because people wanted to suppress what was shown, it was wrong" [Sheppard 1982]. Goodall said this despite his fear about the impact of the film on the community's race relations. Other board members assumed the same position, as did influential members of the community [Sheppard 1982; Davis personal communciation to De Mott and Kreines, 11 October 1984].

Few people in Muncie had seen the film but most had heard about it. Ever since the announcement by Xerox and Grossman, the topic had become the talk of the town. On 12 March, almost immediately after the film was previewed by local school officials, teachers, and parents, the *Muncie Star* carried a long article on reactions from selected interviewers. Jim Hedge, the principal, complained that of all the film taken at pep sessions, athletic events, and other connected activities, only two to two-and-a-half minutes were used. He also said "by no means is the film *Seventeen* a typical portrait of Southside High School." Mrs. Hartling, the home economics teacher, said the film misrepresented her class, showing only five students when she had over twenty, and claiming that she was out of earshot when the rude remarks to her were made. She also said she never had trouble filling her class or with discipline. Michael Gorin, the black sociology teacher, said that "what the film shows is not an honest representation of life at the high school." Carolyn Grieves, Southside's journalism teacher and publications adviser, indicated that she would ask her students to write letters to the editor of the *Muncie Star*, WIPB, and to PBS. The next day she had a dozen letters [North 1982].

One of the letters struck a poignant note. It was from sophomore Tammy Crouch.

> The *Seventeen* segment of the Middletown series in an absolute disgrace to Southside High School students! I do not appreciate being represented to the whole nation as a filthy-mouthed drug addict and alcoholic! I am a straight A student and I don't believe in cussing, taking drugs, or getting drunk.
> What is going to happen in five years when I go and apply for a job that a graduate from Central or Northside has also applied for? I may be better qualified, but the other person may get the job just because I graduated from Southside [North 1982].

The following week Grieves wrote an open letter to Needham which appeared two days prior to his trip to Washington to speak to officials at PBS. In it, she stated her regrets for supporting the station and its telesales. She regretted encouraging her students to help as well, and then stated an opinion representative of education at Southside. "To fully understand our dilemma you must know the school's background. Because of racial problems in the early 1960s, South received a bad reputation. It has been fighting this poor image ever since. We (community, teachers, students, and parents) have worked hard over the years to erase this unfavorable image. We really believe we have made much headway in this area and have changed our reputation....Please do not let one Southside High School girl and her bizarre action destroy the other 1,300-plus students" [Grieves 1982].

On the very day the Muncie delegation went to Washington, Rod Richey, a reporter for the *Muncie Star*, interviewed Davis about *Seventeen*; Davis stoutly defended the film, saying that there had been an "unfortunate misunderstanding" and that he had not intended to hurt anyone in the town. The major confusion, according to Davis was the erroneous belief that he was filming stories that were typical. He denied that he ever used the word typical or that he had said that the project was "to show what religion is like in Muncie, or education or sports." He claimed that he always told the school board he was more interested in feelings than information. Davis also denied that the filmmakers "coached or encouraged" behavior or that the camera inspired exaggerated actions. He praised the participants in *Seventeen* for their vitality which he compared with Holden Caulfield's in *Catcher in the Rye* or Huck's in *Huckleberry Finn*, while suggesting that perhaps Muncie citizens didn't wish those books in their schools. He argued that the Muncie schools received favorable attention in *The Big Game*, and then denied that *Seventeen* was about schools. He expressed his regret that "some of the participants are now uncomfortable about their behavior in the films," but he could understand why they had signed affidavits attesting to manipulation. He described them as being "viciously attacked" and doing what was necessary to protect themselves. He ended his interview with the declaration that he would not willingly withdraw the film and that his major regret was that he might lose the friends he had made in Muncie [Richey 1982].

It was a bravura performance, and it may have convinced some Munsonians about Davis's good faith and the artistic merits of *Seventeen*. In any case, in a lead editorial in the *Muncie Star* the next day, the editor, Larry Shores, who had seen the film when it was first shown, made it the subject of his column. He characterized *Seventeen* as "rough stuff," with profanity, a black-white romance, and with parents and students at their worst. He noted the reaction of the residents who were shocked and made what, in my opinion, was an astute remark: "The problem with *Seventeen* is that it is not typical of Muncie. It is not really typical of anything except a group of unruly students who exceed the limits of acceptable language and behavior in nearly every scene" [Shores 1982b]. Yet, as Shores pointed out, Munsonians believed that Muncie was typical because they had always been taught that it was. Hence, they believed that *Seventeen* was supposed to represent Muncie's schools. Shores admitted he found certain elements surprising: The disrespect students showed teachers, the awe House had in viewing his son, and his fascination "that a collection of unruly, foul-mouthed kids would decide to dress up in formal clothes and attend their high school prom."

Shores then said he could identify with both Davis and Southside students and suggested a compromise solution. PBS should provide an introduction that would offer a frame of reference, that would tell why there were no "good" students portrayed at Southside, and of the controversy the film engendered in Muncie. He concluded that Davis ought to be the one who provided this introduction [Shores 20 March 1982b].

Perhaps the tide in Muncie had turned in favor of the film. In the most amusing letter in the entire exchange, Donald O. Mitchell, a resident of the working-class southside of Muncie, castigated those who had gone to Washington.

> I do not wish to be impertinent. I certainly do not wish to sit in judgement on the self-appointed judges of the morals and image of my community. Indeed, I must admit to being a mere peasant toiling in the fields of Middletown. Alas, no one has interested me with the keeping of that holy grail, 'Image of Muncie.'
>
> However, it is refreshing to know that Knights Slauter, Hedge, Abram, Beasley and Needham have seen fit to appoint themselves 'Image' guardians.
>
> Even as I write, three of them are galloping to the castle Washington to slay the dragon and protect the delicate sensibilities of myself and my fellow peasants!...
>
> Do the situations depicted in *Seventeen* exist in our school system? Of course they do! Are they an unfair depiction of the total system? Of course they are! Who told those lean and hungry fellows that television producers are fair fellows (not lean and hungry) who roam the earth bolstering the local chamber of commerce? Do they still believe in the tooth fairy? [Mitchell 1982].

On 25 March Davis consented to a telephone call-in show on WIPB in Muncie. He had come to town for the viewing of the first segment of the Middletown Film Series, *The Campaign*, which premiered the night before. Some of the questions concerned that film, with a female caller complaining that "It made Muncie look like a bunch of hicks," lacking only a few chase scenes to have been *The Dukes of Hazzard*. Most, however, wanted to know about *Seventeen*. Davis defended the film by saying it was a strong film, "perhaps the strongest in the series." He compared one of his sons who was always taking risks with those individuals seen in the film. He said that the series was lucky to find the students and that he found it incomprehensible that some persons had convinced them that their actions were shameful. He admitted the presence of negative elements but claimed that there were positive ones as well"—the passion and turbulence that surrounds adolescence" [Hawes 26 March 1982; *Muncie Evening Press* 26 March 1982].

Davis was at his best in this appearance. He was smooth-talking, polite, and reasonable. He even took post-show calls. One of the latter was from the mother of one of the girls in *Seventeen* who was upset about being in the public eye because of the controversy. Davis tried to reassure her by comparing her daughter's situation with that of the hostages in Iran, saying that no one would remember her name in a year [Shores 1982b]. Yet his main argument was deceiving, based as it was upon the argument that the Middletown Film Project had never used the word typical nor had it meant to make films claiming typicality. This was a Jesuitical argument since, as we have seen, in the proposals to NEH Davis did argue that Muncie was stereotypically Middle America. This, indeed, was his rationale for the series to the endowment, and it was a rationale that he also conveyed to those of us who were consultants to the project. Further, his argument that the Lynds had never called Muncie typical was also questionable. In the introduction to *Middletown*, they did say that "no claim is made that is a 'typical' city...," but Robert Lynd was somewhat disingenuous about that claim. In a letter to the secretary of the Art Students' League in 1924, he had said "Muncie has been selected from among all American cities of its size for an important research study in American city life. It was selected because it is such a typical healthy small city" [R. Lynd personal communication to Teagarden, 14 May 1924]. It is also true that later on in life he claimed that he was always careful to avoid calling Muncie typical and blamed the Muncie Chamber of Commerce and advertisers for that appellation [Shores 28 March 1982b]. There is not a little irony that Lynd did the same backtracking that Davis was to do as well. Perhaps the opening shot of each of the films, which showed an aerial view of Muncie with credits saying, "Created by Peter Davis, from the Middletown Studies of Muncie, Indiana, by Robert and Helen Lynd," was more appropriate than realized at the time. As Meg McLagan has said: "What Davis fails to address in responding to criticism of *Seventeen* is the fact that implicit in the naming of the series 'Middletown' is an assumption of a privileged point of view 'typical—' Middletown—which directly contradicts the underlying assumption of direct cinema—that each film is a constructed view of reality, a slice-of-life that strenuously avoids making any authoritative claim of this sort" [McLagan 1987:22-23]. McLagan has argued that the question of representativeness is impossible to answer since it involves a statistical not an artistic quality. Film contains a constructed truth made by the filmmaker and, according to Richard Barsam, is disguised self-revelation. "Direct Cinema exists for its own sake as a self-contained universe, we cannot demand that it be true to nature, only that it be true to itself" [McLagan 1987:23].

Davis made some reference to the problem of Direct Cinema or cinema verite, as he called it, in the telecast, but he avoided the question of whether a film in that tradition could capture any "reality" out there. He said that the filmmakers filmed without narration or comment and that the results depended on the viewer [Shores 28 March 1982b]. He said nothing about construction of a film or the function of editing. Instead he located the argument on the grounds of typicality.

Here Davis was on extremely shaky ground. He had dismissed any notion of sociological "truth" coming from careful acquisition of data through the use of social science methodology, but had taken the term *Middletown* as his own divorced from all the layers of meaning it possessed. To address the question of typicality would have involved an analysis of those layers of meaning by the same methods and by the collection of specific data. Davis had made no effort to do that. Instead he went another direction dictated by a different cultural preference, a preference for personal examples and for deviance in a series of idiosyncratic and dramatic episodes done in mainstream television tradition. The problem was not that Davis was confused or deliberately tried to deceive; the problem was that his preference doomed any serious discussion of typicality or of the other sociological questions that had arisen in over fifty years of study of the Muncie community.

Still, on the eve of pulling the segment from PBS, the *Muncie Star* had not condemned the film but had, with reservations, supported its showing. The *Muncie Evening Press* also took the same stance after the fact. Editor Bill Terhune said that he had "mixed emotions" about the cancellation. Its removal from the series relieved certain individuals, but it was "a landmark film that presents real people in real situations." He argued that the foul language that was part of the reason for the film's problems existed in Muncie, and said, "not everybody talks like the Bobbsey twins" [Terhune 1982].

By no means had Muncie rejected *Seventeen* and by no means had the majority of citizens expected Davis to withdraw the film. His action took the community by surprise. Nor were the news releases available to Munsonians much help in determining what had actually happened. The local newspapers carried the PBS announcements that Davis had withdrawn the film after being asked to make certain changes and refusing. Attempts to elicit comments from Davis or PBS accomplished little, although one new issue was raised. Davis claimed that the decision to withdraw had been based on a final version which he had given PBS; on the other hand, Don Egan of PBS's public relations staff said that the system had not received a final version but only a fine cut which lacked titles and closing credits [Hawes 31 March 1982b].

In this case PBS was correct, although it is difficult to see that this minor point could justify the actions PBS took. Presumably the fact that a final version still had to be given to the network meant that further adjustments would not have been out of line. On the other hand, if Davis's position had been sustainable, it would mean PBS had attempted to alter an already completed work.

Since both Davis and PBS refused to comment on the changes requested by the latter, judgements on the merits of the case were difficult to make. Neither of the local papers commented on the issue of censorship nor on the right of privacy being claimed by the participants [Hawes 1982b; La Guardia 1982a]. Only the Ball State student newspaper had a strong reaction, saying "Bull" and attacking PBS, but with mistaken logic and misinformation. The editor asked why the segment had been scheduled if it didn't meet PBS requirements, thus reflecting ignorance of the scheduling procedure. He also claimed charges of filmmakers' involvement were not true, thus showing lack of knowledge of the content of the students' affidavits [*Daily News* 31 March 1982].

The only other Munsonians who commented publicly upon the withdrawal were those who had opposed the showing of *Seventeen*. None of the consultants or Kreines and De Mott were interviewed although all were in town. Brinkman, the attorney for the students' parents, indicated that while PBS had mitigated the damages by its actions, he still did not know whether his fifteen clients would sue. He admitted he had not seen the film but had talked to a large number of people who had and had learned from them what was objectionable. Brinkman said that the filmmakers had been guilty of "libel, slander, invasion of privacy and a violation of a long list of other legal rights." Their worst sin, however, was their deception; "they would say one thing and do something totally different." John Beasley, the school board's attorney, was less bellicose, saying only that he was happy for the kids, while Needham said he wanted to forget the controversy and go back to "running the station" [Hawes 1982b].

National newspapers also took a neutral position. Both the *Wall Street Journal* and *The New York Times* had columns concerning the issue on the day following the PBS announcement. Neither provided much information about why the film was not to be shown. The *Times* did quote an anonymous person who was involved in the controversy (I presume that this was someone from PBS), who said "It's a very difficult issue of freedom of speech versus what these kids might have been doing themselves. There's a possibility that they really could be destroying their lives by saying some of the things they said in the film. In a way, you have to protect them—they're minors after all—from themselves" [Schwartz 1982b].

The *Times'* article also indicated that Davis was searching for another outlet to run the entire series, a real shot in the dark since PBS had already shown one episode and had committed itself to the other four.

Reaction to the withdrawal of *Seventeen* by national newspapers came somewhat later. *The New York Times* sent a reporter to Muncie to sample opinions about the film. He interviewed several persons, including Goodall,

Beasley, and Brinkman, as well as others, Harold Trulock, editor of the *Muncie Evening Press* (wrongly identified as the *Muncie Press News*), and Sam Abram, assistant superintendent of Muncie Community Schools, the highest ranking black in the system's administration. Pictures of Beasley, Brinkman, and Abram accompanied the article which was a rehash of earlier stories, the Davis telecast, and news releases, and which contained egregious errors—misnaming the *Muncie Evening Press* and identifying all of the south side of Muncie as Shedtown. What was new were the comments of Abram who had become the schools' spokesman.

In his quoted comments, Abram said that the information gathered in the affidavits showed the film presented "a distorted view of race relations." He then made a significant error, if the reporter was correct, in illustrating this contention by reference to the white boys gathered in Thomas Park. These young men were supposedly waiting for a black gang member whom they were boasting about attacking. This example was easily refuted by Davis who pointed out the facts that no blacks were shown and that the fight never materialized. (The assumption that the fight would have been interracial was common to many who viewed the film, causing one to reflect on why this particular segment appeared and on the necessity of some kind of contextual explanation.) Abram discounted the problem of interracial dating by saying it was accepted and that no one asked that teachers stop it. He did say, however, that some parents objected and that others became disturbed when they learned from the film that their children were involved. Finally, he ended on an optimistic note; Southside would grow and improve by this experience Sheppard 1982].

A more personal and, to me, more thoughtful consideration of the whole affair was Arthur Unger's piece in the *Christian Science Monitor*. Unger attempted to evaluate the claims of both Davis and the aggrieved parties. He noted that PBS's actions did limit the freedom of the filmmakers, but he also asked if free access meant free license. Since TV, unlike movies in a theater, came into the home, it had a perspective that portrayed "artistic selectivity" as "reality." After viewing most of the segments, including *Seventeen*, his assessment was that "the series seems to be a worthwhile, although flamboyant, effort to upgrade the Lynds' *Middletown*." But he was more harsh on *Seventeen*. "I have seen the original sixth segment and believe that it does a disservice to the youngsters involved, the city of Muncie, and also the filmmakers. It is comparatively easy to exploit adolescents, to encourage them to 'perform.' That may have been the case in *Seventeen*" [Unger 1982].

Beyond that, Unger found that the technique used was problematic. He believed that the division between reality and fiction on TV was so narrow that viewers might, as some already had, regard a cinéma vérité production as being real. The manipulation of scenes by the filmmakers allowed them to present their own vision of the teenage world, overlooking other, different examples. Finally, the question remained whether "public responsibility should override individual freedom." Although Unger failed to answer his own question, it seems obvious that he found public responsibility more compelling [Unger 1982].

Two other comments from national newspapers came down hard on PBS. The reviewer of *Family Business* in the *Washington Post* took time and space to editorialize about *Seventeen*. He said that the Sniders' testimony to the fairness with which they were treated made the claims of the participants of *Seventeen* that they had been manipulated in their actions seem questionable. (He did admit that the two films were made by different film crews which did blunt his critique somewhat.) At the same time, he questioned Grossman's remark that *Seventeen* did not live up to the journalistic standards of PBS by asking what those standards were [*Washington Post* 11 April 1982], a question others had also posed.

Joe Saltzman, associate mass media editor of *USA Today* and chairman of broadcasting, School of Journalism, University of Southern California, reflected on *Seventeen* a year after it was withdrawn. He liked the film and the kids, claiming it had dealt "honestly with teenagers and their feelings." In his view, the failure to show the film was a tragedy because it was an accurate portrayal of one element of Muncie life. He argued that "Everyone in Muncie must know it and anyone watching it must know it." Therefore, it was reality, a rather odd argument for a chairman of broadcasting to make. Because of its power and its reality, the film should have been shown; the tragedy was that PBS knuckled under to pressure and prevented its showing. He even quoted an unnamed PBS official as saying, "If we can't do this kind of documentary, nobody can—and I'd hate to think that nobody can" [Saltzman 1983]. This was a point worth considering, and one that few observers had not noticed or, if noticed, had ignored. The fact was that other documentaries were under considerable political pressure and *Seventeen* was not alone in its particular ordeal. Indeed, three other films had much the same history as the ill-fated Middletown film. They were *Blood and Sand: War in the Sahara*, *From the Ashes...Nicaragua Today*, and *Some of These Stories are True* from the series *Matters of Life and Death*. The history of these films is instructive.

Starting with the last: *Matters of Life and Death* was a major project of CPB. It cost $1,500,000, which bought twenty-two half-hour film segments made by independent producers. When finished and given to PBS by Lewis Freedman, head of the CPB program fund, the films ran into difficulty. PBS officials offered to show only part of the programs during prime time; the remainder would appear at other, less desirable times. Freedman refused to allow this arrangement, took the series to Interregional Program Service, and then resigned [Hulser 1982].

CPB was as obdurate as PBS. One of the segments in its series, *Some of These Stories are True* produced by Peter Adair, met with disapproval after Adair showed the film to CPB in June 1981. The staff asked for some changes which he had made. However, nine months later, CPB informed him the segment was rejected without giving any reasons. According to Kathleen Hulser, the reason was that one of the stories contained an "unflattering anecdote" about Alexander Haig. This story was not libelous; CPB lawyers admitted that but program officials said the segment was of poor quality with bad acting and that it failed to meet the series' theme or conform to the original proposal. The program was unconventional as well, inviting the audience to determine which of three stories was true. CPB actions served to put documentarians on warning; even if they made changes, their work might not be aired [Hulser 1982].

The next film to encounter difficulty was *Blood and Sand: War in the Sahara*, an account of the hostilities between nomadic tribes and King Hassan II of Morocco. Made by Sharon Sopher, the first American journalist to go to the Polisaro camps, the film was critical of U.S. foreign policy in North Africa. Channel 13 (WNET) TV Lab administered the fund which paid for the filming and sponsored the film. In January 1982 PBS staffers previewed a fine cut and were impressed. At that time, Barry Chase, director of current affairs for WNET, scheduled the film for 8 p.m. on Wednesday, 14 April. He gave the filmmakers $21,000 to finish editing the segment, but he also asked for two changes, the deletion of a shot of decaying corpses and of the killing of a goat. On 24 March PBS asked for more changes and announced that *Blood and Sand* would be broadcast at 10 p.m. on 28 April, but would allow member stations to follow the original schedule. PBS's rationale was that the program was not suitable for family viewing at eight because the producer had refused to make the changes it had requested. WNET did not agree with PBS and showed the film at 8 p.m., but other stations opted for 10 p.m. [Hulser 1982; *Broadcasting* 19 April 1982].

The final example involved PBS and NEH. The documentary, *From the Ashes...Nicaragua Today*, was produced by Helena Salberg Ladd with partial funding from the Wisconsin Committee for the Humanities. It was a sympathetic view of the Sandinista government which PBS believed, correctly, would be controversial and unbalanced. As a consequence, it asked for, and WETA-TV Washington, the sponsoring station, agreed to, a discussion program following the screening of the film that would provide balance and update the film which was about a year old. This, however, was not enough. The then chairman of the National Endowment for the Humanities,

William J. Bennett, severely criticized the film, describing it as "unabashed socialist-realism [sic] propaganda" and saying it should not have been given NEH grant funds. This statement, in turn, caused criticism of Bennett; Joseph Duffy, for example, argued that Bennett should not introduce his views into the granting process, an interesting statement from one who had helped politicize the endowment. The criticism prompted Bennett to retreat somewhat and to shift his objection from ideological grounds to one based on the inappropriateness of the film to the humanities [Hulser 1982; *Broadcasting* 19 April 1982].

Media critics commenting upon these examples as well as *Seventeen* saw disturbing trends. By being ultra cautious in anticipating trouble, PBS raised a number of questions about its role in television broadcasting. Created originally only to distribute programs, PBS now was becoming the judge of what it distributed. It not only asked to see unfinished films; it made suggestions about the final product. Was that its mission? If PBS did not show the work of independent producers and experimental filmmakers without fear of controversy, what did it do? If it lost the confidence of these persons, where did it find programs to screen? [Hulser 1982]. *Seventeen* was not alone in raising these questions; it was only part of a larger phenomenon.

Having said that, there are still nagging questions left concerning the problems of *Seventeen* which need to be addressed. These mainly involve Davis and his role.

The first problem is the commitment of Davis to *Seventeen*. I believe that the claims of Kreines and De Mott for complete autonomy cannot be taken too seriously. While Davis was in New York City most of the time that *Seventeen* was being shot, he was in Muncie part of the time and in touch all of the time. He has said that he and the filmmakers were in agreement about the kind of film they wanted to make as early as the spring of 1980. According to him, "We agreed then and we agree now. This was the right way to make this film..." [Davis personal communication to De Mott and Kreines, 11 October 1984]. He assented as the filmmakers chose the school: "When you decided, therefore, to concentrate at Southside, I was ready with strong encouragement. It was a choice I could have easily overruled, not only as a Middletown producer but as a producer of *Seventeen*, but I completely agreed with it" [Davis personal communication to De Mott and Kreines, 11 October 1984]. He also claimed that he "loved" the material that had been filmed in the spring of 1981 so much that he expanded the original length of time allotted to the segment from an hour to ninety minutes [Davis personal communication to De Mott and Kreines, 11 October 1984].

Accepting Davis's claim that he was closely involved at all stages of the making of *Seventeen*, why did he think that the kind of film that was being shaped would be free of controversy and could be shown on public television? He was not unacquainted with trouble, having encountered much criticism over his work in *Hearts and Minds* and *The Selling of the Pentagon*. He also had a less well-known encounter with public television in the 1960s, an encounter that was to presage much that happened with *Seventeen*. Commissioned to do a weekly series about teenagers, Davis made two programs which "dealt too candidly with drugs, profanity, drunkenness, sex and interracial dating at a New York City public high school." The New York City Board of Education pressured Channel 13, the presenting station, to drop the programs. Although the affiliates wished them to continue, Channel 13, not wishing to offend the board, knuckled under. Nor was this the only case; on two other occasions he had films cancelled, once forever. The film owners refused Davis permission to show them at festivals, to have them previewed or even to sue [Davis personal communication to De Mott and Kreines, 11 October 1984].

From this past experience, it is obvious that Davis had a great deal of knowledge concerning acceptability by both public television and the networks. Kreines and De Mott did not, despite their ideological position. Given Davis's knowledge and his control, why did he not suggest to or even compel the filmmakers to either tone down parts that would be controversial or to switch to another story? If he were in control, this would have been possible although, admittedly, it would have created problems.

There are several possible explanations as to why he did not. One could be that Davis believed the film could be shown in the form that was developing without controversy. Perhaps it would serve as a surrogate for the ones which were quashed by Channel 13 twenty years earlier. Perhaps PBS would be less likely to yield to outside pressure than was Channel 13, or perhaps the political climate had changed to become more liberal. Neither of these were astute readings of the situation; and this scenario has to assume Davis was unaware of Reagan's election. A second scenario is that Davis knew that the film would create a scandal, but had no option but to allow the filmmakers to proceed. This explanation would be based upon the facts that the whole project was behind schedule in the spring of 1981, that money was short (as it always was), and that Kreines and De Mott were singularly independent and hardheaded about their films. They had agreed to being removed from one film; would they allow Davis to remove them from another or to dictate the shape or content of the film? Moreover, if a blow-up occurred at that time, a new filmmaker, perhaps Davis himself, would have to shoot and edit another film while *The Second Time Around* was being completed. There was neither money nor time to do this. Given these conditions, might not Davis have decided that he had no choice but to support Kreines and De Mott and hope *Seventeen* could be shown?

There were other complications as well. One was the problem of the cuts requested by PBS. Davis had already agreed to one cut, the turtle-sex segment, thus signalling that he was willing to compromise principle. Why did he refuse to make the additional cuts requested? There evidently was negotiation between Davis's lawyers and PBS that reduced the number of cuts requested from eight to three. The three, as we have seen, were John and Lynn's lingering kiss, "Ron" Massie smoking a marijuana cigarette, and the county fair sequence with mixed couples. According to Davis's account, lawyers for both sides thought the cuts unnecessary and Davis never suggested that he or the filmmakers would agree to them.

On the face of it, Davis's statement seems problematic. If he weren't considering the cuts, why did he tell Kreines and De Mott about the request? Why would he have allowed negotiation if he was not going to make any concessions? The last possibility would have to be based on the telegram Sass sent Davis indicating a compromise. If a telegram were legally binding, however, there would be no reason to negotiate. Instead, a threatened suit ought to have persuaded PBS to honor its agreement.

Further, how important were the cuts requested to the film itself? In my opinion, none of them were crucial to the development of the documentary; and one did involve a moral, if not a legal, problem for the Massies. The kiss scene certainly illustrated the physical involvement of Lynn and John, but that was apparent in many other scenes and had been testified to by Lynn and her friends. The county fair scene was out of sequence, having been shot in the summer after commencement, and added only the information that the white girls would be considered "tainted goods" by white males because of their association with black ones. Again, this wasn't exactly news. The point of "Ron" smoking pot was to indicate his rebelliousness, but that could be seen in his drinking beer at the party. Both reflected upon his parents who, on the basis of filmic evidence, appeared to be contributing to the delinquency of a minor. These scenes were no more integral to the film than was the turtle-sex one. Finally, in my opinion, the film was too long and could have been improved by tighter editing. Why then did Davis stand on principle here but not earlier?

Again, there are several possible explanations for his actions. Perhaps he believed that PBS would agree to show *Seventeen* if he pressed hard with the best lawyer he could get. Perhaps he realized that the affidavits of the participants were too compelling [Davis personal communication to De Mott and Kreines, 11 October 1984]. Perhaps he knew that Kreines and De Mott would not willingly agree to any further cuts.

Davis could have pressed harder and risked a lawsuit. He could have accepted the cuts and then seen what would happen. After all, the lawyers for the school and the parents of students at Southside were not all that formidable, particularly for a New York lawyer who specialized in this type of litigation. Beasley was a member of a firm that practiced business law, a firm that was not one of the most prominent in Muncie. Brinkman was an aspiring attorney, but he belonged to no firm, had little experience, and was scrambling for business. Moreover, given the position of station manager Needham regarding the film, there was little chance it would appear on WIPB. If it weren't shown locally, would a lawsuit even be initiated? I doubted it then as I do now, for neither the school board nor the parents had any money to spare for a major fight.

A final note. The question of who pulled the show is still not clearly answered. The PBS release said Davis withdrew the film. On the other hand, Davis's account is slightly different. "But Grossman kept up his campaign against the film until he had created a sort of open season on *Seventeen* both in Muncie and among his affiliates. He then felt justified in cancelling the broadcast when we (all of us, starting with me) refused to make any further cuts" [Davis personal communication to De Mott and Kreines, 11 October 1984]. Which person did make the decision? Officially it was Davis, but it is obvious Grossman bears major responsibility for the film's removal.

Grossman's motives also must be examined. He and Davis disliked each other intensely, but was personal animus the only, or even the major, reason? Why did he carry his campaign so far? "Legally, the member stations themselves are liable for slander and breaches of equal time rule and the fairness doctrine, so why should PBS feel the need to take prebroadcast responsibility?" [Hulser 1982]. Grossman could have been content with warning the stations or even refusing a prime-time slot, as he did in the case of *Blood and Sand*. He did not; he wanted more. One cannot help agreeing with Davis that Grossman was adamant in his rejection of *Seventeen*. Perhaps Davis recognized that and believed further negotiation futile at the end of March.

The consequences of the public controversy over *Seventeen* were both significant and long lasting. For the series, it meant a notoriety from which it never recovered and a lack of publicity which might have increased its audience and its reputation. For Davis, it meant disappointment and a sense of failure as a producer. For Kreines and De Mott, it meant bitterness and alienation from Davis. It meant fleeing the town under a cloud of suspicion. For Southside, it meant that its efforts to become more respectable had been wasted. For those who appeared in *Seventeen*, it meant notoriety and more shady reputations. For the humanists, it meant some loss of reputation and some moments of anxiety. For Muncie, it also meant a bruised reputation and the knowledge that it would be impossible to make any more films about the town, at least not until the present generation of Munsonians is gone.

On The Air

The first of the Middletown films shown on PBS appeared 24 March 1982. It was *The Campaign*, the pilot film for the series. Despite its enthusiastic reception by NEH and its role in obtaining the funding necessary to make the rest of the films, it was not without controversy. The conflict over *Seventeen* had sensitized PBS to the problem of rough language. As a result, the network sent out two versions of *The Campaign*. One was "an audio-edited soft-feed deleting all expletives" and the other was "an unedited, hardfeed version" [*Muncie Star* 24 March 1982; 25 March 1982]. Stations were allowed to show whichever version they wished. PBS also deleted the promo of *Seventeen* from the previews of coming segments which accompanied *The Campaign*, although that film had not been withdrawn.

WIPB (Channel 49) in Muncie showed both versions of *The Campaign*: one at prime family viewing time and the other late that same night. The station also decided to do follow-ups of all the films. These were to consist of interviews of the participants if possible; if not possible, then interviews with scholars or others knowledgeable about the topic would be used.

Following the showing of *The Campaign*, Larry Dyer, the program director for WIPB, and Ray Scheele, a political scientist from Ball State University, asked questions of Alan Wilson and Jim Carey. The responses were interesting and, in some cases, surprising.

Carey, who was portrayed very sympathetically in the film, had the most doubts about his participation. While indicating that he was going to run again in four years, Carey maintained that he would never again consent to being filmed during a campaign. He gave several reasons why, claiming that filming had hurt his campaign. In the first place, he believed that the Democrats, whom he addressed in both small and large meetings, disliked the constant presence of the cameras and were uncomfortable because of them. In the second place, Carey said the cameras put him "on guard" too much, that he concentrated upon speaking proper English to the detriment of substance until he "finally got to saying what I wanted to say... sometimes I felt sorry about that, too." In the third place, Carey had come to the conclusion that he had revealed too much of his personal life, particularly his feelings concerning his first wife's suicide. Despite these reservations, Carey admitted that the major reason for his defeat was not the film crews but his failure to heal the breach with the county chairman, Rip Nelson, and his subsequent selection of a city committee. He faulted the film for failing to show the impact of that split [*Muncie Star* 25 March 1982].

On the other hand, Wilson was more willing to be filmed, saying that he would do it again—"with some discretion." Wilson admitted to being self-conscious during the early stages, but claimed that he became accustomed to the presence of the filmmakers and felt little intrusion. He also noted that his campaign workers had evicted a film crew at a fund-raising reception because they believed the cameras were too intrusive. Nor was Wilson perturbed by the greater amount of footage shot of Carey, since he thought Carey was a more "interesting character study than I was" [*Muncie Star* 25 March 1982].

The *Muncie Evening Press* conducted a mini-survey the day following the episode and found general agreement among the few individuals interviewed that the film caught the character of each candidate quite well and that, though Carey lost the election, he won in the film. One viewer, Brenda Morris, said that she would have liked to have viewed the film prior to the election. Wilson had appeared friendlier in the actual campaign; the film showed a side of Wilson she did not like and, if she could recast her vote, Carey would get it. Southside teacher Jim Ellis liked Carey's openness which he contrasted to Wilson's guarded and coached answers. Finally, Don L. Osterman, the American Party candidate, criticized the film for ignoring his candidacy and the series for representing Muncie as typical, which he claimed it was not [*Muncie Evening Press* 25 March 1982].

Before the next film was shown, another controversy erupted, triggered by the previews. Even though the promo for *Seventeen* had been withdrawn by PBS, the publishers of *Seventeen* magazine threatened to sue for unauthorized use of the name. "Merrill Panitt, editorial director of *Seventeen* magazine said his publication owns the copyright to the title *Seventeen* and has successfully protected it in court several times." But that was not all, a religious group in Muncie also threatened suit for using its name, *Community of Praise*, on a film which had no connection with it. The group hired a lawyer who expressed its wish to have the name changed [*Muncie Evening Press* 27 March 1982].

The second film to be shown was *The Big Game*. It appeared on 31 March 1982, the same day that Davis withdrew *Seventeen*. The intersection of the two events, in my opinion, was unfortunate. *The Big Game* was one of the weakest films in the series and coming as it did exactly when the furor over *Seventeen* was at its peak meant a double problem for the series. Had *The Big*

Game been shown later, perhaps the series would have had a more favorable reception.

In any case, the follow-up featured both coaches—Norm Held and Bill Harrell—Morrie Mannies, local sportscaster, and Warren Vander Hill, the humanist advisor for the film. Most of the comments in the follow-up were from Harrell who was less than enthusiastic about the screen version. "I was a little disappointed," he said. "For about three months, it seemed like I had a microphone on about all the time.... If I'd known what they wanted, I could have given it to them in about 30 minutes" [*Muncie Star* 1 April 1982]. Beyond the limited results from an extended effort, *The Big Game*, according to Harrell, contained several distortions. It made him seem as if he routinely swore when he rarely did. He did admit that he was a strict disciplinarian, but argued that the film did not put his expulsion of three players into context. He had suspended them for one game, a game at Lafayette, and, in conjunction with their suspension, had given them a curfew. They went to the game and, hence, violated the curfew. This presented Harrell with a choice: either let them run the team or take control himself. He chose to take control [*Muncie Star* 1 April 1982]. In defense of the filmmakers, Vander Hill responded that because of this disciplinary problem, Harrell barred the film crews from shooting for forty-eight hours. This prevented them from providing the context Harrell wanted and, incidently, gave more opportunity to film Held and the Anderson Indians [*Muncie Star* 1 April 1982; 2 April 1982].

Held said little about his appearance in the film except to rebut the claim by Andre Morgan's mother that Andre was being used. He said, "I don't know what they mean when they say a basketball player is being used. Andre has more to gain than anybody if he excels at basketball." Both Held and Harrell praised Rowray as a player, but neither had much insight as to the role of basketball in the larger scheme of things [*Muncie Star* 1 April 1982].

It remained for the dean of Muncie sportswriters, Bob Barnet, to assess the film in terms of what basketball meant to the community. He judged the show to be "expertly done," telling "its story honestly and with commendable professionalism." He was convinced "that all principals with whom he is acquainted—and that includes most of them—came through just as they are in real life." He noted some of the problems connected with high school basketball: the tensions created when athletes were being recruited, the extreme emphasis upon the winning. "Outsiders insist that Indiana high school basketball is somehow different, an appraisal Hoosiers find hard to understand because it is the only kind of high school basketball they have ever known. For better or worse, it is among the best in the land. In a lot of states people don't care that much. One wonders who is right." Norm Held, speaking of the upcoming Central-Anderson battle, said, "If we have over-emphasis, this probably is it. There is always the question, 'Is over-emphasis ever good?' Who knows?" [*Muncie Star* 2 April 1982].

Meanwhile, Larry Dyer, program director at WIPB, had been working hard to create a program to replace the withdrawn *Seventeen*. The gap in the PBS schedule meant an opportunity for the station to originate a program in the series. Dyer received a small grant ($25,000) from CPB to produce a segment designed to place the film series in context and, despite Dyer's denials, rebut the more negative elements [*Muncie Evening Press* 25 April 1982]. He conceived of the program as having an interview format, so his main problem was finding an interviewer of sufficient status to give the program credibility. He tried to interest Walter Cronkite, Dan Rather, and others of the same stature before obtaining Ben Wattenberg, a senior fellow at the American Enterprise Institute and a host of a number of PBS programs. Reputedly, it cost $20,000 of the grant to pay Wattenberg.

On 2 April Davis heeded the protests of the Community of Praise and inserted a disclaimer in the program, a disclaimer that both preceded and followed the segment and that would remain on the screen for at least ten seconds each showing. WIPB, to be quite safe, also arranged for the statement to be read by an off-camera announcer. The statement said: "The title of the following (or preceding) program, and the individuals and events portrayed are not associated with, and should not be confused with, the Community of Praise Inc., an ecumenical Christian organization located in Muncie, Indiana" [*Muncie Star* 2 April 1982]. Davis also agreed that this statement would be added to any promotional or educational materials printed after the agreement. The group, which was mainly composed of Catholics and whose purpose was to support family life and values, then dropped objections to the use of its name.

The follow-up to *Community of Praise* was somewhat unusual in that none of the principal characters appeared nor had any of the Tobeys seen the preview. The explanation for the failure to watch the preview was that Phyllis Tobey had gotten a new job at the Blackford County Department of Public Welfare determining food stamp eligibility and that Phil had to work. There was no explanation as to why they failed to appear for the follow-up, which was shot live at night when neither was working.

Instead, Phyllis was interviewed prior to the screening of the segment and commented upon it via the use of the *Middletown Teaching Notes*. She noted that she had not expected the final scene to be the Full Gospel Businessmen's Fellowship meeting at Muncie's YMCA, but that this was not a matter of concern. She did say that the writer of the notes was more perceptive than she was in doubting the sincerity of Chris's conversion, but that since the film had been shot (February 1981), Chris had become more committed. More than any of the other participants, Phyllis indicated her almost complete trust in the film crew of Leacock and Silver. The Tobeys had agreed to be filmed after being noted by the filmmakers at the Church of the Branches (Haggard's group) in Yorktown and after others had turned Leacock down. Even then, they had little idea of what the filming entailed. "We didn't think anything would come of it," Mrs. Tobey said. "We do not know the scope of what we were part of. We thought it would end up on a late-night, half-hour PBS program" [*Muncie Star* 2 April 1982]. However, she said "We had to trust the Lord and them [Leacock and Silver], and they us; it was a three-way bond" [*Muncie Star* 2 April 1982]. She also commented that Davis told them that everyone would have forgotten their names a couple of weeks after the film was shown and that Silver had reported "the love came through when the film was viewed in the East" [*Muncie Star* 2 April 1982]. Such was the connection between filmmakers and participants that the Tobeys and one hundred other believers had given a going-away party for Leacock and Silver when the two left town.

Despite the Tobeys' claim that they wanted others to see what they believed, neither appeared on the follow-up. It was left to Dr. Haggard, a minor character in the film, to analyze the film with George Jones, Ball State University's religious programs director, who had no connection with the film. Very little of the program focussed on the film itself. Haggard did say that he believed that the film, "made sense," that the filmmakers "allowed thoughts to be completed," but his view was not an insider's one. Haggard spent most of his time describing his reasons for leaving the Presbyterian Church where he was a deacon and beginning the group which he admitted was atypical. "We're an unusual group," he said. "We're just what we are and nothing more. We don't try to sell ourselves; we just try to be an example" [*Muncie Star* 8 April 1982]. Haggard denied he was an evangelist and described his group of about thirty as college–educated professionals who met once a week to seek to gain control over their lives. Jones's contribution was a discussion of the beliefs of the charismatic pentecostal movement. Neither had anything more to say about the Tobeys or the film [*Muncie Star* 8 April 1982].

Whether the Tobeys ever saw *The Community of Praise* is questionable. Three days after the film was broadcast they separated; three weeks later, Phil filed for divorce in the Blackford Circuit Court [*Muncie Star* 22 April 1982]. Although the couple had been married seven years and had seemingly settled down after the first two years when Phil had left five times and after their conversion, it was obvious from *Community of Praise* that tension still plagued the family. Perhaps the public screening of the Tobeys' life was the final straw that broke the camel's back.

Midway through the series, the *Muncie Evening Press* did another mini-survey of local opinion on the three films that had been shown. The paper found six people who had seen all the shows and asked their opinions. One person interviewed was obviously not neutral; she was Lucille Shesler, the mother of David Shesler, one of the protagonists in *The Second Time Around*, which had yet to be shown. She said "I think it's [the film series] great. I think he [Davis] has portrayed exactly what he was after—the drama, the personalities." The others were less enthusiastic. A local housewife said, "I'm not really certain what Mr. Davis wants to show. I watched it, and I found myself wondering why I was watching it. If it has some value, I haven't found what it is yet." The Reverend John McAdams reported that he enjoyed the films and, while he was unwilling to call them objective, believed them to give a "reasonably good picture of Muncie." A black auto worker had an enigmatic reaction, saying "I thought it was blah. It was a tempest in a teapot." Perhaps he was referring to the problem of *Seventeen* or he might have been characterizing *Community of Praise*. A machinist did speak directly about the latter film, commenting "I saw the religion show. I don't believe in that kind of religion, but if that's what they believe in, that's all right." Finally, an unemployed worker found the series very interesting and declared his intention to continue to watch [*Muncie Evening Press* 13 April 1982].

The fourth film to air was *Family Business*; it elicited the most response of any of the segments. The Sniders themselves opted to preview the film despite Howie's concern that some of the scenes might prove embarrassing. In particular, he was worried about the incident in a family card game where Lloyd, the eighteen-year-old, asked for a beer. Giving him the beer would violate Indiana liquor laws, which set the minimum age for drinking at twenty-one. Citing an experience in a hospital in Vietnam where an eighteen-year-old soldier with a missing leg had been refused a beer, Howie decided to risk his license and to give Lloyd the beer.

Of greater concern than the possibility of trouble over serving beer to a minor was the possibility of appearing inauthentic. As Howie said, "We may not look favorable, but that's not the point. The point isn't even whether or not we as a family look as good as we should.... I worried about all of us appearing natural or real. I wanted it to look like the way we were" [*Muncie Evening Press* 18 March 1982].

They were not disappointed. Howie appeared in the follow-up and indicated his belief that the film was "extremely accurate in recording his family's way of life." He had agreed to be filmed, he said, only on the condition that there be no retakes. He re-iterated his trust in Tom Cohen and his belief that Cohen had been extremely close and sympathetic to both him and his family. [*Daily News* 12 May 1982].

The Snider family had very strong feelings about *Family Business*. They all took a holiday from Shakey's to watch the segment at home. The pizza parlor remained open, however, as Howie hired substitutes to work the evening shift. All eight children plus Howie and Judy and Howie's parents, gathered at the Snider house to view the segment. Their responses were extremely positive as scenes triggered laughter and tears. At the conclusion, their comments were as follows:

Howie: It's great. It was just great.
Judy: It was us. I loved it.
Les: Beautiful. It's fit and due for Dad.
Lee: It was excellent.
Larry Joe: Top of the world.
Lisa: I hated to see it end.
Lynn: I'm fascinated by the film work.
Lloyd: Beautiful. Terrific.
Liz: I loved it.
Laraine: I did, too.
Grandpa Snider: I'm overcome.
[*Muncie Star* 15 April 1982].

The emotion felt by the Sniders was somehow conveyed to the viewers as the response began immediately. In the three hours after the telecast, the Sniders received telephone calls from twenty-seven states and Canada. By the next day, the number had grown to over two hundred; by the weekend, the total was over five hundred. The calls came from all kinds of people and for all kinds of reasons. Many of the callers were small businessmen who wished to discover whether Howie was still in business, then to discuss their own problems, and finally to testify as to how the program helped them to greater self-understanding. One such businessman told Howie that he had three sons working for him and that the show gave him insight into how his sons felt. Another call was from a person employed by a loan company who said that he had never realized the impact that his decisions had upon those requesting loans. Still another caller was one of the pizza parlor's co-owners, Chuck Zangus, who reported how much he enjoyed the show, so much that he was moved to tears. The calls were so numerous that the Snider children working the evening shift had to take the phone off the hook in order to wait upon customers [*Muncie Evening Press* 16 April 1982; *Muncie Star* 17 April 1982; *Muncie Weekly News* 22 April 1982].

But that was not all. Howie began to receive letters, some with donations, which he discouraged. Still they came, and Howie decided to send donors a Shakey's T-shirt and to donate excess funds to the Muscular Dystrophy Association in the name of a family friend who had suffered from the disease. Business also boomed. The day following the broadcast was the best Thursday Shakey's had ever had as tourists went out of their way to stop to eat. Howie had customers en route to Michigan and Tennessee detour to Muncie for lunch and even had a couple call from Chicago indicating they were planning on driving to Muncie on Sunday just to eat at Shakey's. The only sour note was that Shakey's corporate headquarters had failed to call despite a suggestion from a public relations expert that Howie should be used as the basis for Shakey's national advertising [*Muncie Evening Press* 16 April 1982; *Muncie Star* 17 April 1982; *Muncie Weekly News* 22 April 1982].

Among the callers who contacted either the Sniders or the local media were television critics from other newspapers. The television critic of the *Minneapolis Star* told Howie that *Family Business* was the best television program he had ever seen. The executive editor of the Athens, Georgia, *Banner-Herald and Daily News* called the *Muncie Evening Press* to determine whether the Sniders were still in business so that he could put that fact in his action line [*Muncie Evening Press* 16 April 1982; *Muncie Weekly News* 22 April 1982].

The following Monday, Howie received even more good news. Henry Winkler, then playing Fonzie on *Happy Days*, called Howie and offered him a contract for a TV series based on *Family Business*. On Tuesday, Winkler announced his intentions in Hollywood; he sent Howie a contract on Thursday. The contract called for a six-month option in return for a payment of $2,500 and permitted another six-month's extension for the same amount. Howie would also receive $5,000 if a pilot film sold and $1,000 per episode if a series were televised. However, the contract did not just benefit Howie; it also called for royalty rights for Davis as producer of the Middletown series. While Howie had other offers, he finally signed with Winkler four months later. Under the contract's provisions, Davis and Howie would share in the proceeds from the TV show although Howie would retain sole merchandising rights to any products associated with it. Howie announced that he would split his share ten ways, with each family member receiving an equal share [*Muncie Star* 23 April 1982; 13 August 1982].

The last film in the series to be shown on PBS was *The Second Time Around*. It was the most intimate segment and the only one directed by Davis himself. David Shesler previewed the movie the day of the showing with his mother and his grandmother, Reva Ray, who came from Tucson. His initial evaluation was that "the segment was more successful than he had anticipated" [*Muncie Evening Press* 21 April 1982].

In the follow up to *The Second Time Around*, Davis participated along with David and Elaine. The moderator was Conrad Lane, an instructor at Ball

State University and a movie buff. In this segment, Davis gave his rationale for choosing David and Elaine without, however, mentioning the abortive effort of Kreines and De Mott. He claimed that he had started out looking for younger participants but had been disappointed with those interviewed. "But the kids we talked to weren't all that interesting. About all they had to say was that they were in love and they hoped everything worked out" [*Muncie Star* 22 April 1982]. Davis then went on to describe the reasons for choosing an older couple. "They're not a typical couple," said Davis. "But they're a couple with far more experience about life, more to say about marriage and marital attitudes that hopefully will relate to young kids and older people in Muncie and throughout the country" [*Muncie Star* 22 April 1982].

The reactions of David and Elaine were equally laudatory of Davis. They testified that he was easy to work with, that they became "relaxed pretty quickly," and that they became friends. Elaine said, "We weren't talking to a camera. We were talking to a friend.... That's one thing I learned from this. You can still trust people" [*Muncie Star* 22 April 1982].

In response, Davis indicated that the Sheslers gave him "too much credit" as all of the other film crews achieved a "similar rapport with their subjects."

Beyond that, the Sheslers showed little insight into the revelations of character which the film provided. Elaine was particularly pleased that the camera had flattered her appearance, saying "I couldn't believe the way I looked in the film. There were no wrinkles, no blemishes." While Davis commented favorably on aspects of the couple's character, Elaine's communication skills, and her openness, he did not mention David's materialism, Elaine's manipulativeness and attempts at dominance, and both their narcissism which the film also showed [*Muncie Star* 22 April 1982].

All of the persons, save Harrold and Held, who appeared in the follow-ups of the films revealed certain common reactions, ones that also characterized those who did not appear, Phyllis Tobey of *Community of Praise* and Lynn Massie of *Seventeen*. In the first place, all had become friends of the film crew and were convinced that these friendships were genuine, not part of an attempt to seduce them into appearing in the films or to suggest certain attitudes or actions. Whether these friendships were genuine or manipulative is difficult to determine. Judging from the remarks of filmmakers, they may have been a combination of both. Regardless of the motivation, the bond between filmmakers and subjects presented a real danger to the latter, leading to the second common experience. All participants had underestimated the kind of exposure that the films would give. None of them appeared to understand before the filming that they would reveal so much of themselves before a large number of persons or that the project was a major one with nationwide exposure. The adolescents in *Seventeen* did not realize this until the controversy arose. Phyllis Tobey didn't realize this until the film was listed in TV guides. Jim Carey did not know what the total impact was going to be until the filming was over. The realization came sooner to Howie, perhaps during the filming, although the full understanding did not come until after the many telephone calls. The Sheslers may never have realized what happened.

Would it have been possible to have made this documentary series without creating a bond between filmmakers and subjects or with the subjects fully understanding what permission to film really entailed? I think not, although I believe that ethical filmmakers have a responsibility to explain to those being filmed the possible consequences. To the extent that I participated in convincing participants to be filmed, I feel I failed to convey the kind of exposure the films would have.

The Second Time Around completed the Middletown Film Series. To fill the hole in the schedule, WIPB had *Middletown Revisited* ready. Station manager Needham and program director Dyer were understandably nervous about the station's first entry into network programming. Dyer, whose brainchild it was, said that the program was not a rebuttal of the series but more of "an addendum to put the shows in their places" [*Muncie Star* 29 April 1982]. As such it should probably have run first, although an earlier screening would have violated cinema direct principles even while providing the context lacking.

In any case, *Middletown Revisited* did not attract the same attention that the series itself had. A number of PBS stations failed to carry it, substituting other programs instead. It was not as dramatic or intense as the films; Wattenberg created an hour-and-a-half interview program with himself as interviewer and narrator. Among those Middletown-connected persons who appeared on the program were Peter Davis, Tom Cohen, Howie Snider, Alan Wilson, Warren Vander Hill, and myself. Wattenberg also interviewed Laurence Martin, pastor of the First Presbyterian Church, who had written a chapter in *All Faithful People*, and Ted Caplow of Middletown III. Finally, he talked with representatives of the local community; these included John Pruis who had been president of Ball State University but who was at the time public affairs director at Ball Corporation, Charles Stroh, president of Muncie-Delaware County Chamber of Commerce, and Hurley Goodall, a locally-elected black representative to the Indiana legislature who appeared in *The Campaign.*

Wattenberg had come to Muncie several days before filming his show to familiarize himself with the community and the studies. Extremely self-confident, Wattenberg persisted in calling his effort the third major study of Muncie, following after those of the Lynds and Caplow. Given the weight he attributed to his own effort, he had to add a new dimension of his own.

That dimension was a discussion of economic trends. Wattenberg began with a synopsis of Muncie as Middletown, of the Lynds' study, of Caplow's effort, and, finally, of the Middletown Film Series. He then drew a comparison of economic conditions in the 1920s, the time the Lynds first visited, and the 1930s, when Robert Lynd returned, with the 1970s when Caplow came to town and with the 1980s when Davis did the film series. The result was to show economic decline. In 1976, Wattenberg claimed, Muncie's unemployment was 6.42 percent; in 1982, it was 18.5 percent [*Muncie Star* 2 May 1982].

The point to this comparison was unclear but it gave Wattenberg a chance to segue to *Family Business*, which he claimed reflected the economic slump in Muncie. It is questionable that this was even a minor theme in the film, but the proposition served as the framework for the interview with Howie, Stroh, and Goodall. All agreed that small business was the backbone of Muncie's economy, although the fact was that the largest employers in the town—Borg Warner, Westinghouse, and Chevrolet—were large corporate entities based elsewhere. Wattenberg tried to lay responsibility for the slump on large corporations. Howie refused to make Shakey's the villain as Wattenberg pressed him to do, saying that he did owe the corporation money.

Then the program directed its major attention to the filmmakers and the films. Wattenberg asked Davis the crucial question about the film series. It was: "How can a series be based on the famous *Middletown* Studies and not call itself typical?" Davis was caught on the horns of a dilemma; the money for the series had been obtained, at least in part, because of the claim that Muncie was archetypical, yet Davis had defended *Seventeen*, and the other films to a lesser degree, with the argument that the persons in the film were not typical [*Muncie Star* 2 May 1982].

Given this dilemma, Davis chose to deny that he had ever said Muncie was typical. "We never use the word typical. Frankly, I find that word kind of boring." Wattenberg then pressed him again, saying "But aren't you really carrying water on both shoulders? Can you really separate the word typical from the word *Middletown?*"

The obvious answer was no, but Davis denied the proposition for the second time, arguing "The Lynds never used the word typical. That's a word that other people have put on it" [*Muncie Star* 2 May 1982].

Here, Davis was wrong, both about the Lynds and about the film series. Although the Lynds did say in *Middletown* that "no claim is made that it is a 'typical' city..." they also state in the same work that "one of two main considerations was that the city be as representative as possible of contemporary American life" [Lynd and Lynd 1956:7,9]. In every grant proposal submitted to NEH, the claim of representativeness, even if not stated in terms of typicality, appeared. This was what the proposals said: "Although the names *Muncie* and *Middletown* refer to the same place (and will be used interchangeably throughout this proposal), they convey different meanings: Muncie is a city of 80,000 in east-central Indiana; Middletown is the code name given to Muncie by the Lynds to indicate its special significance as a town that represents the core traditions of the American experience" [Davis 1980:6]. In his last proposal to NEH, Davis also added that "amid fears that public factionalism and private narcissism threaten to splinter our national identity, these films will show the common ground on which we all stand" [Davis 1980:15].

It was Jesuitical of Davis to deny that the Middletown Film Series had not argued typicality. The idea of typicality permeated the proposals for the film even if the word was never mentioned. Beyond that the name had become so connected with typicality that even if no hint of that quality had appeared in the requests for money, it would still be there.

Tom Cohen, the director of *Family Business* and *The Campaign*, also denied the search for typicality. He said "We didn't want to find a guy who was going to work every day and coming home every night and everything was fine. We wanted someone who was in a crisis, who was being tested" [*Muncie Star* 2 May 1982]. Wattenberg then asked if the use of that criterion did not predispose the filmmakers to emphasize bad news, to be prophets of doom. Again, Cohen denied this was the case, claiming that the people in the film were not losers. He then said that Wattenberg's questions tested him and drew an analogy with the films whose purpose, according to him, was to force viewers to look inside themselves for answers [*Muncie Star* 29 April 1982].

In a sense Cohen's defense was stronger than that of Davis's. In his two films he had no losers; both had traditional happy endings. Carey's supporters assure him that he was a winner in the final scene of *The Campaign* and the Sniders' decision to go on together in business ends *Family Business* on an upbeat note. In the other films, however, the outcome is less clear. Certainly Andre Morgan is not a winner in *The Big Game* and the future of both the Tobeys in *Community of Praise* and the Sheslers in *The Second Time Around* is as questionable in the films as it was in their lives. Finally, in *Seventeen*, almost everyone in the film is a loser, from teachers to teenagers. Only by a twist of the imagination could Lynn Massie be called a winner as Trimmer did in the teaching notes. By almost any conventional standard she was a loser, cutting classes, smoking pot, and lacking any future goals.

Both Cohen and Davis also denied that they were big city liberals who had come to Muncie with preconceived ideas about the town. Davis claimed that Muncie had become a second or third home for many of the filmmakers, saying "We have come to love Muncie. If we came with any biases, we have shed them" [*Muncie Star* 29 April 1982].

Wattenberg pressed Caplow to comment on the film series, which he did, and in a favorable way. He suggested several parallels between his sociological study and the films. While he did note several differences, he argued these were the products of different genres [*Muncie Star* 29 April 1982].

In a final attempt to critique the series, Wattenberg, taking a cue from a letter to the editor in the *Muncie Star*, asked if parts of the series had not made the city look like it was full of "hicks and rubes." Why, he asked, had the series not featured the Muncie Symphony instead of the Muncie Bearcats? Caplow replied that basketball was endemic to the community and other participants agreed although this answer seemed to belie the Cohen/Davis thesis that the important element was that of crisis. Why not a viola player in difficulty? [*Muncie Star* 29 April 1982].

The film ended on a high note and evidently pleased members of the local community. In the following Sunday's *Muncie Star*, the editorial commented that the program was timely and interesting, that the local interviewers dispelled the notion that Muncie was not full of "rubes and hicks," that Alan Wilson "came across as an intelligent spokesman for his beliefs rather than the one-dimensional politician portrayed in the series opener several weeks ago," and that "it was a satisfying way to conclude what has been a hectic but provocative period in the continued sociological examinations of Muncie, Ind" [*Muncie Star* 2 May 1982].

In a limited way *Middletown Revisited* was a reprise of a symposium on the future of the documentary sponsored by *American Film* held in January in New York City, the condensed version of which was published in that magazine in April. The participants included Caplow as the *Middletown III* academic, Davis, Cohen, Leacock, Silver, and Vaughn of the Middletown Film Series, and the following: Jon Alpert, Peter Biskind, Tom Brokaw, Emile de Antonio, Robert Drew, Jean Firstenberg, Richard Lingeman, Alan and Susan Raymond, Julia Reichert, William Rothman, Deborah Shaffer, Morton Silverstein, Helena Salberg Ladd, George Stevens, Jr., Studs Terkel, Alice Trillin, Calvin Trillin, and Jack Willis [*American Film* 1982].

Noticeably absent were De Mott and Kreines or any humanists from the project. The discussion proceeded after participants viewed three of the Middletown films, *The Campaign*, *Family Business*, and *Community of Praise*. Biskind set the stage for the discussion by arguing four propositions which showed that documentary film was in a crisis. They were that documentaries did not earn high ratings and reality programs encroached on their territory; that independent documentaries faced cuts in funding from government agencies; that documentaries had lost their innovative edge gained in the '60s and '70s because of varied techniques, lack of new subjects, and a realization that so-called objective films carried concealed values and hidden points of view; and that the liberal reform impulse behind documentaries was exhausted [*American Film* 1982].

In the exchange, Alpert asked Davis if he had any thoughts about how Munsonians might react to films about them and if they watched documentaries. Davis answered that they did not watch documentaries, with one possible exception, but failed to respond to the first question. Davis also indicated, in reaction to Brokaw's comment that the networks and cable wanted more documentaries, that he had shown *The Campaign* to the networks, that CBS had admired it, that Xerox wanted it on a network, but none would take it because of a rating war and the belief that documentaries would not draw a large audience [*American Film* 1982].

In the discussion of the meaning of Middletown, several interesting points emerged. Caplow said that he had always asked himself "if Muncie is a typical place or an enclave of old-fashioned values." The films convinced him "that these people [Munsonians] are human and American and typical" [*American Film* 1982]. Davis did not challenge this view. Biskind responded that the emphasis on the typical bothered him as he detected an element of liberal voyeurism in the films, particularly in *Community of Praise*. Leacock then said that he and Silver were not interested in typicality. "Typicality would probably end up somewhere between the Methodist church which is a little down, and the Baptist church which is up and we found both types rather boring" [*American Film* 1982].

Of more concern than typicality was the problem of the title of the series and its context. Shaffer said that *Middletown* caused her to think about a comprehensive survey, but that while *The Campaign* was a "wonderful portrait film," it told her little about politics. She asked if it might not have been better to state explicitly that the films were about six moments in people's lives that were inspired by the Lynds. Davis did not agree, using the argument that although they were only inspired by their "grandparents," the Lynds, that the Middletown Film Series should be called *Middletown* because their project was a study similar to the Lynds' [*American Film* 1982].

The biggest problem was, however, context. Ladd said she felt claustrophobia about *Family Business* and *The Campaign* since "not being American, I was very curious about the context." Biskind agreed, saying he wanted the answers to all kinds of questions such as how much unemployment Muncie was experiencing and wondered if the problem was not the cinema verite technique. Drew of course protested that any social analysis would kill a film, but Reichert was not so certain. After praising the films, she added that,

But for the purpose of discussion, I think this is one of the weaknesses of what we call 'verite,' that there's a tendency not to provide a larger context. With all three films, I got very involved in the story of the people; I really cared about them, I wanted to see what was going to happen. But once that's over, you stand back for a moment and think, Why is this guy going to lose his business, maybe, or, why is this guy the mayor? There must be something else going on there.

So you're left with these really big questions which I think the films raise for you. I personally feel that without damaging the artistic integrity or the story line or the drama, you could suggest some of what are the social and political dynamics of life in the Midwest right now.... I think a filmmaker could in some way incorporate these kinds of elements [*American Film* April, 1982].

In response, both Davis and Cohen resorted to the argument that they were artists not journalists, searching for the universal not for detailed description. Cohen even denied that dating a film was important or that outside influences were relevant. Asked about national politics or local economic conditions during the filming of *The Campaign* or *Family Business*, Cohen said these were irrelevant unless the issues were important enough for Carey or Wilson or Howie to mention. Comparing his work to *Death of a Salesman*, Cohen claimed that he could not remember the town in which Willy Loman lived or the economic conditions under which he struggled. The emotional impact was what was significant so his main intent was not to convey ideas but to stimulate emotions. "In journalism you want to know something—for instance, why did Jim Carey lose? That is not as important to me as how you feel about the fact that he lost. And that's what the film's about. It doesn't matter to me *why* he lost" [*American Film* 1982].

In rebuttal, Reichert argued that there needed to be no conflict between drama and conveying information. Citing *Harlan County, U.S.A.*, she praised it for being dramatic but for also telling the history of the town, the history of coal, and of the events in Washington. This was the kind of film she would prefer.

The symposium settled no issues but it did reveal the attitude of the filmmakers somewhat more clearly than did their appearance on *Middletown Revisited*. Davis never denied typicality in the symposium as he did in the film. Both he and Cohen took a position that they were artists not concerned with context or ideas, a position contrary to the central theme of the NEH proposal; and, despite their protests, all filmmakers present, except Vaughn, condescended to the participants. Davis doubted that any of them would watch documentaries, Leacock found Baptists and Methodists "boring, plastic, and predictable," Cohen said all the participants in *The Campaign*, save Carey, were "smaller than life." They defended cinema verite and claimed they could not provide more context because that would violate the principle

of subject centeredness and the flow of actual events [*American Film* 1982].
Yet Cohen used staged events in both films, altered chronology, and pro-
grammed interviews to elicit answers for questions he wished to ask. If the
filmmaker could ask questions about an individual's past, could he not also
ask questions concerning economic conditions or the impact of national politics on local ones? If the subject needed to be nudged in one direction, why
not another?

The critics' reactions to the series were mixed and often reflected the same
issues that had concerned members of the *American Film* conference and
citizens of Muncie. Sometimes there were two diametrically opposed views
carried in the same issue and sometimes reviewers changed their minds as the
film series progressed. In general, the early reviews were more favorable
than the later ones, probably because of the controversy over *Seventeen*.

Harry F. Waters reviewed the series for *Newsweek*, the week the first segment appeared. He did not know that the final episode had been pulled so his
praise of the series proved somewhat misleading insofar as its conclusion
was concerned. He viewed the effort to emphasize human drama as ultimately very successful, saying "However sociologically dubious that decision may seem, it has produced a TV show of uncommon emotional powers."
He then characterized *Middletown* as "combining the intimacy of a Frederick
Wiseman documentary with the poignancy of a Sherwood Anderson story..."
[Waters 1982]. This was high praise indeed since combining the two qualities had been Davis's goal.

Waters compared the film series with *Hometown* and *Middletown Families*, both of which had just been published, and found that they closely
matched. He did not suggest how they matched except to say that Muncie's
political, religious, and familial values had not changed much in fifty years.
How this conclusion could be derived from the films he did not say. He did
say that Davis's cinema verite methodology created a problem. How much
did the filming alter the behavior of those being filmed? He dismissed
Davis's contention that there was little influence and denied his statement
that "They came to regard us [the filmmakers] the way aristocratic European
families regard their servants." From the films themselves he found contrary
evidence. "Teenagers steal furtive glances in the camera's direction, an engaged couple suddenly starts conversing in whispers, the pizza maker's sons
perform put-down routines as if they were auditioning for Norman Lear"
[Waters 1982].

On the other hand, he had no doubts about the credibility of *Hometown*,
despite the fact that Davis borrowed freely from one community to use in the
other, a fact of which Waters was obviously unaware. (Nor did other reviewers catch the parallels in the two, although clues were present. The reviewer

for the *Cedar Rapids Gazette*, for example, praised the chapter in *Hometown* describing activities in a small fundamentalist church which included the exorcism of a fat, pregnant housewife without noting that this kind of scene opened *Community of Praise* when the film was shown several weeks later) [*Cedar Rapids Gazette* 28 March 1982]. Waters felt Davis was least effective when he wrote of events which were foreign to his own social class, a sentiment echoed by the *Cedar Rapids Gazette* reviewer who found "something queerly archaic about a California-born, Harvard-educated New Yorker venturing into hinterlands to find the real America" [*Cedar Rapids Gazette* 28 March 1982].

On the whole, Waters was favorably impressed with Davis's dual achievements. Both book and film combined elements of voyeurism and of nostalgia, but both went beyond these questionable elements to revealing "the enduringly fundamental concerns, passions, rituals and dreams that form the national character" [Waters 1982].

Howard Rosenberg, writing in the *Los Angeles Times* on 24 March had seen only two of the films, *The Campaign* and *Family Business*, when he wrote his review. He was quite impressed, saying, "These may be the real 'Real People,'" and calling *Family Business* "a near masterpiece." He, too, worried about the effect the camera had on the participants, particularly in *The Campaign* when Carey was "always 'on' for the camera and regards it as a tool." He found Carey and Wilson to be stereotypical of the Democratic and Republican parties, thus buying into the filmmaker's vision of what the Muncie parties were. He concluded his review by comparing Wilson's victory with Robert Redford's in *The Candidate*. Perhaps his most valuable contribution was the short afterward in which he reported one of Carey's remarks. After reflecting that he was out of a job, Carey said, "I see from the paper that Fernando Valenzuela signed with the Dodgers for $350,000. Tell him I'll come along and carry his jock strap" [Rosenberg 1982].

One cannot help but be struck by Rosenberg's analysis of the two programs he had seen, an analysis which was almost entirely informed by media considerations. He compared the series to *Real People*, a popular television show of the time. His major concern was the media sophistication of the candidates; he used no other standard to judge the validity or the informational value of the series. His focus was entirely on the films as part of a particular genre.

On the other hand, Ellen Goodman's essay on the family in the *Washington Post* on 1 May was as narrowly focused on print forms as Rosenberg's was on films. She mentioned the public television series only in passing, although the films had already been shown, noting that the Snider family showed passionate intensity. She devoted the rest of her essay to a consideration of Middletown Families, concentrating on the contradiction between Caplow's finding that family life in Muncie was stronger than ever and the perception in the town and in the United States that the opposite was true. Her solution to the dilemma was that Americans had internalized "some primal scene of a family Eden, an ideal of family life." Since none could meet this goal, each individual believes that something is lacking in all families. To illustrate her point, Goodman used passages from Anne Tyler's novel, *Dinner at the Homesick Restaurant*. She then concluded that "although families failed to meet our fantasies, they are complex, powerful, imperfect and their strength is too easy to forget" [Goodman 1982].

The *Washington Post* devoted much space to the series elsewhere; perhaps that was why Goodman did not venture to become more of a film critic. The newspaper had three commentators, each with varying opinions, pass judgement on the series on 24 and 25 March, and was one of the few large metropolitan newspapers to review *Middletown Revisited*.

Michael Kernan began his review of the series with a consideration of the Lynds' books on Middletown, saying that he had forgotten how hostile these volumes were to the community. In particular, he centered upon the penultimate chapter in *Middletown in Transition*, with its portrayal of the meanness of spirit and the contradictions in the Munsonians' world vision. Having done that, Kernan concluded that the problem with Munsonians was "fear of strangers, fear of change, fear of the future, fear of the power of one's own feelings." However, he also believed, without citing any evidence, that Muncie had changed and had become part of the Global Village, while, at the same time, television had brought the myth of Muncie to the world. "That carefree, sentimental landscape of beer ads, the cigarette ads, the telephone ads, the commercial for everything from trucks to gum: that's Muncie's landscape. That's how America sees Muncie, where the sun shines forever and young people laugh and sing while they grab soft drinks from the cooler and clean old-folks smile from their rockers" [Kernan 1982].

Then, using the analogy of the railroad tracks that bisected Muncie, he asked what has Muncie done about its tracks, its connection with the outside world. He contended that "It seems to me that that story, however it came out, would have told me more about Muncie than the Basketball Game, the Election or the other conventional conflicts that Peter Davis used in his insistence on 'drama.' It may sound odd, but the way to achieve universality in art is through the specific, not the general" [Kernan 1982].

Because of the lack of specificity, the series, which involved so much time and effort, left Kernan feeling he was "no nearer to understanding the place than before." In his summation, he argued that the Lynds had given their readers much important information about Middletown but had failed to personalize their findings. He then suggested a counterfactual proposal. Why didn't Davis do an eight-hour series on the Snider family, one which would explore all of the unanswered questions Kernan had about what happened: "Why did Howie stay in his bad location; why did he choose pizza; what did the Sniders' house look like; what did they eat, was his wife a good cook; what were Howie's daughter and his son thinking about when she attacked sexism and he spoke of enlisting?" If Davis had done that, "We really might have come away with a sense of Muncie, of Middletown, and how it feels to live there" [Kernan 1982].

What Kernan had wanted was what I had wanted, to individualize the social data of the kind the Lynds sought out, and in that way to understand the town. Whether that would have been possible using Kernan's novel approach is problematic, but I think it would have been worth a try. In any case, Kernan had recognized what Davis was trying to do: to perpetuate an image of a mythical town, as surely as if he had read the final proposal to NEH. According to Kernan, Davis had succeeded in achieving his goal, however flawed that goal might have been.

In a companion review in an adjoining column, Tom Shales expressed a different opinion, calling the series "a tremendous and important accomplishment" and also "a stirring, even magnificent viewing experience, a vigil at the crossroads that is not only great television, and great American, but great dramaso great as to make many works of fiction with similar themes and settings look trifling and transparent." Shales found little to criticize in Davis's approach or in the films. In his review, however, Shales really only considered two of the episodes, *The Campaign* and *Seventeen*. He liked *The Campaign* immensely because it told the story "so well that it seems to be telling itself, and so filmically that no linear representation of it can do it justice." After giving a synopsis of the film, Shales interjected personal reactions. The story was gripping because "it keeps eliciting unexpected responses with the kind of manipulation that isn't insulting." In particular, Shales liked the film because it brought back memories of city politics in his hometown and of his father [Shales 1982b].

After the accolades for *The Campaign*, Shales recounted the controversy between Davis and Grossman in a truncated fashion, but one that came down decidedly on Davis's side. He then mentioned in passing that *Family Business* would make a hero of Howie Snider before his concluding paean of praise. "What an accomplishment *Middletown* is, and how emphatically it denies that the documentary is a dying form. Only the dull documentary is dying. The CBS News production of *The Defense of the United States* may have been an epic documentary but *Middletown* is a documentary epic. It raises standards by about 75 percent; the filmmaker's cameras seem to be as unobtrusive and revealing as those of filmmaker Frederick Wiseman (*High School, Hospital*) but the films that have resulted are far more accessible and have a much more identifiable narrative shape" [Shales 24 March 1982a].

Shales' plaudits came from a film critic's aesthetic. He was not apparently concerned with problems of representation or with the question of whether the filmmakers had manipulated those involved in the films. He was interested instead in the techniques used, the shaping of the material into a recognizable narrative, in the telling of the story in a gripping and emotionally compelling way. He was not interested in Middletown as such, accepting Davis's argument that the more significant goal was to show individual traumas.

Shales' review of *Middletown Revisited* further reinforced that characterization. In this short piece he was scathing, saying that the purpose of the film was to give "that irritating Ben Wattenberg a chance to discredit *Middletown* [the series] or at least to make it seem boring, but he fails to do either" Shales liked nothing about the program, calling Wattenberg obsessive in claiming Muncie had changed little, describing him as churlish, categorizing the segment as sloppily produced, and questioning the wisdom of PBS in spending the money for the production [Shales 1982b]. Again, he did not question the information conveyed in the film, but was mainly concerned with techniques.

The *Washington Post* was not content, however, with the general overviews of the series provided by Kernan and Shales. Following the showing of *The Campaign*, Richard Cohen commented upon that film for the newspaper. He was critical of the segment for its lack of context, for confusing literal truth with "The Truth." The film failed to inform the viewer that Carey was not the organization's candidate and that the reason Carey lost was that some Democratic voters just stayed home [Cohen 1982]. Because *The Campaign* gave the impression that Wilson had won because he had better advisors and a better image, Cohen felt deceived. Like *Missing* and the docudrama *The Death of a Princess*, *The Campaign* had a "truth-in-labelling problem." Some of it was true, some was part truth, and some was part truth and part fiction. Cohen believed that Davis used this mixture to achieve greater drama, thus giving dramatic values higher priority than journalistic ones. He dismissed Davis's argument that the story should speak for itself, saying that this statement was meaningless if it meant, as it had in the series, that the viewer had vital information withheld. Davis had not given viewers the whole truth [Cohen 1982].

Readers of the newspaper would have been hard put to reconcile the conflicting opinions printed on two consecutive days. Perhaps they could dismiss the contradictions by attributing them to personal differences; astute

readers might well understand that Kernan and Cohen wanted more information from the films while Shales was entranced by the emotional impact of
the episodes.

The mixed reactions seen in the *Washington Post* were not uncommon; in
The New York Times, the same reviewer, John J. O'Connor, changed his
mind as the series progressed, perhaps reflecting the difficulty in deciding
what to say. He did not review *Hometown*, as the *Times* had printed Christopher Lehmann-Haupt's review the week before the film series began.

Lehmann–Haupt's review of *Hometown* was, in general, a favorable one
which lauded the book. According to Lehmann–Haupt, the stories read like
old-fashioned fiction rather than sociology and like passion plays not epipha-
nies. Yet he also found weaknesses. Davis failed to limn the whole community, as he presumably had intended, but had produced instead "a series of
intense individual dramas" [Lehmann–Haupt 1982]. These conclusions, had
they been made of the film series, would not have been inappropriate, and
one wonders if O'Connor ought not have read them prior to writing his film
review just six days later.

At the onset, O'Connor predicted the series would prove as provocative
and controversial as "An American Family" had. After prefatory remarks
and a short history of the project, O'Connor conceded that the films were not
objective, that the filmmakers had emphasized dramatic values. He then reviewed *The Campaign*, accepting the stereotypes projected by the film that
the election was decided by class issues. Questioning the aptness of Davis's
term "found dramas" as implying "more impersonal serendipity than the finished project can justify," O'Connor nonetheless described the documentaries as "brimming with shrewd insights and unsettling observations"
[O'Connor 1982a].

In less than two weeks, O'Connor had changed his mind. In the Sunday
New York Times of 4 April, O'Connor was much more critical, concentrating
upon the question of whether the series could prove equal to the task of portraying a community. What changed his mind? Was it the withdrawal of *Seventeen*? Was it the controversy that had already overshadowed the series?
O'Connor did not say.

He began his review by stating that "found dramas" were no more "found
than a television movie about test-tube babies," before reviewing the history
of cinema verite films and of the project, in which he erroneously identified
Ball State University as Baker State College. While admitting that the programs were "a bit too long," he also described them as "thoroughly absorbing
and illuminating glimpses into ordinary people's lives." He then contrasted
the films unfavorably with the Middletown books which, according to him,
were much more informed and balanced. The films raised more questions

than they answered. They did not justify Davis's claim that they showed America's shared experiences, thus falling short of their promise [O'Connor 4 April 1982b].

O'Connor also reviewed *Middletown Revisited* when it showed on WNET on 3 May. His opinion of the episode was not critical; he mentions the series only to say that it had created controversy; and he supported Wattenberg's conclusion that Davis, in denying typicality to Muncie but at the same time using the title *Middletown*, was "carrying water on both shoulders" [O'Connor 3 May 1982c].

No such change in attitude was noted locally. Editorially, reaction from the start was positive despite the *Seventeen* episode. Bill Terhune of the *Muncie Evening Press* on 6 April, after outlining some of the errors in the films, errors which he described as "minor transgressions," defended the series. He even argued that he was torn about *Seventeen*, for although he was glad no participant was embarrassed because the film was withdrawn, he believed the film portrayed "real people in real situations" and that foul language was part of the American experience. He concluded that the series was a great success and Davis was a brilliant artist [Terhune 1982a].

The least enthusiastic opinion concerning the series came from long-time sports editor of the *Muncie Star*, Bob Barnet, who sometimes wrote for the Sunday editorial page. While he very much liked *Family Business* and found moments of "pure gold" in the series, he decried the attention that researchers had given to Muncie, arguing they had made Muncie a joke by characterizing citizens "as residents of a funny town in which people talk funny and wear funny clothes," and wished that "the Lynds had climbed off the train in some other town." Despite these objections, Barnet concluded that "The *Middletown* study at this point appears to be one of the most decent, careful and accurate ever made of us, but Davis had yielded now and then to the temptation to buy impact with the grimy coin of sensationalism" [Barnet 1982].

Barnet's critique came just prior to a week celebrating Middletown in Muncie. This celebration, which was to coincide with the showing of *Seventeen* but which actually fit with Wattenberg's *Middletown Revisited*, included Ted Caplow who was in town to appear in the last episode and Richard Lingeman, executive editor of the *Nation*, who was in town to give the second annual Center for Middletown Studies lecture. His lecture was entitled "Middletown as a Literary Document"; it preceded a lecture by Caplow to the Friends of Bracken Library on "The Future of Religion in America." Both Caplow and Lingeman autographed copies of their books—*Middletown Families* and *Small Town America*—one afternoon, and both commented upon the just completed film series. Lingeman noted in response to a reporter's question that "a lot of people across the country still think of Muncie as typical"; Caplow called the series fascinating but said that *Community of Praise* was "atypical" as the fundamentalist churches were gaining only a "little bit on the main line churches." Both men stayed in town for a few days, talked to reporters and townspeople, and visited Shakey's Pizza before departing [La Guardia 1982b; *Daily News* 27 April 1982].

The visit had consequences which were to become evident later in the dispute between Davis and De Mott and Kreines. Lingeman, who did not know Davis prior to the film series but who had met him at the *American Film* symposium in January, had become interested in the documentaries and utilized part of his stay in Muncie to sample local opinion. The **Nation** had published a review by Gloria Emerson, a National Book Award winner, of *Family Business* and *The Campaign* the week the latter aired. Her review was enthusiastic, calling the former episode "extraordinary theater" and finding both Snider and Carey to have "an outrageous and stubborn insistence on living intensely." She recommended the series highly and said, "The programs had for me the odd, unexpected effect of making me feel more loving about a country that usually fills me with alarm" [Emerson 1982]. Her piece was not analytical or critical. Instead it was a personal appreciation and reaction.

Two-and-one-half months later, Lingeman did a piece on the film series entitled "Muncie Protects Its Own" for the *Nation*. In it he concentrated on the response of Munsonians to the series, noting at the onset that Munsonians did not react violently to the Lynds' portrayal in contrast with the heated reaction in the upstate New York town featured in *Small Town in Mass Society* and Phillipsburg, Montana, the subject of *Small Town Stuff*. (He failed to mention the angry reaction Muncie had to Margaret Bourke-White's photographs in *Life* in 1937.) He then attempted to discover why this tolerant attitude did not apply to the television shows, and quoted a sociologist who found the suppression of the least flattering film "without stirring up a censorship fight" to be a "remarkable example of community action" [Lingeman 1982b].

Pointing out that Muncie was not as conservative about sex as in the 1920s and that several community leaders wanted *Seventeen* to be aired, Lingeman noted that the driving forces behind the protest were local interest groups whose catalyst was Jim Needham. He gave a short history of the dispute between Davis and PBS based on Davis's perceptions. He discussed the issue of typicality which participants had raised at the *American Film* symposium in January and which Davis had repeatedly encountered in his follow-up appearances in April. For the first time nationally, he repeated the charges of manipulation and unethical behavior made locally against Kreines and De Mott.

Lingeman offered his own version of what happened in the series, a version not unlike that of other media critics. The key was a structural weakness in cinema verite. The absence of any sociological, journalistic, or historical context could confuse or mislead the viewer. Despite his criticism, Lingeman did not attempt to judge what happened. He only concluded that the kinds of scenes captured by the camera's lens were capable of arousing sleepy Munsonians and he warned others to be careful in studying the community [Lingeman 12 June 1982b]. Still, his discursive comments were to enrage De Mott and Kreines as they left Muncie to return to Alabama. Not even an essay favorable to the two filmmakers in *American Film* could compensate for Lingeman's account [*American Film* 1982].

The film series attracted some scholarly attention although, as might be expected, this attention came later, was more detailed, and tried to relate the films to other efforts at studying the community. Two such reviews were by Ralph Janis in the *Indiana Magazine of History* and Howard Gillette, Jr., in the *American Quarterly*.

Janis, who was the executive director of the Kentucky Humanities Council, directed his attention solely to the film and made a number of astute points. He noted that there were few references to either Muncie or Indiana in the films and that had it not been for the introductory music, "My Indiana Home," few would have known it took place in Indiana [Janis 1982:346-47]. As for the protagonists themselves, Janis characterized them as average people, "neither black nor rich, neither fools nor geniuses, neither heroes nor villains." (Janis had not seen *Seventeen*.) They were lower middle-class individuals residing on the "hazy line where white collars show blue." They were similar to the Cramdens and Nortons of the "Honeymooners"; they hadn't made it, but they were coping even though they understood little about what was happening to them. Janis bewailed the decision to withdraw *Seventeen*, which he thought might have balanced out the series by showing other means of coping [Janis 1982:348-49].

On the larger question of what the series (which Janis consistently mislabelled as *Middletown Revisited*) meant, Janis was less sanguine, saying "Despite the series' pedigrees, which include the involvement of fine scholars and the support of the National Endowment for the Humanities and the Indiana Committee for the Humanities, it was clearly not designed to translate scholarly findings for the general public or to provided scholarly perspective on field research done with camera and tape" [Janis 1982:350].

Rather than being a work in the tradition of the Lynds, the series was in the "Tocquevillian tradition," which painted a picture of the town rather than analyzing it. Janis seemed to hint that artistic and analytical success were antithetical, that achievement in one came at the expense of the other. The reason for the analytical failure was the decision not to provide context or commentary, a decision which puzzled Janis. He contended that "talking heads" in documentaries featuring Alistair Cooke and Carl Sagan did not detract from the films but rather added to them, and even speculated that Davis might have refused their use because he feared commentators might either ruin or steal the show. Because of this failure, the series did not reach the height of a *Democracy in America*. Instead, it was what the latter work would have been if Tocqueville had provided no analysis. The lack of context also, in Janis's opinion, accounted for the successful protests against *Seventeen*. Had the scenes in that episode been interpreted, perhaps the protestors might not have been so upset.

In his final summation, however, Janis did judge the series to be valuable. It provided a "compelling and provocative" text which scholars could use to understand the meaning of behavior even though it did not add to the Lynds' work. It enabled him to understand better why Americans related to tales of coping such as "Laverne and Shirley," and said "So long as it is understood as an impressionistic, highly personal revelation of the hearts and minds of a special segment of America caught in the act of coping, its place in the American tradition of self-examination will be neither ignored nor exaggerated" [Janis 1982:350].

Janis's reflections on the film series were diametrically opposed by Howard Gillette, Jr., who reviewed the film series in conjunction with *Middletown Families* and *Hometown*. He was not impressed with either of these books, saying "aided by grants and publicity, these projects have promised much but delivered little, failing to add materially to the legacy they sought to build on in the Lynds' work" [Gillette 1983:426].

He was particularly scathing in his attack on *Middletown Families* which he believed was based upon a principle contrary to Robert Lynd's that social science research should ameliorate society's ills. Gillette, who shares the ideological stance of the Lynds, attacked Caplow and his collaborators for not wishing to change society, for being optimistic about the direction of American society, and for denying the conclusion of the Lynds concerning the growth of class distinctions. He then cited examples where the researchers placed interpretations on data Gillette believed were incorrect [Gillette 1983:429]. Hence, he claimed that the researchers purveyed their own ideology "in ways that separate them dramatically from the Lynds" [Gillette 1983:430]. Gillette's meaning is unclear. Did he mean that the Lynds were non-ideological or did he mean that their ideology was different? The first statement would be naive and the second commonplace; his objection appears to me to be the failure of Caplow and his collaborators to share the Lynds' critique of Muncie society.

In view of this ideological position, one might expect Gillette to like *Hometown* and the Middletown Film Series better, and one would be right. Gillette noted that the stories Davis told of Hamilton reveal the breakdown of the "cohesiveness of the family, the town, and the community," but these stories fail to be as critical as the Lynds were in *Middletown*. Davis had not succeeded in showing fissures in the community as clearly had the Lynds [Gillette 1983:432].

Gillette's analysis of the film series astutely detected the close connection between the series and *Hometown*. Davis's intent was the same, Gillette said, and at least one story was translated from Hamilton to Muncie. (An insider would have seen many more.) In *Community of Praise*, the underlying lesson was that religious faith is all that keeps the Tobey family intact. This lesson echoed one in *Hometown* where the community appears united but is really divided [Gillette 1983:432].

The two films Gillette chose to illustrate his claim that the series came the closest to the Lynds' work were *The Campaign* and *Family Business*. The first, "by revealing the values behind the political structure, pursues its subject with the kind of critical judgement exemplified by the Lynds and confirms the capacity of the film to depict basic elements of culture" [Gillette 1983:433]. The latter episode showed both the strengths and weaknesses of the Schniders' (Gillette's spelling) and combined the two areas of life, family and business, in a way the Lynds would have understood [Gillette 1983:433].

In his conclusion, Gillette said that none of the projects would achieve the Lynds' impact. The film series came the closest because "it best exemplifies the Lynds' capacity to discipline a personal vision of American culture and give it artistic expression." *Middletown Families* was the worst because it failed to criticize American society and did not address the Lynds' vision [Gillette 1983:433]. This conclusion would have come as a great surprise to Caplow and associates who had thought that was exactly what they were doing and from Kreines and De Mott who thought Davis had failed to examine class at all.

The mixed critical reaction to the Middletown Film Series reflected the ambiguities present in those conceptualizing and making the film. Davis had not wanted to film Muncie; he wrote a grant proposal about Hamilton which he could not get funded so he turned it into a book. When filming became possible in Muncie, he transferred his vision of a series on Hamilton to the new locale without sufficiently taking into account the long tradition of community studies. I had wanted a series which was analytical but had no idea how to translate that desire into film. The original intent had changed from my vision to Davis's vision without, however, much recognition of what had happened and with no change of name. At the same time, Davis, like Watten-berg, assumed the Lynds' mantle and proclaimed that he, too, was studying the community.

As a result, the reviewers were confused because of the mingling of two elements: drama and reporting. Their reviews reflected that confusion. Those who disregarded the name of the series and the tradition from which it came saw it as a dramatic triumph, as vindicating the documentary by mak-ing it more interesting. These persons were not concerned about learning anything about the town itself, but were impressed by the intensity and pas-sion of the participants. They were not concerned about the accuracy of the filmmaker's version of events or of the manipulation of participants, both of which they detected. On the other hand, those who wanted more data on the community and more explanation of what happened pointed to the title of the series, its dedication to the memory of the Lynds, and its claim to be another part of the long tradition of community studies as evidence that Davis had failed to make good on his promise. They criticized the series for lacking context, for withholding vital information from the viewer, and for present-ing little historical or sociological data.

The former critics compared the series to films or other television pro-grams in an effort to place it into a visual medium category. The latter com-pared the series to the printed medium, particularly the Lynds' work. Some crossed lines between the two media forms and were critical of the lack of context and pointed to TV efforts that had provided such context. One sug-gested that the significant element in the Lynds' book was the emphasis upon class and culture and, hence, believed that the series was a success because of Davis's willingness to do the same. None believed that *Middletown Revisited* by Wattenberg provided the context needed, except for local critics.

The critics' concerns were not the concerns of the participants. While the critics worried about participants performing for the camera, the participants worried about how they would appear, how their behavior would be inter-preted, and whether the film would be an authentic account of their lives. The critics were interested in the general audience reaction, but the participants seemed to have considered the filmmakers to be their primary audience. They exhibited their lives for the filmmakers who had become their friends. Where this bond had not been established, as in the case of Harrold, there was little insight into that person's character.

The life of the Middletown Film Series did not end in the summer of 1982. It was shown again in the summer of 1983, and won a nomination for an Emmy for the best educational series in 1982, losing to Bill Moyers. The films also appeared on TV screens in many places overseas, among them Hong Kong, Great Britain, and the Netherlands. They even went to more unlikely locales; at a conference in Philadelphia, a doctor from Saudi Arabia told me that he had seen the films there. He did not indicate how he saw them or which ones he saw. Foreign screening varied. Not all the films were shown; the network could choose what it wanted. *Seventeen* was available and was shown. The one least shown was *The Big Game*, which apparently was thought to be the most difficult for foreign audiences to understand. One wonders how much of the films these audiences did grasped, given the lack of context. In my mind, I can see a young man in the Middle East puzzling over the nuances of politics in Muncie. Would they seem stranger to him than to me?

Seventeen Refuses to Die

One of the problems with the Middletown Film Series was the assignments of credits. The pre-film publicity centered upon Davis as the executive producer. This was to be expected, given his prominence and his ability to attract attention, but the stories that appeared in press releases, newspaper columns, and magazine articles did not often include anything about filmmakers or, for that matter, humanists who were also working on the project. For the humanists, this was no big deal; all that was injured was our egos. For the filmmakers, it was more significant. They relied upon publicity to further their careers; it was vital to their advancement. Not to be mentioned was to have serious consequences for relations between Davis and Kreines and De Mott.

Davis claimed that he had planned a publicity campaign for all the films which would have been financed by Xerox. However, when Xerox pulled out of the series, he no longer had the funds to pay for such an effort. Regardless of the reason, the pre-series publicity failed to recognize the efforts of the two filmmakers. This, plus their belief that Davis had sold out to Xerox and PBS, generated much rage.

The hurried exit of Kreines and DeMott out of Muncie did not help either, and the anger of the local community contributed to their sense of martyrdom. Feeling put upon by almost everyone, Kreines and De Mott returned to Huntsville, Alabama, taking the internegative with them. This, in turn, upset Davis, who as head of the Middletown Film Project, was the legal distributor of *Seventeen*. Lacking the internegative, he was unable to make prints for distribution until a year later when he obtained it [Davis personal communication to DeMott and Kreines, 11 October 1984].

Kreines and De Mott further enraged Davis by removing his name and his title as producer from the version of *Seventeen* that they began to show at various film festivals. They also removed any reference to the Middletown Film Series by cutting out the beginning signature and even deleting the Janos Starker credit for playing "On the Banks of the Wabash" [Davis personal communication to DeMott and Kreines, 11 October 1984]. The new credits as they appeared in the 1983 London Film Festival were: "A De Mott/ Kreines Film Production. Produced, directed, photographed, and edited by

Joel De Mott and Jeff Kreines. Production assistant, Peter Esmonds" [*Variety* 1983].

Moreover, Kreines and De Mott prepared a twenty-five-page press release which they distributed when the film was screened. They frequently appeared on stage with the film as well. In both, they were "sarcastic" and "impassioned," attacking Davis, the academic humanists, the *Nation* and Lingeman, *American Film*, the *Journal of Popular Film and Television*, Xerox, PBS, and Larry Grossman [Covino 1984:11]. The press release was a one-sided, highly personal and idiosyncratic view of the events leading to the making and withdrawal of *Seventeen*, which, on many points, was just plain wrong. It was an after-the-fact defense of the filmmakers' integrity, techniques, ideas, and creativity. Unfortunately, this defense often resulted in the denigration of the integrity, techniques, ideas, and creativity of those connected with the Middletown Film Project. To compound the insult, reporters and critics often reprinted segments of the press release or took material from it without investigating the facts of the case or inquiring about them from the others involved in the project.

Their press release entitled "Some Notes on *Seventeen*" began with the statement that "*Seventeen* was eventually suppressed, after an active campaign against the film had been waged..." [Kreines and DeMott n.d.:1]. It first condemned Xerox, which the filmmakers claimed had canvassed stations, NEH, and the Ford Foundation to gain support for cancelling the program despite public television regulations preventing sponsor interference.

They claimed Xerox asked Davis to drop *Seventeen* from the series, a claim that Davis denied, and then had called NEH to discover if the agency would regard Middletown Films as delinquent if it could not deliver the last film. Steve Rabin, the head of the film division, then supposedly said no. Kreines and De Mott believed that this triggered a demand from PBS to move *Seventeen*'s deadline back so that they could not meet it. There is no evidence of any connection between NEH or PBS cited by the filmmakers. PBS was concerned about the film and did ask to see it, but no information was exchanged with NEH. Nor is there any evidence, as claimed by Kreines and De Mott, that PBS knew the other Middletown films averaged a year between completion of shooting and delivery—twice the time available to *Seventeen* [Kreines and DeMott n.d.:1-2]. The evidence does not exist because the statement is not true. *The Second Time Around* was shot after *Seventeen* and it was scheduled to appear ahead of it. Moreover, Kreines and De Mott began shooting at Southside before most of the other filmmakers but took a year to shoot and insisted upon editing their own work. The problem with meeting the schedule was, in part, their own.

They also attacked Xerox for what they claimed was a promise to "mount an extraordinarily elaborate advertising campaign" if Davis would take *Seventeen* out of the series. They even quoted Davis as telling them that if the advertising campaign were laid on, "...it would be like *Brideshead Revisited*—you should be here [New York]—everybody on the subway is holding up the *Times* and the back page is nothing but an ad for *Brideshead*! That could be *Middletown*!" [Kreines and DeMott n.d.:2]. The problem here is that Davis may have said this, but Kreines and De Mott reversed the order of events. Xerox agreed to provide the advertising before the conflict over *Seventeen* began, and withdrew it after the problem arose. It was not a bribe to withdraw *Seventeen*; it was a part of the original agreement. Kreines and De Mott took Davis's side on the controversy with Larry Grossman. They condemned Grossman for characterizing segments of the film as "not acceptable to PBS and ghastly." They denied that Davis had shown *Seventeen* to Xerox as Grossman had maintained, but their denial focused on their own claim of possession. Davis did not have the film; he had the two-and-one-half minute trailer, and "He could rely, additionally, on a fact that probably offered him little comfort otherwise: The filmmakers would have shot anybody—including Xerox's boys—who tried to fuck with their film." Moreover, they argued Grossman conflated corporate values and PBS values by defining "everyday language as words people don't like to hear," and by terming "ordinary boyish behavior 'offensive'" [Kreines and DeMott n.d.:3-4].

Not only did Kreines and De Mott attack PBS; they also blamed both it and Xerox for the affiliates which refused to broadcast *Seventeen* after viewing the satellite feed. PBS discouraged stations from showing the segment while Xerox's actions caused it to eliminate the entire series [Kreines and DeMott n.d.:4-5].

Their special ire was directed at Jim Needham, station manager of WIPB, and at the press which accepted the reasons given of Xerox, PBS, and Davis for the withdrawal of *Seventeen*. They also discounted the two printed accounts of what happened, saying that the piece by Richard Lingeman in the *Nation* was inaccurate and the one by Howard Rodman in *American Film* had been censored.

The filmmakers attacked Needham on all fronts, singling him out as the person responsible for the community's reaction to the film. They characterized Needham as "a longterm advocate of censorship" [Kreines and DeMott n.d.:5]. This is again an overstatement. Needham is a religious conservative and he does not show some programs on the station that he thinks will arouse considerable controversy. On the other hand, the station does broadcast programs that present problems in American society and Needham does not openly advocate censorship.

However, Needham's actions cannot be defended, and were not. The Indiana Association of Press Broadcasters officially censured him for his efforts to rouse opposition to the film by showing it to the school board and then to some teachers and parents at Southside High School. There, Kreines and De Mott are correct.

They were incorrect in their assessment of what the participants in the film said about their involvement. Needham did videotape a questioning session with Lynn and another white girl. The filmmakers said, "Their resistance to the question is goddam heroic," but later reneged somewhat by saying that, "If their resistance is less than wholehearted," there were extenuating circumstances, mainly racism [Kreines and DeMott n.d.:7]. The truth of the matter is that the participants did not resist wholeheartedly; they filed affidavits complaining about the filming process and threatened to sue. They claimed they had been encouraged in certain behavior by the filmmakers, that the filmmakers had arranged the kegger and bought the beer, and that the filmmakers had coached them on what to say.

Obliquely, Kreines and De Mott hint that perhaps there was one participant complaint but attribute it to racial violence in the town, citing the firebombing of a black residence near where one girl in *Seventeen* lived in which "ten whites were implicated in the arson (the house was gutted) but nobody went to trial," and another where a black man was killed by three whites who passed him in a car and randomly shot him [Kreines and DeMott n.d.:7]. What this had to do directly with *Seventeen* is difficult to determine, and even here the facts are wrong. The whites were tried, convicted, and sent to prison in the arson case.

The filmmakers also erred in saying that pressure was also exerted by "parents, lawyers, newspaper columnists, community leaders, and school teachers" to have the students recant [Kreines and DeMott n.d.:8]. Community leaders did not exert pressure. The mayor, Alan Wilson, and one state representative, Hurley Goodall, were in favor of showing the film, as were other people in leadership positions in the community.

The filmmakers were inconsistent on this point. They castigated Lingeman for his emphasis upon the community's part in preventing the airing of *Seventeen* in his "Muncie Protects Its Own," saying he was a naive observer of public television. They also attacked his description of Needham as "Lincolnesque" (a reference to his size) and for his failure to interview them in order to obtain their position. Again, they denied the allegation repeated by Lingeman that parts of the film were staged. "It [*Seventeen*] represents accurately and in detail what it's like to come of age in Muncie as a member of the working class" [Kreines and DeMott n.d.:8].

What really irked Kreines and De Mott about Lingeman's article was his contention that *Seventeen* lacked "sociological, journalistic or aesthetic context" and that the filmmakers "sought only 'interesting' subjects and some kind of coherent story." They countered this argument with the contention that they were filmmakers who were anthropologists and if they had wished no more than interesting subjects or a coherent story they would not have spent two years in Muncie, one of which was devoted to the filming. They objected to being called "big-city filmmakers," to being lumped with the rest of the Middletown crew [Kreines and DeMott n.d.:8-9]. Their arguments here are somewhat forced. Neither Kreines nor De Mott were anthropologists; their description of their origins is disingenuous. "(We moved to Muncie from Alabama—a place everybody rated as provincial, on a par with Tennessee from whose hills and cities many in Muncie had escaped for a better life.)" [Kreines and DeMott n.d.:9]. This overlooks the fact that Joel De Mott came from a prominent academic family in the East (her father Benjamin De Mott is a noted scholar of English at Amherst), and that both Kreines and De Mott attended MIT to learn filmmaking. Finally, the two objected to Lingeman's failure to give them credit for the film and to create the "false impression" that *Seventeen* was Davis's work.

The reason that Lingeman did this, according to the filmmakers, was that he had a personal and financial connection with Davis. He had written one of the *Middletown Teaching Notes* and had "received a hefty sum." The implication was that Lingeman had been bought off [Kreines and DeMott n.d.:9]. Once again, the implication is wrong. Davis had never met Lingeman before Middletown nor had he had any financial connection with him. Lingeman had written critically of an earlier Davis film in *The New York Times*; his work on the *Middletown Teaching Notes* had been commissioned by Joe Trimmer and was paid for out of grants from the Sachem Fund and the Indiana Committee for the Humanities. It had no direct connection with Davis or the Middletown Film Project.

Kreines and De Mott were better pleased with the treatment they received at the hands of Howard Rodman of *American Film*, but then claimed he failed to go far enough. His article responded favorably to the film and accepted the filmmakers' view of Xerox's action in the affairs; but, according to Kreines and De Mott, the editor, Peter Biskind, censored the piece by forcing Rodman to make cuts toning down his favorable review. They claimed Rodman told them of his problems and showed them his original article. Davis has responded to this charge. "Biskind has a different version, saying: The original piece by Rodman was full of unsubstantiated junk and leftist rhetoric. Nothing was edited out of the piece for other than journalistic reasons. De Mott and Kreines have been propagating this false story for some

time. We had the first story on the attempt to suppress *Seventeen* and thought
we were doing them a favor. Now they have this ridiculous vendetta against
me" [Davis personal communication to DeMott and Kreines, 11 October
1984].

Other persons who earned the contempt of the filmmakers were the academic humanists, particularly C. Warren Vander Hill who had written an article, "The Middletown Film Project: Reflections of an Academic
Humanistic," in the *Journal of Popular Film and Television*. Here is what
they said:

> The filmmakers confronted three academic humanists and a President of the
> Middletown Film Project who, together, supported a notion of American life
> based on kitsch and stereotypes (vide their proposal to NEH) and endorsed
> methods of filmmaking that confirmed the kitsch and stereotypes. These meth-
> ods did not represent American direct cinema or acceptable ethnography.
> Since the "academic humanists" were all professors of history and English—
> not a sociologist or anthropologist in the bunch, no one who could even pass as
> a pop culture watcher—and since President Davis had never made a cinéma-
> vérité film, their ignorance deserved some sympathy. But when the ignorance
> became overwhelming—we should adopt it as our own, turn into Hollywood
> Hotel observers of Muncie—it was harder to take. And some of their early de-
> sires were hard to believe—find out about high school life by interviewing past
> class presidents, set out to find in a working–class high school the white boy
> who's going to Harvard (the fact that the guy wouldn't be representative of
> Southside—the school *and* the neighborhood—wasn't the only problem: the
> fact that such a kid did not exist was insurmountable).
> We were always pleasant, I think, though our autonomy vis a vis the aca-
> demic trio and Davis himself remained complete [Kreines and DeMott
> n.d.:11].

The diatribe is wrong on about every count. Kreines and De Mott never
confronted us; as a matter of record, I met them only once and then for coffee
at a local cafe just to become acquainted. Trimmer was the closest of the humanists to them, and he did not confront them. Instead, he aided them as
much as possible, even helping them move into their house in the country.
The criticism of the proposal was unwarranted. It was, in my opinion, a good
one, but all of us realized that the education treatment would probably not be
the story we filmed. Nor were the ideas in it so far-fetched. The filmmakers
created a straw man in claiming that the proposal said we would find a white
boy who was going to Harvard, for nothing in the proposal actually said that
(on the other hand, a boy from Southside who was in school when Kreines
and De Mott were filming did go to Columbia, while other graduates, one a
black girl, went to MIT and Dartmouth). Their putting down of us as not being sociologists or anthropologists or even pop culture watchers was misin-
formed. I participated in the Middletown III project, a major sociological

effort, and held rank as Professor of Historical Sociology at the University of Virginia and have given papers at both popular culture and visual anthropology meetings. Finally, the claim that a person was unrepresentative of Southside implicitly assumes that others were and that only the filmmakers knew those persons who were, a continuing arrogance.

Davis reacted just as strongly as I have to the press release, although to different passages. He particularly rejected the notion that he had not practiced cinéma vérité films by insisting "that the purest examples of Middletown films that were broadcast and were also made in the cinéma vérité manner were *Community of Praise* and *Second Time Around*." He also denied that anyone had asked the filmmakers to "turn into Hollywood Hotel observers of Muncie." The statement that most upset Davis was the one in which the filmmakers claimed complete autonomy, a claim Davis vehemently denied. He was always in charge, he said; he even maintained he protected the filmmakers from interference from the humanists [Davis personal communication to DeMott and Kreines, 11 October 1984]. (This is a curious claim since we were supposed to be collaborators.)

In their press release, the filmmakers attacked the other filmmakers, Tom Cohen, Peter Davis and Jeff Vaughn, for living apart from their subjects. They exempted themselves and Leacock from this failure. The others "...delegated researchers to do their legwork. Then zipped in from New York, approved their subjects—with their preconceptions intact—and filmed for several weeks. Everybody stayed at the Roberts Hotel. A blindered experience" [Kreines and DeMott n.d.:12]. This caused the subjects filmed to regard the filmmakers as "privileged folk" from whom parts of their life should be hidden.

There is some truth in these accusations, although it is outweighed by omissions and exaggerations. The filmmakers did not, with exception of Davis, zip in and film for a few weeks. They did not delegate researchers to do their legwork, although both Cohen and Vaughn had the groundwork for *The Campaign* and *The Big Game* laid out by us.

The greatest omission is failing to describe the Roberts Hotel where those "privileged folk" lived. Kreines and De Mott said, "You lead a catered existence—someone else makes your bed, cleans your mess, cooks your meals and serves you" [Kreines and DeMott n.d.:12]. The reality was that the Roberts Hotel at that time was a fleabag about to be closed. Those guests who lived in it were as decrepit as it was. The film crews rented suites at an incredibly low rate, and installed refrigerators and hot plates to provide some meals, and ate others at cheap restaurants.

Kreines and De Mott portrayed themselves as living where they filmed, which meant they used "the same roads, grocery stores, radio stations, malls, bars, fast-food joints, veterinarians and plumbers as those around you" [Kreines and DeMott n.d.:12]. This was again misleading. They may have used the same facilities as the people they filmed, although even that is questionable, but they lived in suburban south Muncie on a country estate, Good Thunder Farm, which was several miles from Southside High School and that much again from "Shed Town" where most of the action in *Seventeen* was filmed. Their neighbors in this middle-class district where Kreines and De Mott lived described them as "gentry." In point of fact, their living conditions were superior to those living in the Roberts and their location was further removed from "Shed Town."

Next in their press release, they presented a rationale for their filming techniques, arguing against elaborate equipment and large crews and for a one-person rig and self-editing. They claimed that none of the other filmmakers, save Leacock and Silver, observed the same principles. The reason they found their methods to be superior was that these allowed the filmmakers to interact directly with the subjects and not to produce the fictional accounts common in the other tradition [Kreines and DeMott n.d.:13]. "Direct cinema is different. It demands a complicated response to its characters, because as its filmmakers know, real people do not reduce well to simple types, beggars for our sympathy, and direct cinema demands elegant complex structures—so that the flow of reality remains felt, not distorted into the simplistic form of a story that has worked before" [Kreines and DeMott n.d.:13]. Here, I believe that Kreines and De Mott are correct in their articulation of what direct cinema should be, but I also believe that they failed to achieve that goal.

The filmmakers defended their decision to drop footage of the high school wrestler who knew he had to have open heart surgery at the end of the season against Vander Hill's contention that the inclusion of such material might have "muted some of the local criticism." They maintained that this would not have been the case since the person in question was obsessed with sex, so obsessed that he talked of it openly in family conversations. Then, setting up a straw man again, they claimed if this footage had been available to "hired-hand" editors, it would have been included because no editor would have "resisted the kid's *bon mots* just because they have a false sense of the kid's sexual frankness within the family."

The greatest ire directed at Vander Hill by Kreines and De Mott concerned his generic statement about the lack of historical context in all the Middletown films, a statement in which I whole-heartedly concur. Vander Hill said, "We [historians] thought we could make greater contributions to the process of providing an appropriate historical context which would enable the filmmakers to understand best Muncie's unique history... several of the filmmakers had repeatedly displayed their ignorance of American social history in general and Middletown's past in particular... all six films were unfortunately edited in an historical vacuum" [Vander Hill 1982:63].

In their rebuttal, Kreines and De Mott accused Vander Hill of operating in an historical vacuum himself for failing to recognize that their problems paralleled those of the Lynds with *Middletown* and for supporting "the Middletown Film Project's defense" of the organizing concept of Middletown, the class system of Muncie.

The preposterous claim of similarity with the Lynds which Davis characterized as one of the filmmakers' "funnier conceits" was based upon an article, "Robert S. Lynd, John D. Rockefeller, Jr., and Middletown," written by Charles Harvey and published in the *Indiana Magazine of History* [1983]. (Ironically, the basis of this article was a paper read by Harvey in Muncie at a meeting of the Indiana Historical Society during the time, September 1981, that Kreines and De Mott were residents. Needless to say, neither attended the meeting.)

The filmmakers claimed that they were the only ones to realize that they were as much victims of attempted suppression as were the Lynds. In doing so they somewhat distorted the facts of the case. Here are some examples:

> And when Lynd's research emphasized precisely what the Institute wanted to de-emphasize—the existence of a class system—Raymond Fosdick, Rockefeller's boy at the Institute tried to withdraw financing from the Middletown project [Kreines and DeMott n.d.:15].
> The trouble came to head in the spring of 1924, as revealed in several memoranda written by Institute director Galin Fisher for Fosdick and the board. Lynd had returned to New York briefly to negotiate a more specific plan for the study which had to have Fosdick's approval for Lynd to receive further financing. Conflict erupted when Lynd refused to accept clauses inserted in his proposal by the Institute staff which would have tied his work more closely to the churches [Harvey 1983:349].

It is true that Harvey said that Fosdick assumed Lynd might take years to finish and suggested the institute could not finance him indefinitely, and that he suggested that Lynd's stress upon class division was merely a figment of his imagination, but the latter quotation as used by the filmmakers had deletions which change the meaning. Here are the two segments:

> Fosdick suggested that Lynd's stress upon class divisions as the overwhelming reality of Muncie was merely a figment of the imagination... and sought to discredit Lynd's work" [Kreines and DeMott n.d.:15].
> In this way (Fosdick had criticized Lynd for "...looking at the facts of Muncie not as objective phenomena but as they seem to appear through the medium of predetermined principles and theories which may or may not be, fully digested") Fosdick suggested that Lynd's stress on class division as the

overwhelming reality of Muncie was merely a figment of the imagination or an import of alien ideology. He did not, on the other hand, object to Elton Mayo's theorizing about the "bitter reflections on [their] work and situation" by workers whose negative thoughts "issue in social as well as industrial problems." The Memorial [Laura Spelman Rockefeller] financed Mayo's work at Harvard in the late 1920s, and it became basic to corporate personnel programs.

By implying that the established order and its institutions formed the real, hard facts of the city, Fosdick sought to discredit Lynd's work on nonpolitical "scientific grounds" [Harvey 1983:350-51].

Kreines and De Mott maintained that a "Rockefeller consultant at the University of Chicago finally persuaded Rockefeller's agency to cease and desist in all efforts at censorship and allow the work to be published" [Kreines and DeMott n.d.:15]. This was not quite what happened. The Institute never tried to censor the manuscript, although the staff continued to criticize it and they refused to publish it. Ultimately, Alfred Harcourt did [Harvey 1983:350-52].

The facts in the Lynd case are not even as clear as Harvey would have them, for Helen Lynd had a different perspective. Her recollection was that the class issue was not a factor in the institute's decision. She says that the manuscript sat around for a year because the institute thought it was unpublishable because it did not cohere and was irreligious [H.M. Lynd 1983:34, 37-38]. (Harvey did not interview Helen Lynd for his paper although she was still alive at the time of writing. *Possibilities*, her recollections, was not published until 1983 or after his paper was written so he had no opportunity to read her views.)

The facts are further blurred by the filmmakers who presented a false analogy. They equated Xerox with the Institute for Social Research, a dubious equation. In the case of the Lynds, the institute was the primary funding agency and the conflict was an ongoing one. The institute never withdrew money from the Lynds; it refused, for whatever reasons, to publish the results. The results, when published as a book, were edited, and the Lynds had to make substantial reductions and significant revisions in order to please Harcourt, Brace and Jovanovich [H.M. Lynd 1983:40]. In the case of the Middletown Film Project, the primary funding agency was NEH, which contributed about 80 percent of the money and which never, to my knowledge, interfered in any way with the film (the agency does not figure prominently in Kreines and De Mott's demonology). Xerox and PBS provided less than 20 percent of the funding [Davis personal communication to DeMott and Kreines, 11 October 1984; Vander Hill 1982:50]. Xerox withdrew some of its funding and tried to stop the film from showing but PBS, which had little money invested in the project, was the main villain in that episode. To make the filmmakers' analogy fit, NEH should have objected to the film and PBS should have shown it after receiving the cuts it wanted.

Kreines and De Mott emphasized Xerox and the class issue as the main reasons for the withdrawal of *Seventeen* while wrapping themselves with Lynd's mantle to bolster their conviction of a conspiracy against them. The conspiracy was to prevent them from revealing the truth about Muncie and America, that both had class systems. The desire to prevent the exposure of working-class Muncie motivated Xerox to block *Seventeen* after the filmmakers single-handedly decided to "counterbalance the rest of the series," which they claimed ignored class completely. "Therefore—without the support from the Middletown Film Project for their contention that the series was grossly out of balance—the filmmakers of *Seventeen* determined that the protagonists of their film would be working-class, that there would be a large number of protagonists, that the resultant scope and emphasis might counterbalance the rest of the series" [Kreines and DeMott n.d.:16].

The sponsors of course attacked this vision and, according to the filmmakers, mounted a "crusade" to avoid any class reference. The fault for not stopping this plot to silence the truth also lay with academic humanists. "To repeat: in spite of their vaunted knowledge of 'American social history in general and Middletown's part in particular,' the academic humanists offered no objection to a series of work that ignored the Lynds' thesis of class division and the evidence before their eyes that the division still existed" [Kreines and DeMott n.d.:16].

The argument founders for a number of reasons, the most apparent of which is chronology. The proposals to NEH came from the academic humanists before we even knew that Xerox was to be involved. Indeed, I learned of the Xerox involvement only when the problem of *Seventeen* came up in late 1981. It was not Xerox's intention to de-emphasize class; neither was it ours. That was a red herring. Nor were we unaware of class divisions in the community; that there were such divisions was commonplace knowledge.

A second chronological fact that makes the filmmakers' contention more absurd is that, except for *The Campaign*, all of the Middletown Films were shot at about the same time. This means that Kreines and De Mott had no idea about whom the other filmmakers might film. Not a single frame had been shot before the two began on *Seventeen* [Davis personal communication to DeMott and Kreines, 11 October 1984]. Further, since the two did not associate with the other filmmakers except for Leacock and Silver, they did not know what the others were filming. In the case of Leacock's and Silver's film, *Community of Praise*, one of its major protagonists, Phil Tobey, was quintessentially working class, earning a living as an welder and operating a small farm.

More than that, the other films in the series did not ignore class. If anything, the protagonists in them represented the lower part of the social scale.

Ralph Janis has called them lower middle class [Janis 1982:346-51]. I think he was right. In addition to Phil Tobey, Jim Carey can be counted as working class; although he had been a policeman and county sheriff, he was working construction before he ran for mayor. Andre Morgan was from a less than working-class family; his was a poor black, fatherless family with no one working. Howie Snider was a small businessman teetering on the edge of bankruptcy; Alan Wilson was a lawyer who earned $12,000 the year before he ran for office. David Shesler painted signs in city hall while Elaine was a single mother with no job who was surviving on loans and student aid. None could be considered to be connected with big business. All reflected a more complex class situation than the filmmakers had posited. As Davis argued, correctly in my opinion, "'Revelations of a class nature' which you accuse me of ignoring because I wanted to please the sponsors, are in fact contained in every single Middletown film, including the one you worked so well on" [Davis personal communication to DeMott and Kreines, 11 October 1984].

Nor did we humanists ignore class; I, in particular, wished to have included in the film series the findings of Middletown III that the class system in Muncie had changed [Caplow, Bahr, and Chadwick 1982:15]. This wish was contained in the proposals that were sent forth to NEH and presented a more complex view of the stratification in Muncie than the simplistic one presented by the Lynds in *Middletown* and accepted by Kreines and De Mott (Lynd worked out a more complex classification in *Middletown in Transition* but then failed to use it). Muncie had changed a great deal since the 1920s when the Lynds had lumped everyone into the "business class," people who worked with other people, and the "working class," people who worked with things. By this definition, there were seventy-one members of the working class in Muncie out of every one hundred workers in Muncie in 1920 [Lynd and Lynd 1956:22]. By the 1980s, the number of industrial jobs had remained the same but the population had more than doubled. Industrial jobs now constitute only 37 percent of total available jobs. Muncie had become, like much of the United States, a post-industrial society relying more and more heavily on services. The largest employers in town were no longer the industrial plants but rather Ball State University and Ball Hospital. Increasingly, class lines were blurred so that it was difficult to distinguish between persons on the basis of "working class" or "business class." Workers, particularly those who were unionized, earned far more than clerks or nurses or teachers and had a life style which closely resembled the latter. One of the major themes of Middletown III was the convergence of classes, a convergence that I had hoped to show in the films.

This did not appear in the Middletown Film Series because, contrary to the assumptions of Kreines and De Mott, but not to their experience, the humanists had very little say concerning the selection of participants in the films or the form the final films took. We could not object to a series of which we were largely kept ignorant.

The filmmakers also included a selection of reviews of *Seventeen* in their press release to demonstrate how the press had swallowed the business class line. The reviews were uniformly negative. Here they are:

It is the last episode, *Seventeen*, that raises questions about Davis's basic judgement, however. To illustrate his chapter on learning in Muncie, he has concentrated on Lynn Massie and several other seniors at Southside High School....Davis searched not for the best or even typical students, but for the most crudely narrow and foulmouthed ones he could find. They smoke pot in the lavatory, carouse at lowdown beer busts and verbally abuse one of their teachers. What point Davis was trying to make in this disagreeable episode is hard to fathom... [Gerald Clarke *Time* 29 March 1982].

In the final installment, for example, the cameras go to Muncie's Southside High School, presumably to tell us something about education in the city. For the most part, though, the focus is kept on a rather unpleasant white girl who publicly displays her pronounced partiality toward black boys. When not puffing on "pot," she is trying hard to use the most crude street words...They certainly found an outstanding specimen in their high school girl... [John J. O'Connor 1982b].

Navasky blasted the public television people for putting "so much pressure" on Peter Davis that he "felt compelled" to withdraw a segment from a series rather than cut and trim it to satisfy the offended and timid: Navasky is talking about an episode in a series about Muncie, Ind., which trapped blotto teenagers into talking about other teenagers they have seduced, drugs they had taken and rewarding techniques of masturbation [William F. Buckley *Washington Post* 5 May 1982].

Anyone who saw the latest version of the documentary [*Seventeen*] would have little trouble imagining, even if not endorsing, a host of possible objections, from the squeamishly moral to the artistic.... [It] includes, for want of a less prissy term, explicit necking.... Its worst scenes are those where the camera dwells on teenage drug use, drinking and insubordination that are not especially relevant to the narrative... [R.D. Rosen *Washington Journalism Review* June 1982].

A group of marijuana-smoking, beer drinking, foulmouthed youngsters seem to have been induced to reveal what appears to be the worst side of their characters. Teachers are portrayed as ineffective objects of derision. Parents are overly permissive and provide poor examples for the children.... Muncie has every right to object to the obviously unbalanced, perhaps even grotesque, nature of Mr. Davis's coverage.... In addition to language, the social habits and morality in many cases will be objectionable to most viewers [Arthur Unger 1982].

"It's like bringing specimens back from the deep," says Davis, defending [sic, added by Kreines and De Mott to register their disbelief] *Seventeen*. "You can't believe you're seeing it" [Arthur Lubow *People* 29 March 1982].

It is difficult to understand why the filmmakers saw fit to include the negative reviews in their press release, particularly since these reviews cannot be directly tied to the Xerox decision. Kreines and De Mott present no evidence to connect these reviews to the prevailing business class control of the medium. Nor do the reviewers themselves mention any kind of class connection; all comment negatively upon the behavior of the individuals seen in the film. Two previewers found it difficult to understand why the film was structured as it was, to know what the point was.

The whole business of the press release is puzzling. Why did Kreines and De Mott write it? Was it an accurate reflection of what they thought had happened or was it an attempt to place the best face on the whole affair? If it were the former, one must be struck by their ignorance of what was actually being done. If it were the latter, one must wonder at their protestations of purity and adherence to truth in filming. How could one believe that the filmmakers portrayed actual events in *Seventeen* when facts were so cavalierly dismissed in the press release?

It is possible, I suppose, to believe that there was a gigantic conspiracy to block the screening of *Seventeen*, one that extended from Xerox to Davis to PBS down to the humanists, but this pre-supposes that all of these considered *Seventeen* and its fate to be the center of their lives and the focus of all their attention. One would think that without any solid evidence that this had happened, one might question the pattern of thought of someone who believed this.

In any case, one cannot help but be struck by the colossal arrogance of Kreines and De Mott and by their extreme narcissism in dismissing everyone else connected with the project as being incompetent, ignorant, or in league with Xerox. Once they had signed a contract with the Middletown Film Project and its executive producer, and received the money from NEH, they apparently believed that they had no responsibility to the persons who had created the project, no obligation to the series, and that the product they created was theirs alone. They rejected any responsibility to anyone else. One cannot help feeling bitter and asking if they really believed they were all alone in the project, why they had not thought up the ideas and written the grants.

Several final thoughts on the press release. One is that the claims made in it are so extreme and so at variance with what had happened that an impartial observer would doubt that they would be taken seriously. Yet the fact of the matter was that they were. Critics who reviewed *Seventeen* at film festivals accepted the claims at face value and even repeated some of the self-congratulations and self-promotion present in them. The other thought is that the reviews after the press release tended to be much more favorable to the film. Was there any connection between this reception and the press release? Or did the long arms of Xerox not reach into film festivals and art theaters? There are of course alternate explanations; reviewers might have found the film unacceptable for public television but all right for the kind of audience found in the latter venues.

In any case, the private rift between Davis and Kreines and De Mott became public knowledge in March 1983. It came when Kreines and De Mott tried to enter *Seventeen* in a conference on banned films at Filmex (the Los Angeles International Film Exposition).

The organizers of the conference had found plenty of examples from other countries, but were lacking entries from the United States. Barbara Zick Smith, associate director of Filmex and coordinator of the series, decided to include two American films: *Salt of the Earth*, made by the International Union of Mine, Mill, and Smelter Workers in 1953, and *Seventeen*. She admitted in an interview, however, that "*Seventeen* was not a banned film," but said "it was included because it wasn't seen by the people for whom it was intended" [*Los Angeles Times* 27 March 1983].

When Davis discovered that Kreines and De Mott had attempted to enter *Seventeen*, he objected. According to Davis, Filmex director Gary Essart had approached him to receive permission, but Davis had refused because the Middletown Film Project's errors and omissions insurance had lapsed [Davis personal communication to DeMott and Kreines, 11 October 1984]. He lacked the funds to obtain new insurance, so he decided not to risk a suit by either irate Muncie parents or the Muncie Community Schools (Interestingly enough, when interviewed by telephone from Los Angeles, neither Slauter, the superintendent of Muncie Community Schools, nor Brinkman, the lawyer, knew of the controversy, and both indicated they probably would have taken no action had the film been shown.) [*Muncie Star* 27 March 1983].

This information did not change Davis's mind. Essert pleaded for a bootleg print, saying, "If I had the print in my possession, I'd show it and if through some strange circumstance the print comes into my possession, it will be screened" [*Los Angeles Times* 27 March 1983]. It did not and one can only speculate as to why Kreines and De Mott did not offer him their print.

Seventeen finally was shown in a film festival in late 1983, the beginning of a series of appearances in this country and abroad. The show was the London Film Festival. *Variety* reported on the film, giving a thumbnail sketch of the pertinent facts. The credits were not to please Davis. "A De Mott/Kreines Film Production. Produced, directed, photographed and edited by Joel De Mott and Jeff Kreines. Production assistant, Peter Esmonds" [*Variety* 14 December 1983]. *Variety*, however, did note that *Seventeen* was part of the Middletown Film Series which was shelved because of "bad language and immoral behavior depicted in the film" [*Variety* 14 December 1983].

The following year saw Kreines and De Mott on the road showing the film. By this time, Davis had the internegative and he no longer blocked the film's showing. *Seventeen* appeared in the Atlantic Film and Video Festival, 12 April 1984; the Pacific Film Archive, 13 April 1984; Filmex, 7 July 1984; and the Brave New Documentary Series of the American Film Institute, 3 November 1984 [*Muncie Star* 3 November 1984]. When it was shown in Los Angeles at Filmex, a reporter asked Davis why it had not been shown a year earlier. His reply was the same as his previous one; he lacked insurance [*Los Angeles Times* 5 July 1984].

The showing at the American Film Institute alerted Munsonians to the continuing life of *Seventeen*. A Washington law firm representing the Film Institute wrote to Muncie Community Schools' attorney John Beasley informing him that the institute planned to screen the film. Beasley responded by warning the Film Institute that it was possible that the film invaded the privacy of students and added it was not "the content but the procedure we object to" [*Muncie Star* 3 November 1984]. Brinkman, the parents' lawyer, did not respond. The American Film Institute showed the film, and there was no lawsuit. The way was open for *Seventeen* to be seen around the country as long as it was far enough away from Muncie.

The critics were kinder the second time around, and showed the influence of the press release in their critiques. Those least familiar with the circumstances surrounding the making of the film were the most likely to have a favorable opinion.

Following the London Film Festival, two reviews illustrate the difference. The reviewer for *Variety* called the film intriguing but found it troublesome that Lynn "postured" for the camera and said that the film was "episodic" [*Variety* 14 December 1983].

Brian Winston, however, was more enthusiastic about *Seventeen*. Reviewing the tradition in the influential journal *Sight and Sound*, Winston mounted an attack on direct cinema which he said had reached a dead end. He also claimed that only two episodes, *Seventeen* and *Community of Praise*, in the Middletown Film Series qualified as direct cinema. The remaining four were of an ersatz variety called "Vérité." To illustrate his point, Winston claimed *Seventeen* did not use set-up interviews as the other films had. Winston praised Kreines and De Mott for using a one-person rig rather than a large film crew, and for using natural light instead of artificial lighting. He also described the film as the only one "to deal with the working class, white and black." It was the only one which had had "documentary value," as defined by Grierson. At the same time, Winston felt uneasy about the film because "its topic is contentious and its transmission could have haunted the participants." This unease was relieved when he learned from the filmmakers that all the girls had moved away at the same time as the planned transmission [Winston 1983:238]. (It is difficult to know if this statement was true. If they had moved away, they came back soon, as Lynn married Buck in Muncie on 10 December 1983, four days before the London Film Festival showing of *Seventeen*. Moreover, it was not just the girls who would have been haunted. One of the most nervous about the film was the son of a black minister who dreaded the thoughts of his father discovering his secret life. Finally, most of the participants in *Seventeen* remained in Muncie where they are still.)

Michael Covino who viewed the film at the Pacific Film Archive in April 1984 reported on it in the *Express*. He accepted Kreines and De Mott's version of what happened and repeated them in his review. Indeed, much of the review consists of material from the press release. His reaction to the film was enthusiastic, calling it the "best American documentary I have seen in four or five years." He disposed of the criticism that the students were deliberately playing to the camera by saying that if the filmmakers had achieved such "an extraordinary degree of trust, of intimacy, with their subjects that the latter chose to ham it up, it was of little consequence since they were fully aware that they would be on national television." The support for this contention came from Kreines and De Mott, not from anyone else (Again, the affidavits tell another story; the participants speak of scenes that were shot without their consent, and of not realizing the film would be on national TV.) [*Covino* 1984].

Covino filtered the film through his own sensibilities and experiences. *Seventeen* was an authentic look at Muncie's teenagers because his New York City high school was like that—containing an integrated working-class population to whom drug exchanges, heroin busts and murders across the street were commonplace. He apparently thought Muncie was New York City, never considering the possibility, as the Southside parents claimed, that Kreines and De Mott had superimposed their own version of reality on the students.

The curious case of the favorable reviews after *Seventeen* began showing in film festivals illustrates one of the major problems of direct cinema, the lack of context and explanation. The TV critics did not know what to look for in the film; there was no narrative line followed as the camera wanders from one person to another. After the filmmakers explained what they thought they were doing—making a film about the working class in Muncie—then other critics knew what to see. *Seventeen*'s revival in 1984 was, in my opinion, largely a result of Kreines and De Mott's press release and their personal appearance, which made the film understandable. Instead of using pictures to illustrate a text, Kreines and De Mott were using text to explain pictures.

By 1984, Davis had control of the film and was negotiating for its showing in art houses. In early 1985, *Seventeen* moved into the Film Forum in New York City. On 6 February it opened for a two-week run to packed houses. The film's credits had changed again to a compromise position between Kreines and De Mott on the one hand, and Davis on the other. The credits said, "*Seventeen*, directed, photographed, edited and produced by Joel De Mott and Jeff Kreines; also produced by Peter Davis" [Canby 1985a].

The reviewer for *The New York Times*, Vincent Canby, had evidently corresponded with Davis but not with Kreines and De Mott, for he included this curious note: "The idea for the *Middletown* television series came to Mr. Davis, himself a filmmaker (*Hearts and Minds*) when he was gathering material for his *Middletown*-like study of life in Hamilton, Ohio, published by Simon and Schuster in 1982 as *Hometown*. Everyone connected with the *Middletown* television series would like it to be known that the television films are in no way adaptations of the Davis book. They are entirely separate endeavors, Mr. Davis emphasizes, and are meant to 'complement one another'" [Canby 1985a].

This claim was meant to counter the argument of Kreines and De Mott who had said Davis had conflated the two studies. It also bent the truth, since there were elements of each in the other, as we have seen. Some were part of the grant proposal sent to NEH and went no further than that. Others, such as the underlying theme of *The Big Game*, the rivalry between a poor black high school team and a more prosperous white one, remained in the final film, albeit in a transformed fashion.

In addition to staking out a position vis-a-vis the filmmakers, Davis also took one opposed to the humanists. We believed that the idea was at least partly ours and remembered that it was he who rejected the original proposal to film Muncie. Still, Davis's claim was skillfully expressed. He did not say how the idea came to him, or who bore it.

Canby's review of *Seventeen* was enthusiastic; he called it "one of the best and most scarifying reports on American life to be seen on a theater screen since Maysles brothers' *Salesmen* and *Gimme Shelter*" [Canby 1985a]. What impressed him most in his initial review (he was to do three) was that its adherence to the principle of not imposing "some arbitrary order" gave the film a sense of incoherence more resembling human life [Canby 1985a]. He reviewed the film again three weeks later, contrasting it favorably with other films on the same theme because of its "vitality and honesty" and its lack of an "artificial narrative shape" [Canby 1985b]. Finally, at the end of the year, he included it in a list of first-rate "fact" films [Canby 1985d].

What had changed from the critical O'Connor review of 4 April 1982 to the extremely positive review of Canby of 6 February 1985? Both reviewers were highly regarded media critics who enjoyed much respect at the *Times*. Were the diametrically opposed views a result of varying personal aesthetics or a result of three years' difference of time? I cannot help but believe that the latter was the case. By 1985, memories of the rancorous episode had faded, Kreines and De Mott had pushed their press release successfully, and the film had received good notices at the film forums. The film itself was no different, except for minor editing changes, none of which were significant.

In late April, First Run Features signed a contract with Davis to distribute the film. Thus began a series of showings in large cities around the country. Among the cities where the film was to be shown was Cincinnati, Ohio. The Cincinnati Film Society announced it planned to screen *Seventeen* on 10 and 11 May; the announcement reached Muncie, which is only 120 miles from the Queen City, and stimulated local newspaper reporters to inquire about the likelihood of a lawsuit. They asked school superintendent Slauter and attorney Brinkman what action they proposed to take. Slauter indicated he was uncertain but would see what the school board might decide, while Brinkman, characteristically, declined to comment [*Muncie Star* 9 May 1985; *Muncie Evening Press* 9 May 1985]. The Cincinnati Film Society proceeded to show the film; neither the school board nor the parents sued.

The showing of *Seventeen* aroused a latent interest in Muncie, as editorial writers from both morning and evening papers devoted a column each to the question of whether the film ought to be seen by the community. One argued for its showing; the other against.

The affirmative vote was cast by Bill Terhune, a long-time *Muncie Evening Press* employee. Terhune had been present at the screening held by Needham for local media representatives in March 1982, and had believed it should have been shown then. He argued that the behaviors seen in *Seventeen* were not too dissimilar from those of his peers in high school forty years earlier. He admitted that some people would object, but contended that objections could be raised to the other segments in the series. For example, he said some found the winning-is- everything philosophy in *The Big Game* objectionable [Terhune 1985].

On the other hand, Ruth Hillman, a Southside English teacher and sometime newspaper columnist, reacted entirely differently, although with less direct knowledge of the film or its makers. She had failed to see the film when Needham had had a screening for teachers at Southside, and she was under the misapprehension that De Mott was male. Her piece was full of anger, a sense of exploitation and betrayal, and a firm conviction that *Seventeen* should never be shown in Muncie because it invaded the privacy of the students, two of whom she had in class and who expressed great relief when they learned she had not seen the film [Hillman 1985].

To date, the Hillman position has prevailed; there has been no public showing of *Seventeen* in Muncie. After almost ten years, the position of Brinkman, the attorney for the students and parents, remained fixed. In February 1990 the Ball State University Film Committee contemplated a retrospective of the Middletown Film Series and inquired of Brinkman as to the possibility of showing *Seventeen*. Here is his reply:

> The previous position of my clients has consistently been that the film and its contents were obtained by improper and unlawful means. Should the university or its agents show the file [sic], then you [sic] would be an accessory as to certain falsehoods and other unlawful conduct, and we believe there would be economic exposure.
>
> The position of those individuals who are depicted in the film, who [sic] I have lended [sic] assistance to in the past, would be not to show the film. I further would think that the position of the Muncie Community School System would be the same. In the past, they assisted the various individuals and their representatives, and as a result the program was not televised on PBS in this community. Further I would think that showing this film in this community would be disruptive, to say the least [Brinkman personal communciation to Conrad Lane, 21 February 1990].

Seventeen may have still been alive elsewhere, but it was dead in Muncie.

What Happened to Everybody?

One of the questions asked concerning films is the impact that filming had on the lives of those seen in the films and those making them. This chapter struggles with this question and attempts to answer two others: Did filming have an adverse effect upon participants and did any of the filmic lessons learned by the filmmakers carry over into other films or other communication forms? In addition, it examines, perhaps in too much detail, the lives of those most interesting and controversial figures in the Middletown Film Series.

There was life after the Middletown Film Series, both for those in front of and those behind the camera. As might be expected, those behind the camera fared better than those in front, since they were moving upward anyway. However, the participants in the documentary, some of them, achieved more than might have been expected given their social class and life chances.

The three humanists in the project are still at Ball State University. All have advanced in their careers. The most notable advance has been that of Warren Vander Hill. He moved from being Dean of the Honors College to Associate Provost to Provost of the university. Joe Trimmer has continued to teach in the English Department, but has become an authority on writing as process and, as such, is called upon to consult on writing programs at a number of universities here and abroad. I have become the Director of the Center for Middletown Studies while continuing to teach history. For a time I served as an associate editor for the *Historical Journal of Film Radio and Television* and I had a Fulbright appointment to Karl Marx University in Budapest. None of us has been involved in other film projects, although I have made a videotape about Muncie during the 1920s.

Peter Davis has moved from filmmaking into writing. There is evidence that he had already decided on his new career while simultaneously writing *Hometown* and producing the film series. In an interview with the publisher of *Sports Illustrated* given when the magazine printed an excerpt, "A Town Divided Against Itself," from the book, Davis said, "But I always wanted to write, and after *Hearts and Minds* I thought, it's now or never" [Howlett 1982:4]. He expressed the same sentiment the following month in an interview contained in *Publisher's Weekly* [Dahlin 1982:8-9]. A final testament to his resolve is based upon a personal experience. During the filming of the pilot, *The Campaign*, I, along with Trimmer, Vander Hill and Davis, went to the Delaware County Fair to view the traditional beginnings of the campaign. We all stopped at a stand where a man offered to guess our weight, age, or occupation. We opted for occupation, whereupon he successfully identified all except Davis as teachers. He then guessed that Davis worked at the local Westinghouse plant. Davis then identified himself as a writer.

Prior to *Hometown*, Davis had published little. He had reviewed a film, *Paul Jacobs and the Nuclear Gang*, in the *Nation* in 1979, a companion review to one done by Martin Sklar. In it were Davis's reflections on the state of the American documentary film. After completing the film series, Davis embarked upon a full time writing career. He became an editor at *Esquire* and began contributing articles to it on a regular basis.

In these assignments, he displayed many of the same interests and techniques obvious in the Middletown films. He was fascinated by politics and with the lives of unconventional or unusual persons. He probed deeply to ascertain conflicts created by the collision of value systems. In writing, he used the same techniques he had urged upon filmmakers: an eye for striking and revealing detail, prolonged and intensive interviews with a number of persons which could be used to extract appropriate and telling quotations, subtle cutting between different topics and people, and the capturing of personal crises. Unlike his films, however, he interjected personal elements into his writing, so that often his stories became projections of his own psyche.

His first effort at article writing was in the December issue of *Esquire*, one devoted entirely to American heroes. Davis chose as his hero "The Unknown Nonsoldier." The person he identified was John F. Khanlian, a Vietnam protestor who had been a student at Columbia University during the 1968 student riots. Davis began with a generational study going back to Khanlian's Armenian grandfather as well as a description of many of the non-family influences upon him. Davis traced the tensions in Khanlian's life as an adult, particularly those involving his wife and children. The article concluded with these tensions unresolved but with the impression that Khanlian will continue to live out his pacifistic values [Davis 1983:444-48].

Davis wrote his first article on Nicaragua for the *Nation* in early 1984. Entitled "Mirror of Our Midlife Crisis," the essay examined elements in the American character that led to intervention in that Latin American country [Davis 1984:76-88].

In 1987 Davis's second book, *Where is Nicaragua?*, appeared. *Esquire* published an excerpt, "Managua is Waiting," in March, while the *Washington Monthly* included an interview with Davis entitled "If It's Tuesday, This Must Be Managua" in June [Davis 1987b:121-74, 1987d:48-51].

Where is Nicaragua? is a curious book which combines several different genres: travel writing, history, and film critique. Based on many interviews, it also includes an analysis of stock footage of Nicaragua in American-made newsreels. Davis did this in an attempt to get "a feel for the people and terrain of country I had never seen" [Davis 1987a:26-27]. The book had a complex and difficult purpose, according to Davis. "... I have wanted to explore the relationship between Nicaragua and the United States, listen for the meaning as well as the tone of Nicaraguan voices, look for the point and counterpoint of a play that oscillates between forces and tragedy....This book is an attempt to locate context" [Davis 1987:16].

The wheel had gone full circle. From a filmmaker who had argued that he could not show history in film, could not supply context, Davis had become a writer whose mission it was to do just that.

The book is at least partially successful in completing the mission. It shows the images that various persons in each country have of each other and how incomplete many of these are. It takes no position on the images and expresses few opinions, although Davis did conclude that there were missed chances for the United States to befriend the Sandinistas before they became dependent upon the Soviets, for the Nicaraguans to have a powerful friend in the U.S., for American conservatives to see economic progress in terms other than that offered by savings and loan banks, and for the remains of the American Left to test the relevance of the socialist idea.

How much the book was the result of a filmmaker's direct cinema aesthetic was noted by Christopher Lehmann-Haupt who reviewed it in *The New York Times*. After presenting a synopsis, Lehmann-Haupt, although sympathetic to the book, claimed that, "But almost to a fault he [Davis] keeps his feeling and opinions to himself, trying instead to give us a camera-eye's view of Nicaragua." Despite the mild criticism, Lehmann-Haupt concluded that the book was "essential reading" for those who wished to understand the two countries' tragic relations [Lehmann-Haupt 1987].

Another change besides the new emphasis upon context had occurred. The Middletown Film Series had faded from Davis's credits. No longer could one learn of his effort to capture the spirit of Muncie. What he wished to remind readers of was *Hometown, Hearts and Minds* and *The Selling of the Pentagon*.

In June 1984 *Esquire* published Davis's "The $100,000 A Year Woman." This piece begins with an exchange of letters between him and his editorial director, Betsy Carter, about the parameters of the story and the possible candidates for inclusion. Reminiscent of discussions over treatments for films, this dialogue explores the issues to be covered and the advantages and disadvantages of each particular scenario. The body of the article is a detailed examination of a few days in the life of Lisa Wolfson, a young Wall Street trader [Davis 1984b:70-74]. It focuses upon her conflicting desires to have a career and to be married. This account resonates with that of Elaine Shesler in *The Second Time Around*. Both sensitively explore the contemporary world of women, although the former is more instructive because of Wolfson's greater awareness of, and ability to articulate, what she is feeling.

The following year, Davis's contribution was a vignette about his fellow passengers on the Eastern Air shuttle between Washington and New York City. This, like his preceding piece, concerned the life styles of the affluent, but unlike it, "The High and Mighty Crowd" did not treat one individual but rather a group of people. It conveys a series of images of fellow passengers complete with observations on clothing (J. Press and Savile Row) and behavior. Lacking a narrative structure, it paints an interesting group portrait of prosperous and probably influential travelers [Davis 1985:221-22].

Davis's next essay for *Esquire* returned to an earlier pattern, a microscopic look at an untypical American life. In "The Man Who Undressed Men," he examined the photographic images of Bruce Weber, the Avedon of the eighties, who made his reputation by a series of revealing male underwear ads. Unlike *Where is Nicaragua?*, this article contains much of Davis's own experience as well as his fears, revealing his discomfort with androgyny in this passage: "The Calvin Klein model in the underpants is a divine creature and he beckons. Beckoning, he attacks a man's concept of his own sexuality, his own *heter*osexuality" [Davis 1986:441]. This passage also shows the jarring dissonances in language that sometimes characterize Davis's prose, combining as it does the puritanical underpants with the gay divine creature.

Davis continued his examination of the world of gays with an article "Exploring the Kingdom of Aids" the following year in the *New York Times Magazine*. In this essay he created a fictive kingdom based, however, upon impressions he gained from visits to New York gay bars. Like his earlier portrayal of the cabin of the New York shuttle, this is painted with broad strokes; it is landscape rather than portrait. It is context without narrative or character development [Davis 1987c].

Finally, Davis's latest essay, his 1988 account of the Democratic National Convention, a companion piece to one on the Republican National Convention, revealed his distaste for political pieties and the kind of dealing endemic in this very American institution. His view of the convention is very much a personal one. His conclusion that "Dukakis made the news. All Jackson did at this convention was make history" [Davis 1988:131] summed up his clear preference for the latter, although most of the article is written from the viewpoint of a detached observer.

In his writings, Davis has continued the examination of American society and culture that constituted the core of his film corpus. From an anti-establishment vantage point, Davis has meticulously chronicled the foibles as well as the hopes and dreams of those he has chosen as his subjects. His literary efforts have, however, been more subtle and complex, less polemical than his films, less dominated by an effort to persuade or to drive home a point. Perhaps the difference is in the genre, writing accommodating more contradictions; perhaps the difference is in Davis.

There is evidence that Davis may be returning to the world of film. He is currently writing for a documentary on the American underclass which he says will be less "cinéma-vérité" and more informational than the Middletown series [*Muncie Star* 30 April 1989].

Davis has been able to retain a place in the media world, to shed one career and assume another, without a great deal of difficulty. Part of the reason for this achievement has been his position in the intellectual establishment where his anti-establishment position is conventionally assumed, and part is the result of his considerable talent and creativity that cannot be limited to one genre.

The other filmmakers did not change careers. The one exception was Ricky Leacock. Leacock, who made *Community of Praise*, arguably the worst of those films shown on public television and certainly the one most resented by Munsonians who saw it, changed directions according to Mike Zwerin, switching "from teaching to learning, from film to tape, from alcohol to Alcoholics Anonymous and from Richard to Ricky" [Zwerin 1988]. (Zwerin's characterization overdramatizes Leacock, who has always been known as Ricky and who has always been learning.) Leacock continued to teach and to act as head of the Department of Film at MIT until 1988, when he left to work in Paris. He co-directed *Film in Berlin* in 1985. His fascination with cinema direct continued to lead him to try new forms and new ideas as he pared down equipment and project size. In Paris he shot a series of experimental programs for *Océaniques* for the third channel, but he moved further away from commercialism. In an interview with Mike Zwerin for the *International Herald Tribune*, Leacock testified:

> I am no longer interested in big projects. I want to shoot something without worrying whether it's important or not. And it's so easy on tape, the camera is so tiny. In a sense I'm learning to make films all over again. I want to learn what happens if you just shoot something because you like the way it looks. I'm not interested in being 'serious.' I'd like to avoid professional journalism. The word 'professional' has come to have bad connotations. And yet I don't want to compare what I'm doing with home movies because that also has bad

connotations. I don't really know what the hell I'm doing, which is a good sign [Zwerin 1988].

Always uncomfortable with his associate Robert Drew, who wished to make film resembling Robert Capa photographs, Leacock had retreated to a minimalist position, one that stripped filmmaking to bare essentials, all the time resisting the final step to amateurism. His *Community of Praise* had shared certain qualities of home movies, but in retrospect it was still too artificial for him.

While Leacock was moving in one direction, his protege and colleague on *Community of Praise*, Marissa Silver, was going another. Silver came to Muncie when she was only twenty-one, after two years of study at Harvard. She returned to Boston following the completion of the film on religion. There she began to write a screenplay called *Old Enough*, based upon her own adolescent experience when she "met a kid very different from me" who "was rougher, streetier, a lot more sexually savvy than I was" [Maslin 1984]. When she finished, she asked her older sister Dina, who was twenty-six, to produce it. Dina read the script and agreed to do so. She then raised $400,000 through a thirty-five-member partnership, and Marissa began filming in New York City in the summer of 1983 when she was but twenty-three [Maslin 1984].

Old Enough told the story of a summer friendship between two girls, an eleven-year-old and a fourteen-year-old. The cinematographer was Michael Ballhous, who had shot some of Rainer Warner Fassbinder's films. Although *Old Enough* had limited distribution, it received a generally favorable review in *The New York Times*. Janet Maslin said it "has been sweetly directed by Miss Silver, who has a better feeling for filmmaking and for adolescent friendships than she does for the class differences on which the story trades." Maslin criticized Silver for using ethnic stereotypes and for her "extraordinary naivete about how the other half lives," but concluded, "still Miss Silver is a young director who works with a lot of assurance" [Maslin 1984].

Her success with *Old Enough* led to her second film, *Permanent Record*, a story of teenage suicide, made in Hollywood. The film was not very successful, although Siskel and Ebert listed it as one of their 1988 sleepers of the year. David Ansen of *Newsweek* described it thusly: "Director Marissa Silver's sensitive, well-intentioned and beautifully photographed film goes halfway to this goal (to dig beneath sociological cliches and discover the mysterious particularity of art), then loses its nerve and settles for generic uplift." He, however, blamed the screenwriters for the Hollywood ending which appeared to resemble an episode of "Fame" [Ansen 1988].

By 1989, Silver was directing her second Hollywood film, *Vital Signs*, for 20th Century-Fox. The studio brought in Jeb Stuart, who wrote *Die Hard*, to write the script along with Larry Ketron, who was one of the writers of *Permanent Record*, thus showing its commitment to the picture's success. *Vital Signs* breaks Silver's pattern of films about teenagers, but is still about young people, this time third-year medical students [*New York Times* 21 July 1989].

In a curious way Silver had reversed one principle of *Community of Praise* but had retained another, more significant, principle of Davis's. Her first two films had been justly praised for their cinematographic opulence, yet Leacock had taken a minimalist approach in *Community of Praise*. Silver had gone in the other direction. On the other hand, she retained Davis's axiom that the best stories were of individuals at moments of crisis or transition in their lives. Illustrative of that is Silver's reasons for her involvement in *Vital Signs*:

> I guess what interested me was that the story follows five 25-year-olds at a real turning point in their life [sic], as they're moving from youth to adulthood in a very different way. The responsibilities of being a doctor are a lot larger than a lot of young people face, because your mistakes cost lives [*New York Times* 21 July 1989].

Tom Cohen, who directed *Family Business* and *The Campaign*, is still in the film business, despite his expressed desire to write. He has done several commercial bits, the latest of which was a short subject on the making of *Steel Magnolias*, a movie with Dolly Parton, Sally Field, and Shirley MacLaine [*Muncie Star* 30 April 1989]. He has not had the meteoric rise that Silver has had, but he has lacked the former's connections.

Two cinematographers on the Middletown Film Project have done well. John Lindley, who filmed much of *The Campaign* and *The Second Time Around*, has also gone to Hollywood where he shot *Field of Dreams*, one of the spate of recent baseball movies. Although Roger Angell, the noted baseball writer, savaged the film, in part because it was too pretty [Angell 1989:41-56], *Field of Dreams* has a lush quality about it reminiscent of *The Second Time Around*. The old farmhouse and the seemingly too perfect diamond convey a mythical sense just as did the final rally of Carey's supporters on election eve or the march of David and Elaine down the aisle. Both mingle elements of archetypes that transcend time and place, carrying the viewer beyond Iowa cornfields, Muncie fairgrounds, and the Methodist church to a universal American ideal.

Tom Simon, who shot the Anderson part in *The Big Game*, has achieved considerable success in television. He has become the principal filmmaker in the "*National Geographic* Series," which appears regularly on PBS. These episodes display Simon's technical abilities, and are of consistently high quality.

The lives of those who were filmed have changed less dramatically, as might be expected. They were of a different class, lacking access to money or networks for success and not possessing the kind of skills that could compensate for that lack. None had a sister who could raise a half-million dollars, or who knew the rich and famous. Their lives were more commonplace.

For some participants, life has not been easy. Those in *Community of Praise* were particularly hard hit. The veterinarian, Dr. J. Marcus-Haggard, pastor of the Church of the Branches, a nondenominational ministry that cast out demons, died of a heart attack in New York City while attending a religious seminar in July 1982, three months after he appeared in the film.

The Tobeys' marriage broke up before Haggard died. On 10 April 1982, three days after *Community of Praise* aired, Phillip left for the umpteenth time; but, unlike earlier departures, did not return. He went to Kentucky and filed for divorce two weeks later. Eventually he returned to his small farm to reopen his welding shop. He still refuses to comment on the film.

Phyllis, who had been working in the Blackford County Department of Public Welfare as a caseworker, moved to Greensboro, North Carolina, where she obtained a job with an adoption agency. She retains her optimism and her religious faith. She told an inquiring reporter that "Phil divorced me, and I've moved down here and gotten a good job. I've always loved North Carolina anyway, and it was just a good time to start over. I was, of course, broken-hearted over the divorce, but I have a real good quality of life now....It's a whole different atmosphere down here. The Lord has been more than good to my family. There have been some rough times, but the Lord always has seen us through" [*Muncie Star* 30 April 1989].

The children have done better than one might have expected, given their problems. Chris, the oldest son, works at the U-Do Center, a garage that rents tools and gives advice to do-it-yourself mechanics, in Muncie, thus following in his father's footsteps. Rebecca graduated from Purdue in the spring of 1989 with a degree in communications, while Noel, the accident-prone youngest child, went south with his mother and is now taking courses in commercial art at a North Carolina Community College [*Muncie Star* 30 April 1989]. His curiosity and energy ought to make him a success.

Much has happened as well to the Southside students whose fate it was to appear in a film that never appeared on PBS. They, their parents, and Muncie teachers and administrators are still bitter about what happened.

In 1985 the then superintendent of schools, Donald Slauter, said "he still thought 'the whole lot of you [filmmakers] were completely unethical, and... that one cost of all of this *Seventeen* business' was to insure that no one would ever shoot so much as one foot of film, for any reason, in Muncie's schools, unless school officials had the right of final approval" [Slauter personal communication to Vander Hill, 31 May 1985]. Mike Gorin, the black sociology teacher, believed then and now that Kreines and De Mott deliberately edited the film in such a way as to make him and the other teachers look bad. This has not hurt his career, however, as he was promoted to Dean of Men several years later. His colleague, Mrs. Hartling, the home economics teacher, was less fortunate. She retired shortly after the uproar about *Seventeen*, in part because of the controversy, according to Gorin.

In 1989 when reporters tried to interview participants in *Seventeen*, they had mixed results. They were able to interview Shari Massie, Lynn's mother, and Keith Buck, one of the white male students in the film. Lynn refused an interview.

The Massies still live in Shed Town, although Lynn has left home. Jim Massie, Lynn's father, has improved prospects; he was working as a laborer at Attlin Construction when the film was shot, but now he works at Warner Gear, a union shop with decent wages. Tom, Lynn's younger brother, lives at home. He worked for a time at Famous Recipe Fried Chicken, but is now an electrician for Cybertronics.

Lynn married Buck on 10 December 1983, and they had a child, Shontel Nicole, on 26 July 1984. By November, the marriage had broken up. Lynn received custody of the daughter, but Buck continued to support Shontel. In 1985 when queried by a Southside teacher about his reactions to the film project, he is reported to have said, "Who cares about that crap? I'm concerned about supporting my kid" [D. Slauter and C. Siler personal communication to Vander Hill 31 May 1985]. Buck works as a truckdriver for the family business, Muncie Septic Tank Service, run by his mother out of their home in Shed Town. Buck now has a second daughter from another relationship and lives near his father and mother. Lynn has remarried, this time to a Muncie policeman, James R. Peters [*Muncie Star* 30 April 1989], and lives in a middle-class residential suburb on the far west side of Muncie.

Both Mrs. Massie and Buck have very negative feelings about *Seventeen*. Mrs. Massie believes that it had an extremely bad impact on the participants. She has said, "'Bitter' is a mild word considering what they [the filmmakers] did to these kids. I don't want to talk about it because some of the kids are just now getting their lives back together" [*Muncie Star* 30 April 1989].

Buck, though bitter over the distortion he discerned in the editing, is convinced that the film's subjects have done well. He claims that his friends have married, have gotten additional education, and have "become productive members of their communities" [*Muncie Star* 30 April 1989].

Both Lynn and Buck have either changed, or grown older. It is hard to imagine Buck talking about productive members of the community or even thinking in such terms in *Seventeen*. Neither he nor Lynn ever discussed work or marriage in the film, although such discussion may have been edited out. Neither ever expressed any long-term goals, yet both now have children of their own and have accepted some social responsibility.

Southside High School still remains. In his last act as superintendent, Slauter closed Northside High School, the most affluent school in Muncie's "best" residential neighborhood, but he left Southside alone. Basketball coach Robbins has been promoted to principal, thus continuing a Muncie tradition of choosing administrators from the ranks of coaches.

Basketball, however, failed to take either of the stars of *The Big Game* where they wanted to go; both had experiences that could have been predicted from the film. Rick Rowray has achieved middle-class success while Andre Morgan has failed to do so as yet.

Rowray was selected as an Indiana All-Star his senior year, after *The Big Game* was filmed. He was heavily recruited by the University of Kentucky, as seen in the segments with Joe B. Hall, and by the University of Iowa, his father's alma mater. He visited Lexington but didn't like the prospects there too well and hence was receptive to an offer made by Bobby Knight at Indiana University. Knight had just lost a recruit and wanted Rowray to replace him, although Knight had previously expressed no interest. Encouraged by his father, Rowray enrolled at Bloomington.

Rowray did well in his freshman year at Indiana. He played in several preseason games and was listed as a starter for another when he broke his wrist. He sat out the remainder of the season and then transferred back to Muncie to attend Ball State University. His decision not to play for Indiana was a rational one. He knew he would never succeed as a professional basketball player; he was a half-step slow and had trouble going to his left. Given that knowledge, he had no desire to continue in Knight's program, the equivalent of "three years in boot camp" [personal communication with Rowray].

Rowray did not become a basketball star at Ball State; he lacked the ability to break a game open, despite his performance against Anderson in *The Big Game*, and he had health problems. His basketball career was undistinguished, but he did well in his business classes, took a graduate degree, and now teaches marketing at the university where he is a popular and able instructor. He won the College of Business Teacher of the Year Award in 1989. His life has not been without tragedy. His father divorced his mother and moved to Iowa City to become the director of the American College Testing service shortly after *The Big Game* aired.

Andre Morgan has been less successful. A junior at Anderson High School at the time of *The Big Game*, Morgan played well the rest of the 1980-81 season and was himself chosen for the Indiana All-Star team the following year. He did not pay attention to his grades and was a non-predictor so, despite his tremendous physical ability, was not heavily recruited. One school did offer him an athletic scholarship; it was the University of Hawaii which, because of its academic schedule, held out the possibility of athletic eligibility after a successful fall term. Morgan played his first year at Hawaii but had problems. His grades were poor, he quarreled with the athletic department, and he was arrested for drug use. He dropped out of the University of Hawaii, but played for Chaminade for a short time before leaving the island to return to Anderson.

Morgan worked and played basketball for industrial league teams for a time in Anderson. In 1988, Morgan received another chance to play professional basketball. Rob Shoemaker, a former Anderson resident and owner of the Worcester Counts of the World Basketball League, gave him a tryout at the suggestion of Troy Lewis, an Anderson graduate, a Purdue basketball star, and a member of the Counts. Morgan made the team and played the 1989 season [*Muncie Star* 30 April 1989].

The future for Morgan is brighter but it is by no means secure. Morgan recognizes that fact, saying, "The coaches think if I work hard enough and hang in there and continue to improve, there might be a chance for me in the NBA. I had the talent, but everyone has caught up with me. Now I have to develop the skills" [*Anderson Morning Bulletin* 5 August 1989]. Morgan has the ability, but does he have the will? He thinks he does, and he thinks he has changed his attitude toward life.

Unlike Rowray, who was disturbed by the comparison he felt the filmmakers made between a suburban middle-class white and an inner-city black, Morgan believes the film portrays him accurately, saying "That's the way it was at the time. Basketball was my thing back then. All I wanted to do was play basketball. I wish I had focused more on academics. It would have made it easier when I got to college. I might have been able to do something in school" [*Muncie Star* 30 April 1989].

Neither Rowray nor Morgan seem to have been affected much by the film series. The same cannot be said of the Sheslers, the couple featured in *The Second Time Around*. Their story had the most uncertainties in it, since it ended at the beginning of their married life. All the questions asked in the film—whether to buy a house, whether to have more children, whether Elaine would work outside the home, and even whether to stay together—remained unanswered.

The questions seem to have been resolved in a satisfactory way. The Sheslers are still married but their lives have changed considerably. After Elaine graduated from Ball State University with a degree in industrial technology, she hired on with Borg-Warner, the largest industrial plant in Muncie, one that manufactures transmissions and gear cases. She even aspired to a political career, running unsuccessfully for city council on the Republican ticket in the fall of 1983. David continued to work in the traffic department sign painting shop in Muncie.

However, their Muncie residence was short. In July 1984, the Sheslers moved to Tucson, Arizona, where David's aunt and grandmother lived. There they both took jobs; David became a painter at Davis-Monthan Air Force Base while Elaine became an accountant for the Pima County government. They bought a house in Tucson and had no more children. David says "Our life is pretty well settled in; we have 4 acres and a dog. We're kind of comfortable" [*Muncie Star* 30 April 1989]. He failed to add that they still have two sons, Jeffrey who was eighteen and had just graduated from high school in 1989, and Michael who was twenty-two and who works in an amusement park and has aspirations to become a movie stunt man.

The taste of show business that *The Second Time Around* gave the Sheslers has remained with them. In addition to writing short stories, Elaine is modeling, as is David who can be seen in television commercials and movies. In the spring of 1989, the whole family, with the exception of Jeffrey, was in the made-for-television movie, *Gore Vidal's Billy the Kid*. David played a sheriff and bailiff while Elaine and Michael were extras.

Unlike the individuals in *Seventeen*, the Sheslers see their film experience as almost entirely positive. They continue to view the videotape, for varying reasons. Elaine likes to see it after she has fought with David and wants to know why she married him. He just enjoys watching it. Both consider the film to be a perfect home movie, to be viewed together or with friends. As Elaine says, "We get the tape out and review it and feel good again" [*Muncie Star* 30 April 1989].

There is ample reason for the Sheslers to feel as they do. They have achieved their goal of homeownership and have moved into a middle-class way of life. They have survived their second marriage and still have interest, partially stimulated by the film series, that sets them apart from the ordinary. They live in a part of the country where few know about their past and where they are not reminded of their early tribulations and struggles.

But is there life after pizza? Perhaps no one benefited more than Howie Snider from the publicity generated by the Middletown Film Series. Certainly no one enjoyed his movie experience more than Howie did, and no one hopes it will bring him fame or fortune more than Howie still does. He was quite excited and optimistic that Henry Winkler would make a successful TV series.

The Winkler option was backed by Paramount Pictures, which began script development. Paramount sent a writer, Barbara Turner, to Muncie to prepare two scripts. She spent a week, along with a still photographer who took many photos, and wrote the scripts. These proved unsatisfactory to Paramount and Winkler let the project languish. The problem was that Turner's scripts were not funny and that Howie was transformed into a tragic figure [*Daily News* 22 February 1988].

Howie continued to run the restaurant, trying one idea and then another to stimulate the pizza business. He also taught a class in advertising at Ball State University and carried his paper route which he had started in 1979 (he had begun the route to show one of his sons that there were jobs in Muncie). Among the changes he initiated in the restaurant were to discontinue playing the banjo and to create a buffet that featured fried chicken, spaghetti, and lasagna, as well as pizza. Howie also developed a take-in lunch service for near-by Borg-Warner. Business picked up for a time.

On 19 February 1987, Howie disenfranchised his pizza parlor, changing its name to "Howie's Place." His reasons, as expressed publicly, were that "There is no national image for Shakey's. Many people in town thought my name was Shakey. People keep calling me Shakey and my name is Howie....If the national image is not doing us any good, then there's no reason for us to be associated with the franchise. On the other hand, we don't really do the franchise system a lot of good because we're kind of a maverick" [*Muncie Evening Press* 19 February 1987]. At the same time, he admitted that the cost of the franchise was narrowing his profits. He also claimed he could make his own pizza if Shakey would let him sell it. The company did, but business did not improve.

Good news came from the film front later that year. When Winkler's option expired in November 1987, another hopeful producer stepped in, thus continuing the small income Howie had been receiving, and once again raising hopes for a bigger payoff. The producer who obtained the option was Larry Brezner, who had just finished two successful films, *Throw Mamma From the Train* and *Good Morning, Vietnam*. Brezner had tried for an option from Howie in 1982 but Winkler called first. Brezner then waited five years until Winkler's option expired.

Brezner's idea was somewhat different from Winkler who wanted to do a TV series on the Showtime network. Brezner wanted to make a movie which then might become a television series. To begin, he hired Stu Silver to write the script. Silver, who wrote the script for *Throw Mamma From the Train* and who also directed the movie, had written for "Soap," "Webster," and "Brothers."

The basic idea for the Howie movie, which is to be called *Play Indiana* and which is to be released by Orion Pictures, was to produce a film that "is human and warm and hysterically funny" [*Muncie Star* 19 November 1989]. The producer also adds that the movie would emphasize family values. "By traditional standards, one would never call the Howard Snider story a classic success story. But he winds up finding out how important his family is. The process that he goes through is that success" [*Daily News* 28 February 1988].

Obviously the film was to be derivative of several recent films. Silver envisages the film as resembling *Terms of Endearment*, but he also has elements of other successful movies in mind. *Play Indiana*, while referring to Howie's musical antics and based on the state song "Back Home Again In Indiana," is obviously a bow to the 1986 hit, *Hoosiers*. The connection is even more direct in Brezner's preliminary thoughts about who would play Howie. Three names have been discussed; they are Clint Eastwood, Paul Newman, and Gene Hackman, the star of *Hoosiers* [*Muncie Star* 19 November 1989].

There is some question whether the film will ever get made. The announcements of the signing indicated that filming would start in the summer of 1988, but it did not. Later, Howie said that filming would begin in the summer of 1989, but again it did not. Howie is more philosophical this time around. Even though Brezner says the film will be made, Howie says "Maybe it will happen, maybe it won't. Life goes on" [*Muncie Star* 19 November 1989].

And indeed life does go on for the Sniders. By January 1989, all but two of the children had left the pizza business and only one of those still lived at home. Judy Snider was only working half-days instead of seven full days a week. Even Howie had slowed down, expressing a desire "to write and have my garden, and get some peace and tranquility." He also wanted to finish his degrees in journalism and English [*Muncie Evening Press* 5 January 1989].

The handwriting was on the wall for Howie's Place. On 1 March 1989, Howie announced that the restaurant would no longer serve wine or beer in order to discourage alcohol abuse. The unannounced reason was that Howie could no longer afford the liquor license, but Howie put the best side on it that he could. Once again, business picked up for a time. The upsurge was not enough. On 4 July 1989, Howie called it quits after fourteen years in the pizza business. He and his invisible partners had decided that the business could now be sold for enough to recoup their investment [*Muncie Star* 4 July 1989].

At age fifty-seven, Howie is about to enter a new career. He is teaching more classes at Ball State University and hopes that with the finishing of his master's degree in journalism he will become a permanent faculty member. Judy will be content with her grandchildren. The children meanwhile are all grown and on their own, although their lives have not been without problems. Leslie, the oldest son, has been married and divorced twice. He is now living in Gainesville, Florida, and aspiring to be a zoo curator. Lee is married with three daughters. He sells insurance in Muncie. Larry, who was managing Howie's Place, is married and has a son. Lisa works for AT&T in Indianapolis. She is unmarried. Lynn (Lyndon) is a sergeant in the Marine Corps at Cherry Point Marine Air Station in North Carolina which, by coincidence, is where his father once was stationed. He is married and has a son. Lloyd worked part-time at Howie's Place, but his main occupation is now as an emergency medical technician for Delaware County. He got married in late December 1988. Liz married and has two children. She worked as a reporter for the *Muncie Star* before joining the Ball State Public Information Office. Laraine, the youngest, graduated from Ball State in May 1989 with a degree in criminal justice and with hopes of becoming a probation officer [*Muncie Star* 5 January 1989].

The family's reflections on the impact of the film series vary as they themselves vary. Howie claims that the film did not affect his life; although at the same time, he admits to attitudinal changes. He says, "Nothing has changed. If it hadn't been that, it would have been something else. Life's mysterious." Yet he also says that the film made him aware that he was failing to communicate with his children. The film caused him to ask his children if they really felt the way they said they did. Their affirmative answers changed his ways. "I know it improved my relationship with my kids. My communication with my kids had deteriorated because of my obsession with the business" [*Muncie Star* 30 April 1989].

Leslie, speaking for the children, says that the film meant little to any of them. "I don't think any of us, with the possible exception of Dad, really thought it meant much of anything." He also still clings to his stated position that Howie's continuation in the pizza business was a mistake and believes that the audience failed to get the proper message from the film. "For all folks making a normal income, and for all these, excuse me, rich bastards in Hollywood, even people around Muncie, they are all missing the point, that for my entire family, it's been a struggle from day one" [*Muncie Star* 30 April 1989].

Finally, Howie, like Elaine, still has kind words for the filmmaker. He says of Cohen, "I have a great admiration for his talents as a documentary producer and director. I think the best word to describe him is 'sensitive.' He is sensitive almost to a fault" [*Muncie Star* 30 April 1989]. Perhaps Howie's reason for this conviction is similar to Elaine's. For her, Lindley erased the lines in her face and made her more beautiful than she was in life; for Howie, Cohen made him more of a hero than he was, concealing his failures as a businessman and his drinking. Both saw a persona they would have always liked to have been.

One cannot help but believe that Howie's big moment in life was in *Family Business*. His apparently natural tendency to ham it up, to sing and entertain, found expression in the film. His happiest moments were when he was doing his promo over the local radio station or playing the banjo to an appreciative audience. His dedication was never wholly to the pizza parlor; it was but a phase in his life, one that allowed him expression of his not inconsiderable ego and his gregariousness. For this one individual, the film has added to the richness of his life and has provided him with stories which he still tells, while still not altering his economic or social circumstances.

The same cannot be said to be true for Jim Carey. The larger-than-life mayoral candidate whose Irish congeniality highlighted *The Campaign* has risen in the world. In the mayoral election of 1983, a year after *The Campaign* was screened, Carey defeated his opponent, Mayor Alan Wilson, in an election whose results were almost the reverse of that of 1979.

Wilson had proven to be an unpopular mayor, or rather a less than charismatic one. He lost support from nominally working-class, Democratic Southside Muncie when he fought unionization of city workers and he suffered for the Reagan recession of 1982-83 when the unemployment rate in Muncie was as high as 18 percent. His basically shy, introverted personality was not well suited to the rough and tumble of Muncie politics. He recognized the misfit saying, "Politics isn't in my blood the way I think it's in Jim's blood" [*Muncie Star* 30 April 1989].

On the other hand, Carey learned from his defeat. In the 1983 campaign he secured the support of Ira "Rip" Nelson, the Delaware County Democratic Chairman who had opposed him in 1979. With the party united and with a depressed economy in Muncie, Carey was a shoo-in to win. He moved from his position as security guard at Central High School, where his wife was librarian, to the mayor's office.

Wilson, after his defeat, tried to obtain a political appointment as a federal judge. He failed in this endeavor, evidently lacking powerful enough endorsements, although he had been able to obtain Governor Bowen's blessing in the mayoral campaign. He then took a job at a local manufacturing firm, Arrowhead Plastic Engineering, Inc., as a federal procurement bidder. Two years later he returned to the practice of law. He opened an office where he shares a library and secretary with another attorney. He practices general law and acts as a public defender in Delaware Superior Court. He disclaims any desire to run for mayor again saying, "I can't conceive I'd run for anything like mayor again, anything that would require me to give up my law office. City Council might be fun. That's the only thing I'd like to run for, something that might be fun" [*Muncie* Star 30 April 1989]. In 1990, however, he ran for prosecutor and was decisively defeated in the Democratic tidal wave of victory.

Wilson seems to have found a comfortable niche in his life in Muncie. He still lives in the same stone house on Tillotson Avenue with his wife, the director of a home-health care program, and his children. He still sings in the choir of the Presbyterian Church and is content to go his own private way.

Carey has been a great success as mayor, partly because of his own ebullient personality and partly because of extrinsic factors. He has conceived of his role as cheerleader for the city and, with his considerable energy, has achieved much visibility, appearing at almost every public function and many private ones. His major goal has been to reverse the economic decline of the city by promoting its industrial and tourist potential. In this he has been helped by an upturn in the national economy and by efforts by local groups such as the Chamber of Commerce and Horizon 91, an organization whose avowed purpose is to create jobs for the town. The community also added a convention center, and the bankrupt downtown hotel was refurbished and became attractive again (although it went bankrupt again after several years). Carey also benefited from the decision of the Ball Foundation to invest heavily in a new cultural center for the community. The changes in the town helped Carey's image. So successful was he that the Republicans in 1987 could find no strong candidate to oppose him, nominating instead a woman with little political experience who lost badly. By 1989 with the unemployment rate below four percent, Carey seemed unbeatable. Popular opinion had it that he can be mayor for as long as he wants to be.

Not that his political or personal life has been entirely smooth. His administration has been relatively free of scandal with no indictments or trials although he has been the subject of a federal investigation. At the same time, his party's and his own commitment to patronage have raised eyebrows. "Rip" Nelson, the erstwhile county chairman, was allowed to hold two lucrative county positions at the same time until the state forced him to divest himself of one. In one of his capacities as county highway supervisor, the department lost a bulldozer, an embarrassing event. Given the proclivity for patronage, it is not surprising that some city jobs are not done well or that competent people are sometimes forced to leave. Still, even conservative Republicans support the mayor and judge him to be doing well.

Business leaders in the town are most impressed by Carey's drive to improve the town's image, hoping to revive the downtown area. He has torn down or allowed certain downtown buildings to be demolished, thus earning the ire of historic preservationists. He has aspired to build a new city hall but curtailed the city's role in building a new criminal justice facility. The former is part of the plan to change Muncie's image and is voluntary; the latter was mandated by a federal judge. Both facilities have generated considerable opposition because of the manner in which decisions to build them were made and because of the increased taxes they will involve. Carey has not gone unscathed and will probably suffer more wounds when taxes are raised, as they must be. However, the opposition is not organized and is more shrill than reasoned.

Carey is still married to Marilyn, who has taken upon herself the task of planting flowers all over the city. She is not now trying as hard to smooth off Jim's rough corners. Indeed, many of them have already been smoothed away because of all the public appearances of the mayor. He has become a world traveler, flying to Taiwan, Korea, and Japan to encourage business investments from the Far East.

Carey has known more tragedy; he has been as unlucky in private life as he was lucky in politics. After the filming, one daughter committed suicide in California; several years later another was killed in an automobile accident. Only a son remains alive.

Carey and Wilson take different positions on *The Campaign*. In a preview prior to the showing of the segment on PBS, the two were asked if they would do it over. Carey said that he would not allow himself to be filmed again while Wilson said that he wouldn't mind. To an outside observer, it seems apparent that the film treated Carey better than Wilson; he certainly has the audience's sympathy.

Carey exposed himself both physically and emotionally in the film, partly because that was his character. Yet in so doing, he risked revealing his own insecurities and his sense of inferiority because of his lack of education. He admitted that he found the television crew's presence to be nerve-wracking because he had "a tendency to murder the King's English." This problem was compounded by the earthiness of some of his statements and actions. He claims his wife, who objected to the remark he made to his mother-in-law about having sex with her and who also found the topless scene crude, was the most critical of all. Carey defends his behavior, saying that the filmmakers told him to act natural, but he still worries about how others must see him [*Muncie Star* 30 April 1989].

On the other hand, Wilson was not as exposed, probably because of his handlers who protected him from the filmmakers and his own persona which shrank from self-expression. After all, he won the election without exposure; he did not do tricks or alter his behavior. Not that he found the film to be without fault. His sole complaint was that *The Campaign* failed to give a true account of his efforts, that it slanted the victory by showing him going door-to-door only in affluent Northside neighborhoods, while he also worked hard on the Southside. Both men, in general, do not feel betrayed or misrepresented in the film. Carey believes, "It pretty well told the truth on both candidates, their government philosophies and how they felt about Muncie," while Wilson says, "I thought the film captured the essence of a political campaign in Muncie pretty well. I don't think our campaigns are that much different than in other cities" [*Muncie Star* 30 April 1989].

The comments on the film reflect the two men's ways of thinking. Carey is still visceral, worrying about his image and thinking that the campaign showed the political philosophies of both persons, although the latter were mainly conspicuous by their absence. Wilson, on the other hand, is analytical, noting that the camera missed part of his campaign but avoiding any comment on the content.

Were their lives changed by the film? Neither will admit to change, although it seems obvious that the film has benefitted Carey. Like Howie, he relishes the spotlight and is a natural performer. The film gave him an opportunity to demonstrate these talents. It did not, however, change his political career; he would no doubt have won just as overwhelming a victory if he had never been on camera. Nor has being in the film caused him to reflect much on past experiences; he is future-oriented. Wilson appears to have been even less affected. His life is pretty much what it was before he ran for mayor; he is no more or no less successful because of his brief time in the limelight.

What general conclusions can be drawn from the histories of those who were involved in the Middletown Film Series? The first is that none, with the possible exception of those filmed in *Seventeen* and Davis, were negatively affected. It could be argued that Kreines and De Mott were injured, except that prior to *Seventeen* their work was largely seen in alternate cinemas, and that even with the problems, *Seventeen* has had wide distribution. Moreover, even with Davis's career change, the decision to concentrate upon writing to the exclusion of filmmaking was made before the series was finished and may have had nothing to do with the film's reception.

The case is clearer with those who were unfortunate enough to appear in *Seventeen*, not so much the young participants, although they may wince at their juvenile follies, but more the teachers and those other students in the school. These individuals were tarred by being portrayed as incompetent, insensitive, racist, and provincial. While the damage was largely psychological, it may have had an economic impact as well. Certainly, the whole Southside community suffered a continued loss of esteem.

On the other hand, no one in the films seems to have gained very much from their appearances either. Perhaps Howie will some day be richer because of *Family Business*, but don't count on it. Perhaps the Sheslers have become more media involved because of *The Second Time Around*, but that is not certain either. Jim Carey is certainly more polished and sophisticated than he was in *The Campaign*, but this may be the result of six years as mayor.

Those who've had the negative experiences have tried to block these out from public exposure; those whose experiences have been more positive are more likely to reminisce, but none will admit that the experience had much of an influence upon them.

Looking beyond the impact of the film on individuals to the lives themselves, one finds more optimism about Muncie's and America's future. All the films tried to capture individuals in crisis; none portrayed anyone who was a sure winner. Indeed, some (especially those in *Seventeen*) appeared to be certain losers. No one was rich or especially talented, Andre Morgan excepted. At best, the participants were somewhat above average in status; at worst, they were on the edge of the bottom. Ten years later, however, they were living better lives, or at least more conventional ones; they had jobs and homes; they were more settled. Some were divorced; but given their personalities and those of their former mates, this was probably for the better. None had made spectacular improvement, but there was measurable advance in some of their lives.

Perhaps the reasons for this were the general improvement in the economy of Muncie or the ten years' experience after the films were made. In any case, almost all seemed more comfortably middle class, with the possible exception of Buck and Morgan.

The more difficult question to answer is whether they have grown in insight and awareness as a result of being filmed. Has the experience of being subjected to the scrutiny of the camera helped them to examine their lives? There is no unambiguous answer. Perhaps another series about the same people now might provide one.

For those who pointed the camera and directed the filming, the series was but a step up in a professional career, unless like Leacock or Kreines and De Mott, their choices led elsewhere. Leacock wanted to go back to essentials, to become a minimalist, and he did. Kreines and De Mott scorned commercialism and were not asked to join the ranks of those who were interested in making money. For the others, the series provided an opportunity to learn new skills or to hone old ones. In this sense, it was a valuable school.

Does this mean that the series was ultimately exploitive? The answer is not a simple one. In one way it was. The filmmakers benefitted while the participants did not. The participants risked exposing themselves and in return received only a chance to see themselves on the television screen. The filmmakers got paid, earned reputations or enhanced those they already had, and made contacts that were valuable for the future. The humanists were also paid, got to add another item to their vitas, and to present papers at meetings or to write articles for scholarly journals.

In a way it was not. For some of the participants, Howie especially, this experience was a high point in lives devoted to work and to other mundane activities. It was a time to be creative, to act and fantasize, and, at best, to reveal emotions that would have otherwise been concealed. Although some of the fantasies, the creativeness, and the emotions were contrived, they were not, in my opinion, out of character. In the end, there was a psychic reward.

To the final tally sheet must be added the worth of the series to the larger society. Despite individual reward or penalty, the series remains one of the most compelling looks at a community in our time.

Reflections and Conclusions

The Middletown Film Project is fading into the past, if it has not already gone. Remaining are the six films themselves and the hundreds of hours of outtakes in the archives of the Center for Middletown Studies. What has been learned from the project?

Does the experience argue against federal support for filmmakers? I do not believe so, despite the recent furor over the Mapplethorpe photographs and the funding of their exhibition by the National Endowment for the Arts. The controversy over *Seventeen* did raise questions concerning NEH's support of filmmaking, and that fact, combined with the reduced federal funding of NEH in the 1980s, meant the decade was not one of plenty for documentarians.

What the failures, and the successes, of the series do reveal, however, are the inherent weaknesses of NEH's film funding. The problem is not that federal funding automatically means federal control. Indeed, the opposite seems to have been the case in the Middletown experience. Of all the entities involved, NEH made the least attempt to dictate content. Compared to Xerox and PBS, NEH was the one large institution which came out of the affair without looking a little foolish.

There are problems in federal funding. One of the most obvious is that NEH's mission is to further the humanities which, according to its definition, does not include filmmaking. The latter is the province of NEA. Therefore, in order to fund films, NEH requires that they must have humanities content. That content must originate with professionally trained humanists: anthropologists, historians, philosophers, or literary critics. On the other hand, any project hoping for funding must persuade NEH of the high quality of the film, so that to compete necessarily means the collaboration of a professional filmmaker. Although I believe that collaborations between filmmakers and humanists are difficult, if not impossible, to effect, the success of *The Civil War* both as an artistic effort and as received by the public seems to prove me wrong. Perhaps the reason for this success was the passion of Ken Burns for the Civil War or perhaps it was the fortunate personalities of the humanists, in particular Shelby Foote.

Given that this discovery is unlikely, a collaboration between filmmakers and humanists seems inevitable, and this inevitability means trouble, mainly because of differences in attitude. Filmmakers, from my experience, tend to be aggressive and self-confident to the point of egotism, and to be dismissive of others who are not. They, like Davis, say, give us the money and we'll give you the story. In addition, they have learned to be deceptive while appearing to be honest, and to take little on trust.

Humanists, on the other hand, tend to be less aggressive and self-assertive, to be less certain of what they are doing, to be less decisive and more likely to see complexities. They have a greater commitment to process than to product, more concern with ideas than images, and are somewhat naive in dealing with high- roller filmmakers and executive producers. As a result, they favor more research and less filming, more meaning and less appearance.

Can the two work together? It is possible, but two particular difficulties must be overcome. On the one hand, the two should fully understand each other's roles and expectations. This we never did; for our part, we trusted that Davis would do the right thing without realizing that even if he did, that was a poor excuse for failure to plan exactly what responsibility each party had, what kinds of control, if any, we had over the content of the films, and what exactly were the categories reserved exclusively for the filmmakers. As a result, we, with the exception of Trimmer, found ourselves to be peripheral to most of the project, a symbol of which was a gradual retreat of our names in the film credits until *Seventeen*, when all but Trimmer's were gone.

On the other hand, the example of *The Adams Chronicles* should be avoided. There, NEH insisted that other historians check scripts after they had been written and edited. This complicated the project and delayed it considerably, causing the project director to vow never to apply again. I sometimes feel that way; yet on occasions, I think humanists could have been more involved. I was given an opportunity to help edit one of the films after I had threatened to resign from the project, but I do not consider that it would be useful for an untrained humanist to help edit or to have a veto on the finished film. I believe that such contingencies can be avoided if collaborative agreements were carefully written and well understood. One way to accomplish this would be to insist that humanists be given contracts, just as the filmmakers were, detailing duties and obligations.

Despite these proposed reforms, there seems to me to be no way for NEH to prevent another *Seventeen*, even if it wished to do so, except by intimate knowledge of the filmmaker's work and trust in his/her integrity. Even that will not always suffice.

I am less optimistic about the ability of direct cinema to survive as a documentary technique. Here, I agree with Winston's argument that direct cinema has reached a dead end, although I disagree with him that Kreines and De Mott approached that ideal very closely.

In any finished film, time is compressed. *The Campaign* runs approximately eighty-nine minutes; the actual events pictured cover a four-month period. *Seventeen* takes about ninety minutes; it was supposedly shot over a nine-month period. This means it is impossible to film every event in the period; it also means that some filmed events must be cut; and that the remaining ones be placed in order by editing. Despite Canby's description of *Seventeen* as being not naturally coherent, the film does have an aesthetic order imposed by the filmmakers who altered chronological sequences and, according to the participants, manipulated certain behaviors. All films, even supposedly direct cinema, are distortions of actual events created by filmmakers and editors. In part, the quarrel between Davis and Kreines and De Mott was over the degree to which such filmic intervention took place.

Every film then is narrativized by those who make them. In that sense, every film is fictive. Here, the insights of Hayden White concerning historical writing as contained in *Tropics of Discourse* [1978] can be applied equally to film. All films are, in this sense, literary creations composed of story elements drawn from the past. They not only provide models, but are also metaphorical statements enabling readers to find meaning in their lives and those around them. Films resemble fiction because they share the same structure. In the end, films illustrate White's dictum "that we can only know the actual by contrasting it to the imaginable."

Direct cinema is thus doomed to failure from the start because of scrambling of sequence, time compression, and other editing devices. The only possible way to escape the dilemma is to do what C-Span attempts when it turns the camera on to capture a complete record of all that happened in the order that it happened. For most viewers, that is unsatisfactory and boring.

What does that mean for documentary film? It means, I think, that since intervention is impossible to avoid, it should be done honestly and openly with the full knowledge of the viewer. It means the willingness to use talking heads, to have narrators or not to have them, to include musical background or to leave it out (early talkies dispensed with the music associated with silents because it was unnatural, while now even documentaries use music to heighten tension or signify mood changes).

It also may mean a movement further in the direction that Kreines and De Mott and Leacock argued the documentary should take, toward home movies or home videos. If coherence is not significant, if the one-person rig is to be used, and if a strong story line is not essential, perhaps the professional documentarian should step aside for the gifted or not so gifted amateur; after all, what are the two most significant functions of a professional filmmaker?

They are the filming of events and the editing of the film. A skilled amateur could, with practice, produce a film of acceptable quality, particularly if the emphasis were on the subject and not the technique. The matter of editing, however, is less simple. This step involves more knowledge and experience on the part of the editor. Could a skilled amateur do the job? I believe it is possible by using either one of two alternatives: paying a professional editor, or editing it oneself as best one could. The first alternative would result in a more structured narrative; the second would sacrifice coherence for greater authenticity.

But making a film is not the same as getting it shown, as Kreines and De Mott discovered. The major role of the producer, in this case Davis, was to get the film distributed and advertised. He was highly successful in persuading PBS to place the series on the schedule, to obtain a sponsoring station, and to find underwriters to advertise it. The whole package, however, fell apart with the problem of *Seventeen*, as we have seen, and Davis was unable to put it back together.

The secret of Davis's success as promoter was twofold; the series was a costly one and Davis had an excellent reputation as a filmmaker. He was able to exploit these strengths and to sell the project. Could a skilled amateur do as well? I think the answer here is clearly no. A humanist trained in filmmaking would lack entry into the small network of film producers. He/she could learn filming techniques at almost any major university and could make decent films. He/she could not, however, expect to attract a national audience, given the prevailing system.

The present situation, however, is changing. Public television is coming to resemble major network television; the latter is losing its audience, either as viewers become bored or are attracted to more specialized cable channels. All want more good material; perhaps a program on the best home video documentaries might prove as popular as the current funniest home videos are now.

Even if national exposure is not possible, there are opportunities for local and regional showing. Local television stations, both public and private, need programs and will accept efforts of persons untrained in filmmaking. WIPB broadcast a videotape, *My Grandfather's Middletown*, which a colleague and I made with a small grant ($2500) from the Indiana Committee for the Humanities (now the Indiana Humanities Council), a videotape which was essentially a slide-show of historic photographs along with a narrator. It was well received, enough so that it was re-run. It was also nominated for a Barnouw award.

Scaling down expectations also has the added advantage of scaling down costs. Large-scale film projects are inordinately expensive, and funding one or two major projects quickly exhausts the media budget for NEH. On the other hand, smaller projects can be done much more cheaply. For the cost of one Middletown Film Series, two thousand *My Grandfather's Middletown*s could be made. Or to use another measure of opportunity cost, the money expended for *Seventeen* which was never shown on public television would have paid the cost of another study of Muncie (Middletown IV ?). If this study would have been as productive as Middletown III, it would have had considerable impact on the intellectual community, an impact which, I believe, would have been much more lasting than that of *Seventeen* had it been shown. Given a choice between the two, I would have chosen another study of Middletown, one which would focus upon the ethnography of the various sub-cultures in the community and on the history of the town which badly needs to be written.

Having said this, I must also say that I still consider the Middletown Film Project to be a valuable contribution to community studies. It is, in its own way, as much a landmark as was *Middletown* or *All Faithful People*, and, like the two books, will be more valued as time passes and the stories of Howie Snider, Jim Carey, and Lynn Massie lose their freshness and novelty. What remains will be a visual record of how Munsonians behaved and thought at the beginning of the decade of the 1980s. As American values and practices shift, those of the past will come into sharper contrast and will define both the content and direction of social change. By looking at them, we will see how far we have come.

Appendix

All the films in the Middletown Film Series may be obtained from the National Endowment for the Humanities except for *Seventeen*. They may also be gotten from state humanities councils, either from their media collections or borrowed from the National Endowment for the Humanities or from the Indiana Humanities Council. There is no charge for this service and study guides are available from the same sources. Selected Offices of Cultural Affairs at U.S. consulates overseas can provide films for interested viewers there.

Seventeen is available commercially. The distributor is:

First Run / Icarus Film
153 Waverly Place
6th Floor
New York, NY 10014

Filmography

I. Middletown Series. Peter Davis, Producer.

The Campaign. Tom Cohen, Director; John Lindley, Camera; Tom Cohen, Sound. PBS, 9PM, 24 March 1982; 90 minutes. Featured Jim Carey and Alan Wilson.

The Big Game. E.J. Vaughn, Producer-Director; Paul Goldsmith, Camera; Ron Yoshida, Sound. PBS, 9PM, 31 March 1982; 60 minutes. Featured Andre Morgan and Rick Rowray.

Community of Praise. Richard Leacock and Marisa Silver, Filmmakers. PBS, 9PM, 7 April 1982; 60 minutes. Featured the Tobeys: Phil, Phyllis, Chris, Rebecca, and Noel.

Family Business. Tom Cohen, Director; Tom Hurwitz,Camera; Peter Miller, Sound. PBS, 9PM, 14 April 1982; 90 minutes. Featured the Sniders: Howie, Judy, Leslie, Lloyd,Loraine, Larry, Lisa, Lee, Lyndon, and Lizbeth.

Second Time Around. Peter Davis, Director; John Lindley, Camera and Co-Director; Larry Loewinger, Sound. PBS, 9PM, 21 April 1982; 60 minutes. Featured David Shesler and Elaine Ingram.

Seventeen. Joel De Mott and Jeff Kreines, Filmmakers. Never shown. Scheduled for PBS, 9PM, 28 April 1982; 90 minutes. Featured Lynn Massie.

Middletown Revisited. Larry Dyer, Producer, Filmed by WIPB. 9PM, 28 April 1982; 90 minutes. This was a fill-in for *Seventeen* which was narrated by Ben Wattenberg, who interviewed local residents as well as Ted Caplow, Peter Davis, and Tom Cohen.

II. Follow-up Videos. Larry Dyer, Producer.

The Campaign. WIPB, 10:30PM, 24 March 1982; 30 minutes. Featured Jim Carey, Alan Wilson, and Ray Scheele.

The Big Game. WIPB, 10PM, 31 March 1982; 30 minutes. Featured Bill Harrell, Norman Held, Morrie Mannies, and C. Warren Vander Hill.

Community of Praise. WIPB, 10PM, 7 April 1982; 30 minutes. Featured George Jones and J. Morris Haggard.

Family Business. WIPB, 10:30PM, 14 April 1982; 30 minutes. Featured Howie Snider.

Second Time Around. WIPB, 10PM, 21 April 1982; 30 minutes. Featured David Shesler, Elaine Ingram, and Peter Davis.

III. *Interview with Peter Davis*. WIPB, 9PM, 21 April 1982;60 minutes. Featured Davis in a call-in format.

All of the above videos are held in Educational Resources at Ball State University. All the outtakes of the Middletown Film Series are held in Special Collections for the Center for Middletown Studies at Ball State University.

References

Allen, Frederick Lewis
    1961   *Since Yesterday*. New York: Harper & Brothers; Bantam.
    1964   *Only Yesterday*. New York: Harper & Row; Perennial Library.
American Film (June 1982).
Anderson Morning Bulletin (5 August 1989).
Angell, Roger
    1989   The Sporting Scene: No, But I Saw the Game. *New Yorker* (65):41–56.
Ansen, David
    1988   Teens, Tentons, and Hypsters. *Newsweek* (111):62
Baer, Diane
    1989   For Snider Family, There Is Life After *Family Business*. *Muncie Evening Press* (5 January).
Bahr, Howard M.
    1980   Change in Family Life in Middletown, 1924–77. *Public Opinion Quarterly* (44):35–52.
    1982   "The Perrigo Paper": A Local Influence Upon *Middletown in Transition*. *Indiana Magazine of History* (78):1–25.
Bahr, Howard M., Theodore Caplow and Geoffrey K. Leigh
    1980   The Slowing of Modernization in Middletown. In *Research in Social Movements, Conflicts and Change*, Louis Kriebergh, Editor. Greenwich, CT: JAI Press.
Barnet, Bob
    1982   All Together Now: Let's Be Typical! *Muncie Star* (18 April).
Barnouw, Eric
    1974   *Documentary: A History of the Non–Fiction Film*. New York: Oxford University Press.
Berger, Peter
    1984   Review of *All Faithful People*. *America* (150):36–37.
Berman, Ronald
    1979   Art vs the Arts. *Commentary* (November):46–52.
Binford, Karen D.
    1971   An Analysis of the Effect of Intelligence on the Relationship between Socio–Economic Status and Academic Advancement. *Sociological Focus* (4):27–37.
Bodnar, John
    1980   Immigration, Kinship and the Rise of Working Class Realism in Industrial America. *Journal of Social History* (14):45–65.
Borenstein, Audrey
    1978   *Redeeming the Sin: Social Science and Literature*. New York: Columbia University Press.

Brown, Richard H.
  1976   Social Theory as Metaphor. *Theory and Society* (3):169–97.
Brownell, Blaine
  1972   A Symbol of Modernity: Attitudes toward the Automobile in Southern
            Cities in the 1920's. *American Quarterly* (24):20–44.
Canby, Vincent
  1985a   Screen *Seventeen*: A Look at American Life. *New York Times* (6 Febru-
            ary).
  1985b   Growing Up Misunderstood in Today's America. *New York Times* (25
            February).
  1985c   Documentaries on Cinematic Horror. *New York Times* (21 June).
  1985d   Vivid Joys Among the Vast Array of Failures. *New York Times* (29 De-
            cember).
Caplow, Theodore
  1975   *Toward Social Hope*. New York: Basic Books.
  1979a   The Gradual Process of Equality in Middletown: A Tocquevillean
            Theme Re–examined. *Tocqueville Review* (1).
  1979b   The Measurement of Social Change in Middletown. *Indiana Magazine
            of History* (75):344–57.
  1981a   The Future of Religion in Middletown. Paper read at the annual meeting
            of the Society for the Scientific Study of Religion, Baltimore, Maryland.
  1981b   The Sociological Myth of Family Decline. *Tocqueville Review*
            (3):349–69.
  1982a   Christmas Gifts and Kin Networks. *American Sociological Review*
            (14):383–92.
  1982b   Looking for Secularization in Middletown. Talk at the annual meeting of
            the Friends of Bracken Library, Muncie, Indiana.
  1982c   The Myth of Family Decline and Its Benefits. *Christian Science Monitor*
            (19 April).
  1982d   Religion in Middletown. *The Public Interest* (68):78–87.
  1983   Response to the Comment by Miller and As in "Avoiding Bias in 'Deriva-
            tive Samples': A Neglected Issue in Family Studies." *American Socio-
            logical Review* (48):876.
Caplow, Theodore and Howard M. Bahr
  1979   Half a Century of Change in Adolescent Attitudes: Replication of a Mid-
            dletown Survey by the Lynds. *Public Opinion Quarterly* (43):1–17.
Caplow, Theodore, Howard M. Bahr and Bruce A. Chadwick
  1981   Piety in Middletown. *Transaction Magazine* (18): 34–37.
  1982b   *Middletown Families*. Minneapolis: University of Minnesota Press.
Caplow, Theodore, Howard M. Bahr, Bruce A. Chadwick, Rueben Hill
            and Margaret Holmes Williamson
  1983   *All Faithful People*. Minneapolis: University of Minnesota Press.
Caplow, Theodore and Bruce A. Chadwick
  1979   Inequality and Life Styles in Middletown, 1920– 1978. *Social Science
            Quarterly* (50):367–86.
Cedar Rapids Gazette (28 March 1982).
Christian Century (31 August, 31 October 1977).

Coben, Stanley
    1975   The Assault on Victorianism in the Twentieth Century. *American Quarterly* (26):604–625.

Cohen, Richard
    1982   Whose Truth? *Washington Post* (28 March).

Colson, Elizabeth
    1976   Culture and Progress. *American Anthropologist* (78):261–71.

Condran, John G., Dwight W. Hoover, Bruce Meyer, Paul Mitchell, and C. Warren Vander Hill
    1976   *Working in Middletown*. Muncie: Indiana Committee for the Humanities.

Coughlin, Ellen K.
    1982   Middletown Much the Same After 50 Years Finds, But Sociology Greatly Changed. *Chronicle of Higher Education* (24):19–20.

Covino, Michael
    1984   Missing: The Strange Case of *Seventeen*. *Express* (13 April).

Cox, Don
    1985   Storytelling and *Family Business*. Direct Cinema Class, N.Y.U. (Fall 1975).

Cunningham, Bob
    1986   *History of Muncie: City Elections, 1905 Through 1986*. Muncie: Privately printed.

Dahlin, R.
    1982   Publisher's Weekly Interviews. *Publisher's Weekly* (221):8–9.

Daily News (27 April, 12 May, 16 June 1982).

Davis, Peter
    1979   The Sorry and the Pity of Non–Fiction Film. *Nation* (228):277–78.
    1980   Grant proposal for Middletown Film Series to the National Endowment for the Humanities, 16 February.
    1982   *Hometown*. New York: Simon & Schuster.
    1983   The Unknown Nonsoldier. *Esquire* (100):444–48.
    1984a   Mirror of Our Midlife Crisis. *Nation* (238):76–88.
    1984b   The $100,000 a Year Woman. *Esquire* (101):70–74.
    1985   The High and Mighty Crowd. *Esquire* (103):221–31.
    1986   The Man Who Undressed Men. *Esquire*: 338–47.
    1987a   *Where Is Nicaragua?* New York: Simon & Schuster.
    1987b   Managua Is Waiting. *Esquire* (107):171–74.
    1987c   Exploring the Kingdom of Aids. *New York Times Magazine Section* 31 May:32–36.
    1987d   If It's Tuesday, This Must Be Managua. *Washington Monthly* June:48–51.
    1988   When Atlanta Burned. *Esquire* (110):126–31.

De Mott, Joel
    N.D.   Notes on one-person shooting.

Devolution at NEH: Politics and the National Endowment for the Humanities. *National Review* (28):92–93.

Dixon–Goist, Park
    1977   *From Main Street to State Street: Town, City, and Community in America*. Port Washington, N.Y.: Kennikat Press.

Documentaries Make Waves at PBS
1982   *Broadcasting* (19 April).

Does Documentary Have A Future?
1982   *American Film* (7):57–64.

Elder, Glen A.
1982   A Third Look at Middletown. *Science* 21 May: 854– 57.

Emerson, Gloria
1982   Muncie Business. *Nation* (234):379–81.

Etzkowitz, Henry
1979–80 The Americanization of Marx: *Middletown* and *Middletown in Transition. Journal of the History of Sociology* (2):41–57.

Fisher, Galen M.
1924   A History of the Small City Study. Unpublished paper, Institute of Social and Religious Research, Rockefeller Institute, New York.

Flink, James A.
1972   Three Stages of American Automobile Consciousness. *American Quarterly* (24):451–73.

Fox, Richard Wightman
1983   Epitaph for Middletown: Robert S. Lynd and the Analysis of Consumer Culture. In *The Culture of Consumption*; Richard Wightman Fox and T.J. Jackson Lears, Editors. New York: Pantheon Books.

Francisco, Brian
1989   Carey and Wilson on *The Campaign. Muncie Star* (30 April).

Frank, Carrolyle M.
1974   Politics in Middletown: A Reconsideration of Municipal Government and Community Power in Muncie, Indiana, 1925–1935. Unpublished PhD dissertation, Ball State University.

Freedman, Estell B.
1974   The New Woman: Changing Views of Women in the 1920's. *Journal of American History* (61):372–93.

Gillen, John
1957   Research Reviews: The Application of Anthropological Knowledge to Modern Mass Society. *Human Organization* (18):24–29.

Gillette, Howard
1983   Middletown Revisited. *American Quarterly* (35):426–33.

Goheen, Peter N.
1974   Interpreting the American City: Some Historical Perspectives. *Geographical Review* (64):362–84.

Goldberg, Vicki
1986   *Margaret Bourke–White: A Biography.* New York: Harper & Row.

Goodall, Hurley and J. Paul Mitchell
1976   *A History of Negroes in Muncie.* Muncie: Ball State University.

Goodman, Ellen
1982   The Family: A Double Message. *Washington Post* (1 May).

Gordon, Milton M.
1958   *Social Class in American Society.* Durham, N.C.: Duke University Press.

Grieves, Carolyn
1982   *Seventeen* Damages South. *Muncie Evening Press* (16 March).

Guterbock, Thomas M.
1980   Social Class and Voting Choices in Middletown. *Social Forces* (58):1044–56.

Haddan, J.K.
1980   H. Paul Douglass: His Perspective and His Work. *Review of Religious Research* (22):66–88.

Hall, Linda
1972   Fashion and Style in the Twenties: The Change. *The Historian* (34):485–97.

Handlin, Oscar
1979   *Truth in History*. Cambridge, MA: The Belknap Press of Harvard.

Harvey, Charles E.
1983   Robert S. Lynd, John D. Rockefeller, Jr. and *Middletown*. *Indiana Magazine of History* (79): 330–54.

Hawes, G.K.
1982a   *Middletown* Cast Confronts Its Creator. *Muncie Star* (26 March).
1982b   *Middletown* Director Withdraws *Seventeen* From PBS Series. Muncie Evening Press (31 March).

Herbers, John
1982   How They're Doing in Muncie, IN. *New York Times Book Review* (18 April).

Hillman, Ruth
1985   Our Neighborhood. *Muncie Star* (14 May).

Hoover, Dwight W.
1976   Were There Any Old People in Middletown? Paper read at the Conference on Human Values and Aging, New York.
1978a   Planning grant proposal for forming a federation of state humanities councils to the National Endowment for the Humanities, 5 March.
1978b   Research and development grant proposal for Middletown film to the National Endowment for the Humanities, 19 February.
1978c   Script development grant proposal for a Middletown Film Series to the National Endowment for the Humanities, 23 August.
1983a   Is Modernization a Useful concept in Historical Writing? Middletown as a Case Study. Paper read at the annual meeting of the Indiana Association of Historians, Bloomington, IN.
1983b   *The Second Time Around* as Compared to *Middletown Families*. Paper read at the Annual meeting of the American Studies Association, Philadelphia, PA.
1986   Politics as Usual in Middletown, 1983–1986. Paper read at the annual meeting of the Great Lakes American Studies Association, Adrian, MI.
1987a   Censorship or Bad Judgement? An Example from American Public Television. *Historical Journal of Film, Radio and Television* (7) 2:161–74.
1987b   The Long Ordeal of Modernization Theory. *Prospects* (11):407–451.
1987c   The Middletown Film Project. *Journal of Film and Video* (39) 2:52–65.
1987d   *Seventeen*: The Genesis of the Idea and the Continuing Reaction. In *Visual Explorations of the World*, Jay Ruby, Editor. Aachen, Germany: Edition Herodot.
1988   The Political Process: Can It Be Captured on Film? *Social Science Perspectives Journal (2)*.

1989   My Grandfather's Middletown. *History Teacher.*
Horizon (October, 1977).
Howlette, P.G.
   1982   Letter from the Publisher. *Sports Illustrated* (1 March).
Hulser, Kathleen
   1982   Is Public TV Doing Its Job? *Nation* (234):582–86.
Humanist at the Humanities
   1977   *New Republic* (177):7–10.
Inman, Julia
   1982   Seventeen Program Will Not Air. *Indianapolis Star* (31 March).
Issarie, M. Ali and Doris A. Paul
   1979   *What Is Cinema Verite?* Metuchen, N.J.: The Scarecrow Press.
Jacobs, Lewis
   1979   *The Documentary Tradition.* New York: W.W. Norton, Inc.
Janis, Ralph
   1982   Middletown Revisited: Searching for the Heart of Mid–America. *Indiana Magazine of History* (78): 346–51.
Jay, Martin
   1973   The Dialectical Imagination: A History of the Frankfurt School and the Institution of Social Research. *Boston: Little, Brown.*
Jensen, Richard
   1979   The Lynds Revisited. *Indiana Magazine of History* (75):303–19.
Joe Duffy's New Job
   1977   *Christian Century* (31 August).
Kasen, Jill H.
   1980   Whither the Self–Made Man? Comic Culture and the Crisis of Legitimation in the United States. *Social Problems* (28):131–48.
Kernan, Michael
   1982   America's Cautious Myth of Itself. *Washington Post* (24 March).
Kolin, Melvin L.
   1976   Social Class and Parental Values: Another Confirmation of the Relationship. *American Sociological Review* (41):527–37.
Krebs, Michele
   1985   How the Auto Forever Changed Lives: The Story of Middletown, U.S.A. *Automobile News*, Centennial Celebration Issue.
Kreines, Jeff and Joel De Mott
   N.D.   Press Release.
La Guardia, Joan D.
   1982a   TV Producer Withdraws Controversial *Seventeen. Muncie Star* (30 March).
   1982b   Family, Religion Have Changed Little Here. *Muncie Evening Press* (27 April).
   1987   Howie to Shake Off "Shakey" Name, and Maybe Do Away with Pizza Too. *Muncie Evening Press* (19 February).
Lazersfeld, Paul
   1975   Remarks Read at the Memorial Service of Robert S. Lynd, Columbia University, 28 February 1971. In *Sociology and Public Affairs: The Chicago Schools.* James T. Carey, Editor. Beverly Hills: Sage Publications.

Leacock, Richard
  1959   La Camera PassePartout. *Cahiers du Cinema* (16):37–38.
  1961   For an Uncontrolled Cinema. *Film Culture* (22):23– 25.
Lehmann–Haupt, Christopher
  1982   Books of the Times. *New York Times* (18 March).
  1987   Books of the Times. *New York Times* (6 April).
Le Masters, Ron
  1989   Both Men Winners in *The Big Game. Muncie Star* (30 April).
Lindt, Gillian
  1979–80 Robert S. Lynd: American Scholar–Activist. *Journal of the History of Sociology* (2):1–12.
Lingeman, Richard
  1981   The Family is Alive and Well in Muncie. *Chicago Tribune* (3 May).
  1982a   The Campaign. In *Middletown* Teaching Notes *22 March: 2*
  1982b   Muncie Protects Its Own. *Nation* (234):722–27.
Long, Laura
  1989   Love Is Better Second Time Around. *Muncie Star* (30 April).
Los Angeles Times (27 March 1983; 5 July 1984).
Lucas, Deborah
  1989   Students, Others Still Bitter Over *Seventeen. Muncie Star* (30 April).
Lynd, Helen M.
  1983   *Possibilities.* With the collaboration of Staughton Lynd. Bronxville, N.Y.: Friends of the Esther Rauschenbush Library.
Lynd, Robert
  1921   But Why Preach? *Harpers* (142):81–85.
  1924   Letter to Miss Stella Tegarden, Secretary, Art Students' League (14 May).
Lynd, Robert S. and Helen M.
  1929–56 *Middletown: A Study in Cultural Conflicts.* New York: Harcourt, Brace, Jovanovich, 1937; Harvest Books, 1965.
  1937–65 *Middletown in Transition: A Study in Cultural Conflicts.* New York: Harcourt, Brace, Jovanovich, 1937; Harvest Books, 1965.
Lynd, Staughton
  1979–80 Robert S. Lynd: The Elk Basin Experience. *Journal of the History of Sociology* (2):13–40.
Madge, John H.
  1962   *The Origins of Scientific Sociology.* New York: The Free Press of Glencoe.
Mamber, Stephen
  1974   *Cinema Verite in America: Studies in Uncontrolled Documentary.* Boston: The Massachusetts Institute of Technology.
Mandel, Leon
  1977   *Driven: The American Four–Wheeled Love Affair.* New York: Stein & Day.
Marcorelles, Louis
  1964   The Deep Well. *Contrast* (3): 246–49.
Maslin, Janet
  1984   Screen: *Old Enough. New York Times* (24 August).

Dwight W. Hoover

Mayer, Jane
  1982   Producer Pulls Show Off Public Television Rather Than Cut It. *New York Times* (31 March).
Maynard, Greg
  1989   Couple Divorce, But Faith Endures. *Muncie Star* (30 April).
McLagan, Meg
  1987   The History of *Seventeen* and the Middletown Film Project. Ethnographic Film Class, New York University (Spring).
McPherson, J. Miller
  1981   Dynamic Model of Voluntary Affiliation. *Social Forces* (59):705–28.
McQuade, Donald
  1982   Community of Praise. In *Middletown* Teaching Notes *(22 March)*.
Miller, Judith Droitcour and Ira H. Cisin
  1983   Avoiding Bias in "Demographic Samples": A Neglected Issue in Family Studies. *American Sociological Review* (48):874–76.
Miller, S.M.
  1979–80 Struggle for Relevance: The Lynd Legacy. *Journal of the History of Sociology* (2):58–64.
Mitchell, Donald O.
  1982   *Seventeen. Muncie Star* (22 March).
Moffett, Al
  1981   The American Family Is Alive and Well. *Saturday Evening Post* (March).
Mooney, Michael
  1980   *The Ministry of Culture.* New York: Wyndham Books.
Morrisey, Charles T.
  1985   Oral History and the Boundaries of Fiction. *Public Historian* (7):41–46.
Moxley, Lucina Ball
  1986   *Reflections of Lucina: The Best Years.* Indianapolis: Privately printed.
Mulcahy, Kevin V.
  1982   Government and the Arts in the United States. In *Public Policy and the Arts*, Kevin V. Mulcahy and C. Richard Swaim, Editors. Boulder, CO: Westview Press.
Muncie Evening Press (10 May 1932), (12 June 1935), (9 December 1948), (18 March 1982), (25 March 1982),(26 March 1982), (27 March 1982), (13 April 1982), (16 April 1982), (21 April 1982), (23 April 1982), (25 April 1982), (28 April 1982), (9 May 1985), (19 February 1987), (5 January 1989).
Muncie Star (10 October 1937), (9 March 1959), (7 December 1972), (8 December 1972), (14 December 1972), (4 November 1979), (11 November 1979), (12 March 1982), (19 March 1982), (24 March 1982), (25 March 1982), (31 March 1982), (1 April 1982), (2 April 1982), (8 April 1982), (13 April 1982), (15 April 1982), (17 April 1982), (22 April 1982), (29 April 1982), (2 May 1982), (12 May 1982), (13 August 1982), (23 March 1983), (27 March 1983), (3 November 1984), (9 May 1985), (4 April 1989), (30 April 1989), (11 November 1989), (30 November 1989).
Muncie Weekly News (22 April 1982).
Muncie's Blackboard Jungle
  1982   *American Film* (7):10–13.

National Review (19 August, 9 December 1977).

New Republic (20 August 1977).

New York Times (24 August 1984), (21 July 1989).

Newsweek (31 October 1977)

North, Juli
   1982   PBS *Seventeen* Segment Fills Southsiders with Anger, Dismay. *Muncie Star* (12 March).

O'Connor, John J.
   1982a   TV: Middletown in Video Verite. *New York Times* (24 March).
   1982b   When a Documentarian Tries to Play Sociologist. *New York Times* (4 April).
   1982c   TV: "The Letter" by Maugham. *New York Times* (3 May).

Parker, Steve
   1988   Film to Showcase "Howie's Place" Owner. *Ball State News* (22 February).

Parkinson, Leon
   1978   Comment and Opinion: Our Town. *Muncie Evening Press* (28 June).

People (29 March).

Peterson, Ivar
   1982   In a "Typical" U.S. Town, Revolutions Come Slowly. *New York Times* (7 February).

Polsby, Nelson W.
   1959   The Sociology of Community Power. *Social Forces* (37):232–36.
   1960   Power in Middletown: Fact and Value in Community
Research. *Canadian Journal of Economics and Political Science (26):592–603*.
   1967   *Community Power and Political Theory*. New Haven: Yale University Press.

Populism as Elitism
   1977   *Newsweek* (31 October).

Rance, Mark
   1986   Home Movies and Cinema Verite. *Journal of Film and Video* (38):95–98.

Rapp, Rayna and Ellen Ross
   1983   It Seems We've Stood and Talked Like This Before: Wisdom From the 1920's. *Ms* (11):54–60, 92.

The Real America in the Story of a Family That Works
   1982   *Washington Post* (5 April).

Richey, Rodney
   1982   Producer of Documentary on Muncie Reacts to Reactions. *Muncie Star* (19 March).
   1989a   It's Still "Howie's Place." *Muncie Star* (30 April).
   1989b   It's the End for "Howie's Place." *Muncie Star* (4 July).
   1989c   Play It Again Hollywood. *Muncie Star* (19 November).

Rights and Wrongs of Scholarship: NEH
   1977   *Horizon* (October)

Roof, Wade C.
   1984   Review of *All Faithful People*. *Science* (17 February).

Rosenberg, Howard
   1982   Reality TV from Middle America. *Los Angeles Times* (24 March).

Rossi, Peter H.
  1983   The Muncie Papers: Some Comments on the "Middletown Series." Paper read at the Community Section Meeting of the American Sociological Association, Detroit, Michigan.
Saltzman, Joe
  1983   The Children's Hour. *USA Today* (3 May).
Schwartz, Tony
  1982   Final PBS *Middletown* Segment Is Withdrawn. *New York Times* (31 March).
Searching for the Mythical Middle America
  1982   *Cedar Rapids Gazette* (28 March).
Shales, Tom
  1982a   TV's Stirring Vigil at the Crossroads. *Washington Post* (24 March).
  1982b   *Middletown* Revisited. *Washington Post* (28 April).
Sheppard, Nathaniel, Jr.
  1982   Muncie Finds Film on Students a Distorted Mirror. *New York Times* (11 April).
Shores, Larry
  1982a   *Middletown* Bits and Pieces. *Muncie Star* (2 March).
  1982b   An Untypical Television Show. *Muncie Star* (28 March).
Small Cultural Disaster: Search for a New Chairman
  1977   *National Review* (9 December).
Smith, Mark C.
  1979–80 Robert Lynd and Consumerism in the 1930's. *Journal of the History of Sociology* (2):99–119.
  1983   *Middletown*, Community Studies, and 1920's American Social Science. Paper read at the joint meeting of the Midcontinent and North Central American Studies Association meeting, Iowa City, Iowa.
  1984a   Fifty years of an American City: Stability and Change in Middletown. *Indian Journal of American Studies* (14):57–65.
  1984b   From *Middletown* to Middletown III: A Critical Review. *Qualitative Sociology* (7):327–36.
  1985   Rejoinder to Theodore Caplow. *Qualitative Sociology* (8):63–64.
Snider, Howie
  1989   Personal Appearance at NEH Seminar, "Values in Small Town America" (26 July).
Stein, Maurice
  1960   *The Eclipse of Community*. Princeton, N.J.: Princeton University Press.
Strasser, Susan M.
  1980a   An Enlarged Human Existence? Technology and Household Work in Nineteenth–Century America. In *Women and Household Labor*, Sarah F. Berk, Editor. Beverly Hills, CA: Sage Publications.
  1980b   *Never Done: A History of American Housework*. New York: Pantheon Books.
Terhune, Bill
  1982   Cheers for Peter Davis: Middletown Films A Plus for City. *Muncie Evening Press* (6 April).
  1985   Looking Back on It: Why All the Fuss Over Seventeen? *Muncie Evening Press (16 May)*.

Thernstrom, Stephen
    1964   *Poverty and Progress: Social Mobility in a Nineteenth Century City.* Cambridge, MA: Harvard University Press.
    1968   Notes on the Historical Study of Social Mobility. *Comparative Studies in Society and History* (10): 162–72.

Titus, A. Constandina
    1981   Local Government Expenditures and Political Attitudes: A Look at Nine Major Cities. *Urban Affairs Quarterly* (16):437–52.

Trachtenberg, Alan
    1982   Family Business. In *Middletown* Teaching Notes *(22 March)*.

Trillin, Alice
    1982   Second Time Around. In *Middletown* Teaching Notes *(22 March)*.

Trimmer, Joe
    1982   *The Big Game.* In *Middletown* Teaching Notes (22 March).

Unger, Arthur
    1982   PBS's cancelled "Middletown" segment: was its "slice of life" spiced up? *Christian Science Monitor* (5 April).

Vander Hill, C. Warren
    1982   The Middletown Film Project: Reflections of an "Academic Humanist." *Journal of Popular Film and Culture* (53):48–65.

Vanek, Joann
    1980   Household Work, Wage Work, and Sexual Equality. In *Women and Household Labor*, Sarah F. Berk, Editor. Beverly Hills, CA: Sage Publications.

Van Gelder, Lawrence
    1984   At the Movies. *New York Times* (21 July).

Variety (14 December 1983).

Washington Post (11 April 1982)

Waters, Henry F.
    1982   Pulse of the Heartland. *Newsweek* (99):50–51.

Wattenberg, Ben
    1984   *The Good News Is the Bad News Is Wrong.* New York: Simon & Schuster.

Weales, Gerald
    1984   Review of *Middletown Families.* New York Review of Books (26 April).

Wertheim, Arthur Frank
    1976   Radio Comedy and the Great Depression. *Journal of Popular Culture* (10):501–19.

Whyte, William Foote
    1984   *Learning from the Field: A Guide from Experience.* With the collaboration of Kathleen King Whyte. Beverly Hills, California: Sage Publications.

Wilson, William H.
    1974   *Coming of Age: Urban America, 1915–1945.* New York: John Wiley & Sons, Inc.

Winston, Brian
    1983   Hell of a Good Sail....Sorry No Whales. *Sight and Sound.* Autumn 1983:238–43.

Dwight W. Hoover

Yau, Esther C.M.
1983   *Middletown*: Direct Cinema as a Document of Socio–Cultural Reality. Paper read at the Popular Culture/American Culture Association meeting, Wichita, Kansas.
Zimmerman, Paul
1974   Review of *Hearts and Minds*. *Newsweek* (3 March).
Zwerin, Mike
1988   Leacock Returns to the Home of Cinema Verite. *International Herald Tribune* (25 November).

Index